The Joseph Winterbotham Collection

AT THE ART INSTITUTE OF CHICAGO

The Art Institute of Chicago

MUSEUM STUDIES

VOLUME 20, NO. 2

The Art Institute of Chicago
MUSEUM STUDIES
VOLUME 20, NO. 2

*The Joseph Winterbotham Collection
at The Art Institute of Chicago*

Foreword   100

A Living Tradition: The Winterbothams   102
and Their Legacy

LYN DELLIQUADRI, *The Art Institute of Chicago*

The Joseph Winterbotham Collection   111

MARGHERITA ANDREOTTI, *The Art Institute of Chicago*

Checklist of the Joseph Winterbotham   182
Collection, 1921-1994

SOPHIA SHAW PETTUS, *The Art Institute of Chicago*

Selected References and Index   189

Foreword

JAMES N. WOOD

Director and President

In 1921, during the Art Institute's fledgling years, Joseph Winterbotham had a remarkable and far-sighted idea for bringing European painting to Chicago. Mr. Winterbotham was a businessman and not a collector of art, but he traveled widely, often to Europe, and understood the importance of fine art to the cultural life of a community. The plan he formulated in the first decades of the twentieth century was greeted with an enthusiasm that still endures as we approach the century's end. It has provided the Art Institute with an increasingly valuable group of late nineteenth- and twentieth-century paintings, many of which stand among the masterpieces of the museum's holdings.

The Winterbotham Plan was unique in its day, and, to my knowledge, there was no other major museum that had a comparable arrangement. In the following essay, "A Living Tradition: The Winterbothams and Their Legacy," the Winterbotham family and plan are discussed in detail. Suffice it to say here that the plan began with a gift of $50,000, which was to be invested and maintained as principal; its interest was to be used for the purchase of paintings by European artists. The key stipulation of the plan was that initially only thirty-five paintings should be purchased. Once that number was attained, which occurred in 1946, any work could be sold or exchanged for a work of superior quality and significance to the collection. In this way, Joseph Winterbotham created a living tradition—a collection of paintings that in the course of sixty-five years has continually changed in scope and improved in strength.

The Winterbotham Plan has come to be known as the Art Institute's first commitment to the acquisition of modern art. Although Joseph Winterbotham indicated only that acquisitions be of works by European artists, the first painting bought under the plan—Henri Matisse's 1919 canvas *Woman Standing at the Window*—set the stage for a collection with a decidedly contemporary complexion. Between 1921 and 1929, ten of the thirteen paintings then acquired for the Winterbotham Collection had been created in the twentieth century. The remaining three were by Post-Impressionists, artists central to the development of Modernism, and included the Art Institute's first painting by Paul Gauguin, *The Burao Tree (Te Burao),* which has remained in the Winterbotham Collection to the present day. This trend in selecting contemporary paintings seemed to have met with the approval of the collection's founder; shortly before he died, he wrote to the museum's vice-president, "I congratulate the Art Institute and myself on the fine discrimination you have heretofore exercised in selecting paintings."

In the course of the first fourteen years of purchasing under the Winterbotham Plan, a committee of Art Institute trustees often made selections on the advice of members who traveled frequently to Europe and were well acquainted with the galleries of Paris and London. As time passed, the considerable involvement of Joseph Winterbotham, Jr., in this selection process justified a reconstitution of the Winterbotham Committee to include a family member, one trustee, and the museum's director. After Joseph Winterbotham, Jr., died, he was succeeded by his niece Rue Winterbotham Shaw, a central figure in Chicago's art world for many decades; and she, in turn, was succeeded by her son Patrick Shaw, who represents the family today.

By 1947, when the group of thirty-five paintings was finally in place, the first exhibition of the complete collection was mounted. At this time, it became clear that the pictures would be better displayed if they were interspersed among the museum's growing holdings of nineteenth- and twentieth-century European art. The Gauguins, Cézannes, van Goghs, and the great Toulouse-Lautrec bought for the Winterbotham Collection found their natural places next to the Impressionist and Post-Impressionist paintings that had been given in subsequent years by some of the Art Institute's other major patrons. The Cubist works by Picasso and Braque, the Modigliani portrait, the monumental early Chagall, and the Surrealist canvases by de Chirico, Dali, and Tanguy gravitated to their rightful positions among the museum's burgeoning twentieth-century acquisitions. It was the recognition of this fact that moved Joseph Winterbotham, Jr., to propose, in 1945, a change in his father's original provision for a room devoted to the permanent exhibition of the Winterbotham Collection. He suggested, instead, that the thirty-five paintings be brought together for exhibition one month a year.

Since then, the annual gathering of the Winterbotham Collection has been accompanied by a regular reassessment of the whole and its parts. Over the years, various members of the Winterbotham family have offered or bequeathed paintings to the collection—Joseph Winterbotham, Jr., being a particularly active and generous donor. Opportunities arose to purchase important works by such modern pioneers as Miró and Delaunay, and later it was deemed wise to increase the collection's scope by adding works of more contemporary masters; thus came examples by Balthus and Jean Dubuffet. Witnessing the collection's changing composition has been a stimulating experience for both the curatorial staff and the public. As the years have passed, however, and finer and finer paintings have entered the group, fewer and fewer have been considered for replacement or exchange.

It is inevitable, given the nature of the Winterbotham Plan, that the group of thirty-five paintings now comprising this special collection will undergo further change. Nevertheless, we are exceedingly proud of the shape and quality it has taken in the course of its sixty-five-year history, and we have sought, with the publication of this issue of *Museum Studies,* to honor the Winterbotham Collection, its founder, and the family that has nurtured it to its present distinction.

❊   ❊   ❊   ❊   ❊

This issue of *Museum Studies* was made possible through the financial support of the Winterbotham Fund. I wish to thank the staff members of the Art Institute who contributed to this endeavor. I am particularly indebted to Margherita Andreotti and Lyn DelliQuadri for writing so well on the Winterbotham Collection. I am also grateful to Ann Wassmann, who designed this issue with her usual intelligence and flair; Courtney Donnell, whose research was the basis for much of the material assembled here; Sophia Shaw Pettus, who revised and compiled the checklist and bibliography; Michael Sittenfeld, who edited this issue and guided it to completion; Manine Golden, who supervised the production of this issue; Mary Bodach, who assisted in the preparation of the manuscripts; Tonje Kilen, who contributed to the bibliographical research for this project; Cris Ligenza, who typed the manuscripts; and Annie Morse, who compiled the photographs published here. Finally, I want to thank Catherine Bock-Weiss, Douglas Druick, Gloria Groom, and Charles Stuckey for their thoughtful comments on Ms. Andreotti's manuscript.

The paintings in the section "The Joseph Winterbotham Collection," pp. 111-81, are ordered chronologically according to their date of execution. For each painting in this section, the title in the original language, if it is known, is given in parentheses after the English version.

A Living Tradition:
The Winterbothams and Their Legacy

LYN DELLIQUADRI

The Art Institute of Chicago

By the 1920s, less than a century after its founding, Chicago had been transformed from a prairie swampland to an exuberant industrial and cultural metropolis. Skyscrapers, stockyards, steel mills, streetcars, wharves, warehouses, locomotives, automobile-clogged streets, and lake-going vessels laden with grain and coal announced an unprecedented prosperity. There was opera, theater, a symphony orchestra, Jelly Roll Morton and Louis Armstrong; the literary achievements of Carl Sandburg, Sherwood Anderson, Theodore Dreiser, and Edna Ferber; the newly opened Field Museum of Natural History; and The Art Institute of Chicago, whose Italian Renaissance facade was already blackened and stained from nearly three decades on Michigan Avenue. Some sources attributed the city's wealth and progress to "prairie energy." Frank Lloyd Wright, himself endowed with it, remarked, "The real American spirit . . . lies in the West and Middle West, where breadth of view, independent thought, and a tendency to take common sense into the realm of art, as in life, are more characteristic."[1] Of such a spirit the Winterbothams were made.

Joseph Humphrey Winterbotham (fig. 1) was born in Columbus, Ohio, in 1852. He settled in Joliet, Illinois; married Genevieve Baldwin of New Haven, Connecticut; and raised four children. The Winterbotham family moved to Chicago in 1892, where Joseph Winterbotham became engaged in various successful business enterprises. During the course of his life, he organized no fewer than eleven corporations, including cooperage manufacture, moving and transfer, and mortgage financing. A practical-minded man, he sent his sons, John and Joseph, Jr., to Yale, and his daughters, Rue and Genevieve, to Europe. After his wife died in 1906, he lived in an apartment in the Virginia Hotel, a building at the intersection of Ohio and Rush Streets that was considered one of the first and finest of "modern," luxury apartment dwellings. Europe, with its rich cultural texture, seems to have cap-

tured his fancy, and he enjoyed frequent travel there, sending back photographs of himself stepping into Venetian gondolas and browsing in Parisian quarters. By all accounts, he was intelligent and witty, without pomposity or pretension. He remained close to his family, brought his sons into his businesses, encouraged his daughter Rue in her passionate involvement with the arts, and regularly invited his grandchildren for Sunday breakfast at the Virginia Hotel.

Rue Winterbotham (figs. 2–3) inherited the independence and energy of her father and undoubtedly helped shape his taste in and commitment to art. She was an accomplished linguist and talented interior decorator. With her husband, musician and composer John Alden Carpenter, she spent a great deal of time in Europe, becoming acquainted with the avant-garde artists, dancers, and composers of the early twentieth century.

Since the Chicago of the World War I era had few art galleries and the Art Institute's collection at that time was largely dependent on the taste of its benefactors, who preferred earlier artistic expressions, Rue Winterbotham Carpenter took it upon herself to establish a Chicago outpost for contemporary art. In 1916, more than a decade before the opening of New York's Museum of Modern Art, she helped found the Arts Club of Chicago, which continues to this day to be a center for the exhibition and discussion of current artistic activity. Rue's father and brothers were among the club's first members. Two years later, she became its president, retaining the office until her death in 1931. She designed the interiors of the club's several locations and took on its mission of fostering and developing the highest standards of art. She organized first showings in Chicago of drawings by Pablo Picasso; sculpture by Auguste Rodin, Gaston Lachaise, and Constantin Brancusi; paintings by Georges Braque, Marie Laurencin, and American modernists Arthur B. Davies, John Marin, Morton L. Schamberg, Charles Sheeler,

and Joseph Stella. During her tenure, Rue Winterbotham Carpenter produced an astonishing list of one-man exhibitions by European artists Joan Miró, Georges Rouault, Jacques Villon, and Fernand Léger—all little known in America at the time. Broadening the scope of the club's activities, she also invited to perform there Sergei Prokofiev, Igor Stravinsky, Martha Graham, Harold Kreutzberg, and Leonid Massine, who made his debut as a soloist for an Arts Club audience.

It was in this atmosphere of artistic profusion and excitement that, at the age of seventy, Joseph Winterbotham conceived a plan in 1921 for assisting the Art Institute—one of the youngest of America's great art museums—in building its permanent collection of European paintings. Previously, in 1890, the museum had purchased a group of Old Masters from the Prince Demidoff Collection, sold that year in Paris, which comprised works by Rembrandt van Rijn, Jacob van Ruisdael, Meindert Hobbema, and Adriaen van Ostade. El Greco's masterpiece *The Assumption of the Virgin* had been bought in 1906, and a Gustave Courbet landscape and Henri Fantin-Latour's famous *Portrait of Edouard Manet* had been acquired, as had the Henry Field Collection of Barbizon pictures by such mid-nineteenth-century French artists as Camille Corot, Jules Breton, and Jean François Millet. Following European precedents, an entire gallery was devoted to plaster-cast copies of Classical, medieval, and Renaissance sculptures and architectural fragments, giving midwestern visitors a concept of the roots of Western European art. However, despite the 1913 exhibition of the revolutionary "Armory Show," there were few examples in the Art Institute of works produced by the contemporary art movements that had been underway on the Continent since the turn of the century. Although the great French Impressionist and Post-Impressionist paintings, for which the Art Institute has become renowned, had been regularly exhibited, they had not yet been con-

tributed to the museum by Chicago collectors Bertha Honoré Palmer, Frederic Clay Bartlett, and Mr. and Mrs. Martin A. Ryerson, who gave them in subsequent years—1922, 1926, and 1933, respectively. The only works of twentieth-century art by 1921 that were among the museum's holdings were portraits and landscapes primarily by American artists in the previous century's academic tradition.

Joseph Winterbotham did not offer the Art Institute works of art from his own collection—no evidence exists that he even collected art—but, rather, he offered the museum the opportunity to buy paintings that it wanted and needed to broaden the scope of its holdings. His initial 1921 gift was $50,000, which he stated was to be invested, with the interest to be used "for the purchase of works of art painted by European artists of foreign subjects."[2] He designated that the collection of paintings purchased with these funds should eventually number thirty-five, and that no more than $2,500 should be expended on any one. However, once a collection of thirty-five was accumulated, any picture could be replaced by one of better quality, for a sum greater than $5,000. By making this later stipulation, Winterbotham made clear his intention to insure that "the purchase of paintings, as time goes on, is toward superior works of art and of greater merit and continuous improvement."[3] A letter to Winterbotham from Art Institute president Charles L. Hutchinson reveals the warm reception to his unique and farsighted offer: "The terms of your splendid gift to the Art Institute have been announced to the Board of Trustees, and I am writing to tell you that the gift has been accepted with great enthusiasm. . . . There can be no doubt that your gift, which makes possible building up of this much needed section of our collection, will have far-reaching value in the development of the museum toward a more adequate and well-balanced representation."[4]

The original terms of the deed of gift gave the respon-

FIGURE 3. Constantin Brancusi (French, born Romania, 1876–1957). *Portrait of Rue Carpenter,* 1926. Black chalk on paper; 64.5 x 45 cm. The Art Institute of Chicago, Gift of Mrs. Patrick Hill in memory of her mother, Rue Winterbotham Carpenter (1981.302). Rue Carpenter played a key role in bringing an exhibition of Brancusi's work, the largest until that time, to the Arts Club of Chicago in 1927.

sibility for the selection and purchase of paintings to the trustees or their appointed representatives. The early commitment to buying European art of modernist persuasion was more the result of the individuals upon whom these responsibilities devolved than of a formal indication by Winterbotham. A new director and curator, Robert B. Harshe, was an amateur painter and believed in a strong museum emphasis on European modern art; and trustee Frederic Clay Bartlett, also a painter, traveled widely and, with his wife Helen Birch Bartlett, was forming an extraordinary collection of avant-garde art, which included examples by Pablo Picasso, Henri Matisse, André Derain, Amedeo Modigliani, and late work by Paul Cézanne, Vincent van Gogh, Paul Gauguin, and Henri de Toulouse-Lautrec, as well as Georges Seurat's monumental *A Sunday on La Grande Jatte—1884*.[5] Robert Harshe and Frederic Bartlett, along with Charles Hutchinson and Martin Ryerson, eagerly began buying for what would be called the Joseph Winterbotham Collection.

They lost no time in making their first purchase, a Matisse canvas painted in Nice in 1919 entitled *Woman Standing at the Window* (fig. 4), which not only represented that artist for the first time in the Art Institute, but was among the first works by Matisse in an American museum. Early in 1922, they purchased two works by contemporary German and Austrian artists Max Clarenbach and Julius Paul Junghanns, whose paintings had been shown at the 1914 Carnegie Institute International Exhibition. Although these two paintings and others acquired during the early years of the collection's formation did not pass the test of time and were subsequently replaced by finer pictures, it was the special feature of the Winterbotham gift to take such risks. It must have lessened the burden felt by the early executors to know that their purchases were not necessarily irrevocable. They could pick from the current art of the day and bring to

the Midwest examples of the most recent European artistic activity. If, in time, their choices proved to be of lesser interest, other pictures of greater significance to the museum's overall collections could take their places. Thus, implicit requirements for constant reevaluation and gradual growth—in quality rather than quantity— were integral parts of the Winterbotham Plan. To provide a complete picture of the collection's changing composition, a chronological list of all of the paintings acquired for it is included at the end of this issue (see "Checklist of the Joseph Winterbotham Collection, 1921–1994," pp. 182-88).

Impatient to see the collection grow, on three occasions Joseph Winterbotham, hearing of impending visits to Europe by Art Institute trustees, sent checks to buy paintings. For one check, given in 1922, he specified that the painting to be purchased "be of superior excellence, of a beautiful landscape."[6] This charge was dispatched with the acquisition of the Art Institute's first painting by Gauguin, a lyrical landscape of 1892 entitled *The Burao Tree (Te Burao)* (p. 131). In 1923, the Arts Club, which administered a gallery in the museum between 1922 and 1927, mounted an exhibition of paintings by

Jean Louis Forain, from which the Art Institute purchased Forain's *Sentenced for Life* (p. 141), one of the artist's characteristically insightful works of social commentary. During the next few years, a painting by Leo Putz, an Austrian colorist living in Munich, and another by Gauguin, the ravishing 1890 *Portrait of a Woman in front of a Still Life by Cézanne* (p. 129), were added to the collection, bringing the number of works to seven. Shortly before he died in 1925, Winterbotham experienced the great satisfaction of seeing Toulouse-Lautrec's arresting and unconventional composition of 1887–88, *Equestrienne (At the Circus Fernando)* (p. 125), added as the collection's eighth picture. Earlier that year, the canvas had been shown in Chicago's first exhibition of paintings by that artist, also organized under the aegis of the Arts Club.

After their father's death, Rue Carpenter and John Winterbotham augmented the principle of his gift to $70,000. Six more paintings were acquired in 1929. Five of them were purchased in Europe by Frederic Clay Bartlett, who wrote back to the director that he had wrangled with the dealers to reduce their prices in order to meet Winterbotham's original $2,500 per-painting terms. "I think we must try very hard to change the terms of the gift, otherwise as things are going, we could never get together a collection worthy of Mr. Winterbotham's aim," he lamented.[7] Nevertheless, he returned to Chicago with a still life by Georges Braque (p. 155) and four

other works by artists he thought quite promising: Jean Lurçat, Charles Dufresne, Jean Marchand, and an Australian-born Frenchman named Edouard Goerg, whose work he liked so much that he bought one of his paintings for himself. The final acquisition of the year, André Dunoyer de Segonzac's *Summer Garden (The Hat with the Scottish Ribbon)* of 1926, had been initially purchased by Rue Carpenter and then was bought by the museum for the Winterbotham Collection, bringing the number of works to a total of fifteen at the close of the decade. Of these, five—two by Gauguin and one each by Forain, Toulouse-Lautrec, and Braque—have been of such enduring significance and value that they are still part of the collection and mark an extraordinary period of vitality and experimentation, both by European artists and by the Art Institute.

In 1935, Joseph Winterbotham, Jr. (fig. 5) suggested that the composition of the Winterbotham Committee be changed to include the active participation of a family member, along with the museum director and a trustee. Highly qualified to represent the family, this younger son of the original benefactor had assembled his own worthy collection of European and Asian art. In fact, the Arts Club opened its new quarters in the Wrigley Building in 1936 with an exhibition of paintings and drawings from his collection. At the time the younger Winterbotham assumed a position on the Winterbotham Committee, he also proposed an amendment to the 1921 deed of gift that formalized an emphasis on contemporary art, stating: "No picture is to be purchased for the Winterbotham Collection executed by an artist who has been dead over ten years—only foreign, contemporary, living artists' work to be purchased."[8]

During the 1930s, because of the worsening political situation in Europe, trips there became less frequent. Chaim Soutine's 1929 canvas *Small Town Square, Vence* was bought in Paris in 1931, but, soon after, the

FIGURE 4. Henri Matisse (French, 1869–1954). *Woman Standing at the Window,* 1919. Oil on canvas. Private collection. This painting, which is no longer in the Art Institute's collection, was the first work purchased for the Winterbotham Collection. Acquired in 1921, it was the first work by Matisse in the Art Institute's collection and one of the first works by the artist in an American museum.

FIGURE 5. Joseph Winterbotham, Jr., late 1940s. A discerning collector of European and Asian art, this younger son of Joseph Humphrey Winterbotham (fig. 1) had a prominent role in acquiring twentieth-century works for the Winterbotham Collection. Photo courtesy of the Winterbotham family.

Winterbotham Committee began to look to the New York galleries, which were representing more and more European artists, many of whose work had been banned by the Nazis. Soon after it was constituted, the new committee bought pictures by Raoul Dufy, Derain, Karl Hofer, Matisse (p. 135), Modigliani (p. 151), another by Soutine (p. 161), and a third version of Marc Chagall's *The Praying Jew* (p. 149), painted in 1923 and exhibited at New York's Museum of Modern Art in 1932. Joseph Winterbotham, Jr., donated the collection's first Surrealist example, a mysterious canvas by Salvador Dali entitled *Shades of Night Descending,* which was later traded for Dali's *Inventions of the Monsters* of 1937 (p. 169). With the help of the committee, Daniel Catton Rich, the director of the Art Institute from 1938 to 1958, engineered a number of remarkable purchases for the collection: Giorgio de Chirico's haunting early canvas *The Philosopher's Conquest* of 1914 (p. 147); Oskar Kokoschka's color-saturated 1919 landscape *Elbe River near Dresden,* which had been confiscated in Austria, but was smuggled out of the country to a New York art dealer; and Picasso's Cubist *Fernande Olivier* of 1909 (p. 139), formerly among Gertrude Stein's famed collection of early twentieth-century art. The committee decided to loosen the restriction on purchases of only European art after several exhibitions in the United States of the exciting work of Mexican muralists and painters José Clemente Orozco, Rufino Tamayo, and Diego Rivera. During the 1940s, paintings by each of these artists were acquired, with Rivera's *Mother Mexico* of 1935 coming as a gift from Joseph Winterbotham, Jr. In deference to the collection's original conception, these pictures were replaced many years later by works of European artists. In 1946, with the purchase of Yves Tanguy's Surrealist landscape *The Rapidity of Sleep* (p. 177), painted the previous year, the Joseph Winterbotham Collection finally achieved its designated goal of thirty-five paintings.

The complete Joseph Winterbotham Collection was shown as a group for the first time in 1947 (see fig. 6) in a special month-long exhibition. An illustrated catalogue, written by Katharine Kuh, who would shortly become the Art Institute's first Curator of Modern Painting and Sculpture, was published in conjunction with the exhibition. One of Joseph Winterbotham's original stipulations had specified that, once the collection was complete, a room should be equipped for its permanent installation. In 1945, his son modified this directive to require only an annual showing of the group.[9] During the rest of the year, each painting was placed where the museum deemed it could be shown to best advantage, among other works of its type or period. Every year, for many years, the collection was mounted together at regular intervals. On one occasion in 1949, a selection of twenty-four paintings was requested by the Dallas Museum of Fine Arts for exhibition at the Texas State Fair, under the title "The Joseph Winterbotham Collection of Twentieth-Century European Paintings." The paintings have never again traveled together as a group, in part because they are integrated prominently within the museum's collection of late nineteenth- and twentieth-century art, and their absence would be keenly felt.

The time had now arrived when, according to the deed of gift, exchanges and replacements in the collection could be made with the objective of improvement. As mentioned earlier, the elder Winterbotham foresaw the necessity of providing more money for this purpose and required that each replacement cost no less than $5,000. An astute businessman, he seems to have anticipated the upward spiral of the art market. The first opportunity to make an exchange came in 1949, when Joseph Winterbotham, Jr., offered to sell to the Art Institute, for a modest sum, one of the centerpieces of his own collection, El Greco's *The Feast in the House of Simon* (c. 1610–14). In making this generous offer,

Winterbotham rescinded his earlier amendment requiring the purchase of only contemporary art and proposed a return to his father's broader stipulation.[10] Thus began an era of major contributions to the collection by the Winterbotham family, replacing pictures of lesser quality purchased in the 1920s and 1930s. Fernand Léger's *The Railway Crossing* (Preliminary Version) of 1919 (p. 157), originally purchased by Rue Carpenter, was given in her memory by her daughter Mrs. Patrick Hill in 1953. Also, in 1953, the Art Institute acquired van Gogh's *The Drinkers (after Daumier)* of 1890 (p. 127) from Winterbotham, Jr., and accepted his gift of Cézanne's *Apples on a Table-cloth* (c. 1886–90); when he died at age seventy-six, in 1954, he bequeathed the major portion of his private collection of European and Asian art to the Art Institute. A total of eight works were eventually added to the Winterbotham Collection.

Rue Winterbotham Shaw (fig. 7), granddaughter of the elder Joseph Winterbotham, had assumed the mantle of her aunt Rue Carpenter as president of the Arts Club in 1940, and she was the natural heir to her uncle's position on the Winterbotham Committee. In both realms, she provided firm and perspicacious leadership. She had studied painting with Walt Kuhn in New York and with Nathalie Gontcharova in Paris. After settling in Chicago with her husband Alfred Phillips Shaw, a prominent architect, she followed in the art activist footsteps of her predecessors. For thirty-nine years (1940–79), as president of the Arts Club, she directed a program of exhibitions, lectures, and concerts that assured and maintained the club's international reputation. A tireless defender of the

avant-garde, she brought to Chicago its first exhibitions of works by Max Ernst, Hans Hofmann, Jacques Lipchitz, Wifredo Lam, Arthur B. Davies, Jackson Pollock, Isamu Noguchi, Robert Motherwell—only a few in a lengthy list of adventurous shows. She counted among her close friends many great artists, composers, and authors in both the United States and Europe, including Marianne Moore, Virgil Thompson, and Alexander Calder. One of Calder's finest stabiles, commissioned by her in the early 1940s, still can be seen in the Arts Club foyer. When the club moved to its present day location in 1951, members could boast of an interior designed by Ludwig Mies van der Rohe, for Rue Shaw had persuaded the great architect of the International Style, who was teaching in Chicago at the Illinois Institute of Technology, to donate his services. The club's modernist elegance reflected the taste, gentility, and integrity that Rue Shaw brought to her work, earning her a reputation as the most esteemed and influential member of the Chicago art community.

At the time Rue Shaw began to represent the family on the Art Institute's Winterbotham Committee, the collection was taking a direction quite different from one that emphasized contemporary European art. Along with other committee members—Daniel Catton Rich, trustee Leigh Block, and Katharine Kuh—Mrs. Shaw believed that the collection would be enhanced by adding to it some of the predominantly nineteenth-century paintings included in her uncle's bequest. The first group of additions consisted of Cézanne's *House on the River* (1885/90; p. 121), van Gogh's masterful *Self-Portrait* (c. 1886/87; p. 123), Odilon Redon's luminous *Sita* (c. 1893; p. 133), and a canvas thought to be by Gauguin called *Of Human Misery*. Four other pictures from Joseph Winterbotham, Jr.'s bequest were brought into the collection several years later; these included an undated pastel by Matisse called *Dancer in Red;* Edgar

FIGURE 6. Left to right: Mrs. Joseph Winterbotham, Jr., Mrs. Rue Winterbotham Shaw, Miss Rue Diana Hill, and Joseph Winterbotham, Jr., at the first exhibition of the Winterbotham Collection at the Art Institute, 1947.

Degas's *Portrait after a Costume Ball (Portrait of Mme Dietz-Monin)* of 1877/79 (p. 115); a landscape by a student of Gustave Courbet named Marcel Ordinaire, which was thought to be by the master; and a portrait by Edouard Manet entitled *Young Woman* (c. 1879). The composition of the Winterbotham Collection thus began to appear as one featuring key artists and styles in the history of modern art. To further develop this new direction, Katharine Kuh was able to find and propose the purchase of three important paintings by early twentieth-century pioneers: Oscar Kokoschka's 1908 *Commerce Counselor Ebenstein* (p. 137); Joan Miró's 1918 *Portrait of Juanita Obrador* (p. 153); and Robert Delaunay's 1911 *Champs de Mars: The Red Tower* (p. 143). A. James Speyer, who succeeded Kuh as Curator of Twentieth-Century Painting and Sculpture and as a Winterbotham Committee member in 1961, continued to look for paintings that would highlight the major accomplishments of twentieth-century art. In the ensuing years, Speyer suggested the purchase of Ben Nicholson's *November, 1956 (Pistoia)* of 1956; Balthus's *Solitaire* of 1943 (p. 175); Dubuffet's *Genuflection of the Bishop* of 1963 (p. 179); and, in 1970, René Magritte's *Time Transfixed* of 1938 (p. 171). In 1973, the committee added a painting by Claude Monet, *Etretat: The Beach and the Falaise d'Amont* of 1885 (p. 119), that had been given earlier to the Art Institute by Rue Shaw's mother, Mrs. John H. Winterbotham.

For fourteen years the composition of the collection remained the same. Since 1987, however, the Winterbotham Committee has made a series of purchases and changes that have added eight new paintings to the collection. Patrick Shaw, the son of Rue Shaw, joined the committee in 1979 as the representative of the Winterbotham family; the other current committee members are James N. Wood, director and president of the Art Institute, and

Stanley M. Freehling, who succeeded James W. Alsdorf as chairman of the museum's Committee on Twentieth-Century Painting and Sculpture in 1990. This committee has greatly enhanced the Surrealist component of the collection, adding Yves Tanguy's untitled screen of 1928 (p. 167), one of the masterpieces of this artist's career, as well Max Ernst's *The Blue Forest* of 1925 (p. 159) and Paul Delvaux's *The Awakening of the Forest* of 1939 (p. 173). The committee acquired Lyonel Feininger's 1911 *Carnival in Arcueil* (p. 145) after the rediscovery of a group of important paintings from this artist's early career. Two other paintings purchased during this time by the committee—Max Beckmann's *Reclining Nude* of 1927 (p. 163) and Gerhard Richter's *Christa and Wolfi* of 1964 (p. 181)—add considerably to the Art Institute's holdings in twentieth-century German art. Finally, the addition of two earlier paintings—Gustave Courbet's 1862 *Reverie (Portrait of Gabrielle Bourreau)* (p. 113) and Arnold Böcklin's 1883 *In the Sea* (p. 117)—can be seen, in part, as reflecting the committee's continuing desire to represent nineteenth-century art in the collection.

In the nearly seventy-five years of its existence, the Joseph Winterbotham Collection has taken on various forms, each attempting to fulfill the objective of its creator to give the Art Institute a group of European paintings of the highest quality. So astute were many of the early choices that fourteen of the original group of thirty-five paintings remain in the collection.[11] Guided by the capable hands and unfailing generosity of succeeding generations of the Winterbotham family, the Joseph

Winterbotham Collection now contains some of the signal works in the museum's permanent holdings of nineteenth- and twentieth-century art. Yet, according to the terms of this farsighted gift, the current composition of the collection is not immutable. It will continue to be reassessed on a regular basis and, undoubtedly, opportunities will arise to make advantageous exchanges. There seems to be little question that the collection's future will be just as it was envisioned by its founder; and because of that vision, visitors to the Art Institute will continue to enjoy outstanding examples of European art.

Notes

1. Quoted in Emmett Dedmon, *Fabulous Chicago* (New York, 1953).

2. Joseph Winterbotham Deed of Gift to The Art Institute of Chicago, Apr. 9, 1921, The Art Institute of Chicago Archives (hereafter referred to as AIC Archives).

3. Ibid.

4. Charles L. Hutchinson to Joseph Winterbotham, Apr. 18, 1921, AIC Archives.

5. For a discussion of Frederic Clay Bartlett and the Helen Birch Bartlett Memorial Collection, which was given to the Art Institute in 1926, see *The Art Institute of Chicago Museum Studies* 12, 2 (1986), which is devoted entirely to this collection.

6. Joseph Winterbotham to Charles L. Hutchinson, June 8, 1922, AIC Archives.

7. Frederic Clay Bartlett to Robert B. Harshe, June 5, 1929, AIC Archives.

8. Joseph Winterbotham, Jr., modification to Deed of Gift, Nov. 25, 1935, AIC Archives.

9. Joseph Winterbotham, Jr., to Chauncey McCormick, Mar. 17, 1945, AIC Archives.

10. Joseph Winterbotham, Jr., to Chauncey McCormick, Sept. 27, 1949, AIC Archives. El Greco's *The Feast in the House of Simon* was later moved from the Winterbotham Collection into the general collection of the Art Institute.

11. The fourteen paintings from the original group of thirty-five that remain in the Winterbotham Collection are: Forain's *Sentenced for Life*, Gauguin's *The Burao Tree (Te Burao)* and *Portrait of a Woman in front of a Still Life by Cézanne*, Toulouse-Lautrec's *Equestrienne (In the Circus Fernando)*, Braque's *Still Life*, Dufy's *Open Window, Nice*, Soutine's *Dead Fowl*, Matisse's *The Geranium*, Chagall's *The Praying Jew*, Modigliani's *Madame Pompadour*, de Chirico's *The Philosopher's Conquest*, Picasso's *Fernande Olivier*, Dali's *Inventions of the Monsters*, and Tanguy's *The Rapidity of Sleep*. Seven additional paintings from the original group remain in the Art Institute's permanent collection: Albert Besnard's *By the Lake*, Edouard Georg's *The Epicure*, Karl Hofer's *Girls Throwing Flowers*, José Clemente Orozco's *Zapata*, Rufino Tamayo's *Woman with Bird Cage*, El Greco's *The Feast in the House of Simon*, and Marcel Ordinaire's *Landscape*.

The Joseph Winterbotham Collection

MARGHERITA ANDREOTTI

Associate Editor

The Art Institute of Chicago

MARC CHAGALL. *The Praying Jew,* 1923 copy of a 1914 work (pp. 148-49).

GUSTAVE COURBET (French, 1819–1877)

Reverie (Portrait of Gabrielle Borreau), 1862

Oil on paper mounted on canvas; 63.5 x 77 cm

Signed and dated, lower left: *G. Courbet /.62.*

Joseph Winterbotham Collection, 1987.259

Gustave Courbet is known primarily as an uncompromising Realist who loudly proclaimed his independence from the past and scorned the idealizing tendencies of both Classicism and Romanticism. As this lushly painted portrait reveals, Courbet was far from the purist that he claimed to be. His style here is clearly indebted to the Spanish and Venetian artists whom he had studied as a youth in the galleries of the Louvre. He was also not above conferring to this portrait a distinctly Romantic aura through the figure's pose and setting, and through the use of a vaguely allegorical title. Courbet's vaunted Realism is most evident in the vivid portrayal of the girl's idiosyncratic features—the flaring eyebrows; the large, almond-shaped eyes; the strong nose; the thin lips, animated by a hint of a smile; and the pointed chin.

The portrait's sitter was the fourteen-year-old daughter of Laure Borreau, a woman who was apparently Courbet's lover. The artist painted at least four portraits of the girl's mother. Until fairly recently this was thought to be another portrait of the latter, both because of the close family resemblance between mother and daughter and because the girl was made to look considerably older than her actual age through the artist's dramatization of her pose and setting.

Courbet's vigorous painting technique is especially obvious here in the landscape and in the figure's dress. The paint is forcefully and heavily applied, often with a palette knife, as in the background, or with loose, confident brushstrokes, as in the area of the dress. The most sensitively painted areas are those of the girl's face, neck, arm, and hand, which present a smoother, more nuanced technique for rendering the warmth and softness of her flesh. A romantic mood, perhaps inspired by the girl's budding womanhood, is established by the dark foliage on the left, the glowing reds and pinks of a sunset on the right, and a glistening expanse of water beneath it. The girl's dark brown hair falls freely over her shoulders.

Pensively, she inclines her head and rests it on her hand. A delicate pearl pendant in the shape of a cross hangs from a gold chain around her neck. A black lace shawl and the black accents of her dress give her an almost Spanish air. In this warm portrayal, Courbet showed a taste for rich, resonant color, dramatic contrasts of light and dark, and a technique possessing all the self-assurance and flair that characterized his own personality.

EDGAR DEGAS (French, 1834–1917)

Portrait after a Costume Ball (Portrait of Mme Dietz-Monnin), 1877/79

Distemper, with metallic paint and pastel,
on canvas; 85.5 x 75 cm

Signed, lower left: *Degas*

Joseph Winterbotham Collection, 1954.325

In discussing this painting, art historians have often focused on the relationship between Edgar Degas and his subject, Adèle Dietz-Monnin, wife of a prominent French businessman and politician. It is clear from a letter to Mme. Dietz-Monnin, which Degas probably never sent, that difficulties arose between them in the course of painting the portrait. According to family tradition, she rejected the portrait because she thought it made her look drunk or like a prostitute. The portrait seems to have been originally intended as a form of payment for money lent to Degas by members of her family. Although areas of the portrait have a sketchy quality, Degas considered the painting sufficiently finished to sign it and submit it to the 1879 Impressionist Exhibition under the title *Portrait after a Costume Ball (Portrait après un bal costumé)*.

Whatever the precise nature of the disagreement between the artist and his subject—information about the circumstances surrounding the portrait remains insufficient to reach firm conclusions—this painting in many respects exemplifies the kind of subject drawn from modern life that inspired so many of Degas's best works. As is typical of him, the sitter is shown in an unguarded moment. There is a spontaneous, utterly unposed quality to her expression and posture that belies the many studies (several survive) and sittings that undoubtedly preceded it, as well as the carefully calculated decision to show the woman at this particular moment of the evening's event and in "costume" rather than street clothes. With great originality, Degas chose to focus on the complex moment of transition from a highly public event, the costume ball, back to private life. Without embellishment and sentimentality, he captured the tired expression on the woman's face, the exhaustion underlying the perfunctory smile and listless wave of the hand, the relaxation of her public persona as her shoulders slump and her whole body sinks wearily into a chair at the end of a long evening. Lights and shapes bounce off the mirror behind her and appear as indistinct patches of color at right and left, suggesting the blurred effect of the surroundings on the sitter's tired senses.

In accordance with his taste for technical innovation and experimentation, Degas used several media in this portrait, as well as a highly varied and improvisational kind of brushwork. He tailored his medium and technique not only to the impromptu nature of his subject, but also to rendering a great range of textures—the reflective surface of the mirror; the gold of the mirror's frame and of the chairs at left; the satiny sheen, dominated by icy pinks and greens, of the woman's dress and bonnet; and the fur of the brown boa as it snakes its way down her dress.

ARNOLD BÖCKLIN (Swiss, 1827–1901)

In the Sea (Im Meere), 1883

Oil on panel; 86.5 x 115 cm

Signed on the harp: *AB*

Joseph Winterbotham Collection, 1990.443

Although Arnold Böcklin's work was widely admired in the 1880s and 1890s, his reputation waned rapidly after his death with the ascendancy of Impressionism and the French-centered conception of the development of modern art. Today's more comprehensive and complex understanding of European art of the nineteenth and twentieth centuries has led to a new appreciation for his work. Böcklin is now recognized as an important contributor to an international Symbolist movement (he lived alternately in his native Switzerland, Germany, and Italy), and he is also acknowledged for influencing a large number of artists, many of whom are now counted among the pioneers of modern art, such as Edvard Munch, Vasily Kandinsky, Paul Klee, and Giorgio de Chirico (see p. 147). De Chirico was especially impressed by the type of painting for which Böcklin became best known—eerily mysterious landscapes punctuated by an occasional lone figure, such as *Villa by the Sea* (which exists in numerous versions dating from the 1860s through the early 1880s) and *Island of the Dead,* his single most famous painting (which likewise exists in several versions dating from 1880 onward). The haunting silence of these pictures can be clearly felt in de Chirico's own enigmatic works.

In the Sea belongs to a type of painting that, at least superficially, has little in common with the work just described. In pictures such as this, Böcklin featured groups of mythological figures, from centaurs to mermaids, depicting them with a lusty energy and earthy realism clearly at odds with the idealizing tendencies of nineteenth-century academic art (compare, for example, Adolphe William Bouguereau's *Bathers* of 1884 in the collection of the Art Institute). The mermaids of *In the Sea* are plump and fleshy; the tritons border on the grotesque, the one at center sporting a bulging belly, the two at right featuring large, protruding ears. Rather than the idealized inhabitants of a rarefied, classical world, these uninhibited figures seem almost coarse. The faces of the mermaids and the large harp-playing triton at center are distorted by loud singing or shouting. At far right, the heads of two other tritons emerge from the water, eager to join in the fun.

Although thematically and compositionally very different from the desolate landscapes exemplified by Böcklin's *Island of the Dead,* these mythological pictures are, upon close inspection, no less disquieting. The more we look, the more uneasy we become about certain details, which seem to throw into question the nature of this boisterous scene. We are struck, for instance, by the equivocal expression of the triton at center, as he looks upward toward the mermaid who is thrusting herself upon him with wild, predatory abandon. Is the triton merely startled or does his expression bespeak anxiety, even fear? Are the sirens benignly playful, or is there something frenzied in their actions and expressions, reminiscent of their reputation in Greek mythology for luring sailors to their death with their singing? We are likewise reminded of the dire fate of the lyre-playing Orpheus, torn to pieces by wild bacchantes. The composition's icy colors, dominated by shades of green and purplish red against a turbulent sky and glassy sea, further contribute to the vaguely ominous mood. The picture thus takes on a distinctly Dionysian character, suggesting the intoxicating and potentially destructive force of unbridled nature and evoking an amoral world in which there is no boundary between play and aggression.

CLAUDE MONET (French, 1840–1926)

Etretat: The Beach and the Falaise d'Amont, 1885

Oil on canvas; 69.3 x 66.1 cm

Signed, lower right: *Claude Monet*

Gift of Mrs. John H. (Anne R.) Winterbotham

in memory of John H. Winterbotham;

Joseph Winterbotham Collection, 1964.204

By the time this picture was painted, the Impressionists had begun to rethink the style that had marked the heyday of their movement in the 1870s. While Camille Pissarro would come under the influence of Georges Seurat's theories and Pierre Auguste Renoir changed his style to include monumental figures, Claude Monet focused with ever increasing tenacity on his original goal of painting "directly from nature, striving to render my impression in the face of the most fugitive effects." In an effort to achieve an accurate impression rather than a composite effect, Monet had by then adopted a method of working simultaneously on a number of canvases depicting the same subject. He changed canvases every time the light changed substantially and returned to a particular canvas on subsequent days when he thought the effect of light corresponded to that work. The writer Guy de Maupassant observed Monet working in this way at Etretat in 1885 and published his recollections the following year:

I often followed Claude Monet about in his search for impressions. He was no longer a painter, actually; he was a hunter. He walked along, trailed by children carrying canvases, five or six canvases representing the same subject at various hours of the day and with varying effects. He would pick them up or drop them one by one according to how the sky changed. And face to face with his subject he would sit and wait, watching the sky and shadows, gathering up a falling ray or passing cloud in several dabs of the brush and . . . setting it down on his canvas with great alacrity. I once saw him catch a sparkling shaft of light on a white cliff and fix it to a rush of yellows that gave an eerily precise rendering of the blinding ineffable effect of its radiance.

This painting seems indeed to have been achieved through such a process. The artist focused here on one of his favorite subjects, the white cliffs near the town of Etretat on the coast of Normandy, where Monet vacationed frequently between 1883 and 1886. Monet viewed this scene from a distant vantage point that enabled him to encompass a vast expanse of beach, water, and sky, as well as the cliffs. These rise with rugged majesty from a curving span of beach dotted with boats and brightly colored sails. The water's surface is broken by the orange sail of a solitary boat, the horizon line animated by a bank of scudding clouds. The scene is drenched in what appears to be the early afternoon sun, since the shadows cast by the cliffs are short, indicating that the sun is overhead. Monet's brushstrokes are bold, quick, and confident, the surface of the painting often showing heavily impastoed areas, as he records the scene before him rapidly, in a constant race against time and its inevitable effects on conditions of light and atmosphere. Pinks and blues predominate, richly modulated with touches of yellow, green, purple, and white. This is in many respects a quintessential Impressionist picture, with all the freshness, vividness, and pleasure we have come to associate with that style of painting.

PAUL CÉZANNE (French, 1839–1906)

House on the River, 1885/90

Oil on canvas; 51.5 x 61 cm

Bequest of Joseph Winterbotham, 1954.304

One of Paul Cézanne's major contributions was a heightened awareness that, for the artist, painting involves a personal struggle to find pictorial equivalents for what he or she wishes to represent, whether it is the natural world that so obsessed Cézanne or any of the many other subjects, both real and imaginary, that have occupied modern artists. Passionately engaged in this struggle, Cézanne developed a method of painting that became legendary. He constructed his pictures purposefully and doggedly, shuttling between the canvas and "the motif" (as Cézanne referred to his subject), making endless adjustments to the painted surface to bring it in line with what his mind and eye perceived in the scene before him. An unfinished picture such as *House on the River* is thus of special interest, not only because it has the appealing freshness of a drawing or watercolor, but also because it opens a door to the mysteries of the artist's celebrated method, giving us valuable insights into the stages of the pictorial process leading up to his finished canvases.

Especially evident here is Cézanne's habit of working on most areas of the canvas at the same time, with the exception of the edges, which he sometimes left unfinished even in a canvas he considered final. This picture also shows very clearly the building up of the surface through patches of color rhythmically applied in a manner that was much imitated by his admirers. A closer inspection reveals, however, that this characteristic application of paint encompassed a wide variety of brushstrokes. Quivering outlines delineate the tree trunks and branches. Wide, patchy strokes establish the broad masses of foliage, while blocks of color define the openings in the house and their reflections on the water's surface. The color scheme is also modulated with great subtlety, as it progresses from the cool, shaded areas of the water and river bank, dominated by dark greens and browns, to the lighter, airier, partially sunlit areas of the foliage and house, treated in pale shades of blue or silvery green.

Structurally, the composition is largely determined by the parallel bands of water and riverbank. As is typical of Cézanne, their boundaries avoid the strict geometry of a rigidly parallel alignment: as the band of water widens toward the right, the riverbank narrows, following a gentle slope. Countering this horizontal emphasis are the verticals of the trees, which echo each other in their forked growth and taper upward, dissolving into the unpainted areas of the canvas. Although unfinished, there is a balance to the entire composition that reflects Cézanne's constant concern with the internal dynamics of a picture, with maintaining at every stage of a picture's development a condition of internal harmony between its different parts. This is one of the many ways in which Cézanne made visible one of modern art's major tenets, that a work of art is not a servile reflection of the outside world, but an independent entity with its own laws, its own inner reality.

VINCENT VAN GOGH (Dutch, 1853–1890)

Self-Portrait, 1886/87

Oil on artist's board mounted on
cradled panel; 41 x 32.5 cm
Joseph Winterbotham Collection, 1954.326

This small but mesmerizing painting is one of about two dozen self-portraits that Vincent van Gogh painted after his arrival in Paris in the spring of 1886. It reflects the influence of the paintings he saw in Paris by the Impressionists and Post-Impressionists. In contrast to the long, sinewy brushstrokes that characterize his late works such as *The Drinkers (after Daumier)* (p. 127), van Gogh here employed short, brisk strokes and dabs of pure color, a kind of modified Divisionism clearly inspired by the work of Georges Seurat, whose masterpiece, *A Sunday on La Grande Jatte—1884* (1884–86; Helen Birch Bartlett Memorial Collection, The Art Institute of Chicago), was on view that year at the Salon des Indépendants, Paris. But unlike Seurat's painting, which has lost some of its original brilliance because of the artist's use of unstable pigments, this portrait seems to have preserved all the freshness of the day it was painted. The bright palette contrasts markedly with the sober expression on the artist's face—the intense, direct gaze; the heavy, worried eyebrows; the downward turn of the mouth—which suggests both the penetrating seriousness with which van Gogh viewed the world and the fiercely passionate temperament that often exasperated those who knew him.

Van Gogh was thirty-three when he painted this self-portrait. Driven by a generous and idealistic nature, he had embarked on a long succession of failed occupations, from art dealer to teacher to lay preacher in the Belgian coal-mining district, turning finally to art as a full-time pursuit in 1880. Van Gogh's mental illness and tragic end have often monopolized viewers' attention, making it difficult to "see" his work clearly. But as this remarkably vivid portrait attests, van Gogh was first and foremost an exceptionally gifted artist who could work to brilliant effect even within the confines and self-imposed discipline of a style not entirely his own.

HENRI DE TOULOUSE-LAUTREC (French, 1864–1901)

Equestrienne (At the Circus Fernando), 1887–88

Oil on canvas; 100.3 x 161.3 cm

Signed, lower left: *T-Lautrec*

Joseph Winterbotham Collection, 1925.523

This painting, which was widely admired at the time of its creation by artists such as Georges Seurat, has remained one of Henri de Toulouse-Lautrec's uncontested masterpieces. Although Toulouse-Lautrec was only twenty-four when he painted it, he already possessed a dazzling talent as a draftsman and a keen eye for boldly simplified forms, qualities that were to reach their most distilled form in the famous posters of his later years.

Thinly and rapidly painted, this picture has the confident, improvisational quality of a drawing. Its subject is the Circus Fernando, one of the first permanent circuses in Paris, which provided rich inspiration to many artists, both before and after Toulouse-Lautrec portrayed it. Here the artist has concentrated not on rich color harmonies and a seductive subject (as in Pierre Auguste Renoir's *Two Little Circus Girls* of 1878–79, inspired by the same circus, which is now in the Potter Palmer Collection of The Art Institute of Chicago), but on an incisive recording of movement and form, and on the often unflattering but revealing physical idiosyncrasies of his subjects. From Edgar Degas, Toulouse-Lautrec inherited a connoisseur's eye for gesture and expression, as well as a taste for unconventionally cropped compositions. Especially striking in this painting is the unorthodox cropping of the clowns and the heads of several of the spectators. Toulouse-Lautrec drew inspiration for the flat, linear simplification of forms against a solid ground, as in the figure of the ringmaster at left, from Japanese prints, whose influence was by then ubiquitous among the Impressionists.

The right half of the painting is dominated by the dramatically foreshortened form of a horse, his powerful rump prominently and irreverently presented to the viewer. The horse's tail billows in a manner that wittily echoes the flapping tails of the ringmaster's jacket. The equestrienne perches on the horse's saddle, readying herself for an acrobatic jump through the hoop held by the clown who is partly visible at top. The arch of the circus ring is echoed in the impetuous curve of the ringmaster's body, as he advances forcefully toward the horse and rider, and in the curve of his whip, which visually links the two main protagonists of the scene. Throughout, the artist shows himself a keen observer of his human subjects, attuned to their every quirk. The pointed portrayal of the figures often verges on caricature, as in the almost brutish determination on the face of the ringmaster, the forced, brightly painted smile of the horsewoman, and the jagged silhouette of the clown at left.

VINCENT VAN GOGH (Dutch, 1853–1890)

The Drinkers (after Daumier), 1890

Oil on canvas; 59.4 x 73.4 cm

Joseph Winterbotham Collection, 1953.178

This haunting painting dates to the last year of Vincent van Gogh's life—he was to die of a self-inflicted gunshot wound on July 29, 1890. In May of the previous year, the artist had voluntarily committed himself to the Asylum of Saint-Paul in Saint-Rémy, a small town near Arles. He stayed in the asylum for a full year, suffering intermittent seizures and working between bouts of illness. According to van Gogh's letters to his brother Theo, the artist based this picture on a print after a drawing by Honoré Daumier (fig. 1) while he was in the asylum in late January or early February 1890. In a letter of February 10, 1890, van Gogh reported to Theo that he found making the copy "very difficult." Certainly, it must have been a considerable challenge to render the black-and-white print in the very different medium of oil painting.

The subject of Daumier's composition may have also aroused some ambivalence in van Gogh. On the one hand, it focused on the life of humble people going about their daily activities, a subject that had engaged him from his earliest days as a painter. Van Gogh's devotion to the poorest members of society had been expressed, even before the decision to become a painter, in his stint as a lay preacher in the Belgian coal-mining district. And van Gogh's first great painting, *The Potato Eaters* of 1885, had focused on a group of peasants, lovingly portrayed in all their earthy coarseness, partaking of a simple meal. The figures in this painting—gnarled and weathered in the case of the three men, almost grotesquely chubby in the case of the child—are imbued with a certain crude vigor that is indeed reminiscent of the deliberate "roughness" with which van Gogh rendered his peasant subjects in earlier works.

On the other hand, Daumier's fig-

ures are not peasants; they are laborers in Paris's industrial suburbs. From a letter to Theo of June 1889, it is clear that van Gogh, although an admirer of Daumier's "drawing," did not consider Daumier's subjects to be as "serene and pure" as the beloved peasants of his own earlier work, whose poverty was redeemed by constant contact with nature. It is perhaps for this reason that van Gogh somewhat softened in his own rendering the dire expression of the man on the left. There is real pathos in the way van Gogh depicted these four ungainly figures, spanning the ages of man—from childhood, through maturity, to old age—and real desperation in the avidity and concentration with which they drink, as if to quench a spiritual as well as physical thirst.

By adding the landscape to Daumier's original composition, van Gogh introduced an opposition between industrialized suburb and countryside, between the corrupting forces of civilization and the restorative powers of nature. To the far left are belching factory chimneys; to the far right, barely visible, because of the pale colors used—pale pinks, blues, and greens—is a flowering orchard or garden, symbol of the natural world that is so clearly absent from the withered lives of these people.

FIGURE 1.

Charles Murand (French, active 1860–1881), after drawing by Honoré Daumier (French, 1808–1879). *The Drinkers*, 1862. Wood engraving. New York, The Metropolitan Museum of Art, Harris Brisbane Dick Fund, 1928.

PAUL GAUGUIN (French, 1848–1903)

Portrait of a Woman in front of a Still Life by Cézanne, 1890

Oil on canvas; 65.3 x 54.9 cm

Signed and dated, lower right: *P. Go. / 90/*

Joseph Winterbotham Collection, 1925.753

Paul Gauguin's life rivals that of Vincent van Gogh as the stuff of legend. In 1883, he left his job as a stockbroker and, eventually, his wife and five children to take up a nomadic, often impoverished, existence as a full-time painter. His "escape" from civilization included increasingly prolonged stays in such exotic places as Martinique, Tahiti, and finally the Marquesas Islands, where he died in 1903. While still a stockbroker, Gauguin had assembled a pioneering collection of Impressionist paintings, among them five or six canvases by Paul Cézanne. His favorite was apparently the still life partly visible in this picture, known as *Fruit Bowl, Glass, and Apple* of 1879/80.

In this densely composed painting, Gauguin pays tribute to Cézanne not only by including one of his works in the background but also by emulating Cézanne's manner throughout the picture. In many areas of the portrait, especially the dress and hand, Gauguin adopts the rhythmic, parallel, patchy brushstrokes typical of the older artist. Cézanne's influence also seems apparent in the laborious, tightly woven construction of the composition, in which the woman's head seems almost embedded in the still life. An X-ray examination of this painting has revealed that Gauguin did indeed labor over many of its details, from the position of the woman in the chair—she was originally seated further back—to the relationship of her hands, which were at one point clasped in her lap, somewhat in the manner of existing portraits by Cézanne of his wife.

Gauguin's own personality is most evident here in the emphasis on rich harmonies of closely related colors (the picture is dominated by blue and its derivatives, purple and violet) and on the fluid outlines of the forms of the chair and woman's dress. This self-conscious orchestration of colors and forms became even more evident in Gauguin's later works, in accordance with his belief that lines and colors, in a manner closely akin to music, carry intrinsic expressive qualities, independent of naturalistic objectives. Gauguin was also one of the first to turn to a wide variety of non-Western sources for inspiration in his effort to imbue painting with renewed mystery and to forge alternatives to naturalism. Some of the flatness and linear emphasis in this portrait reflects Gauguin's interest in Japanese prints. Ironically, it is because of this quality that Cézanne once disparagingly referred to Gauguin's works as "Chinese images."

The identity of the sitter of this portrait has long been debated and still remains uncertain. The picture was once thought to have been completed in Brittany, but it has since been suggested that it may instead have been painted after Gauguin's return to Paris in November of 1890 during his stay with Emile Schuffenecker, a close friend and supporter. This hypothesis finds support in the characteristics of the woman portrayed. With her elongated, refined hands and cinched waist, she seems more like a city dweller than one of the earthy peasant women found in Gauguin's Breton canvases.

PAUL GAUGUIN (French, 1848–1903)

The Burao Tree (Te Burao), 1892

Oil on canvas; 68 x 90.7 cm

Titled, signed, and dated, lower right:

TE Burao P. Gauguin 92

Joseph Winterbotham Collection, 1923.308

This picture was painted in Tahiti where Paul Gauguin had moved in 1891, impelled by a desire to escape the stifling effects of civilization and by the attractions of a simple, inexpensive way of life. The influence of Paul Cézanne, so evident in the earlier *Portrait of a Woman in front of a Still Life by Cézanne* (p. 129), is still apparent here in the use of rhythmic, parallel brushstrokes for certain areas of the foliage. But far more dominant is an emphasis on the undulating, linear patterns formed by the branches piled up in the foreground, and on the silhouettes of certain forms, such as the tree trunk looming at the left edge of the picture and the solitary dog on the right.

The mood of this picture is somber. The sky is cloudy, the water is slate gray. From the dense shadows of the foliage in the background emerge a hut and a robed figure at far right. The foreground presents an intricate barrier of dead branches, tree trunks, and seaweed. A lone dog wanders through the debris, possibly sniffing for prey. The picture's mood foreshadows the more explicit mystery of later works such as *Day of the Gods (Mahana no Atua)* of 1894 (now in the Helen Birch Bartlett Memorial Collection of The Art Institute of Chicago), in which the silhouetting and patterning of forms increasingly takes on a life of its own, in accordance with Gauguin's passionately held belief that lines and colors are in themselves expressive.

A comparison with Claude Monet's landscape *Etretat: The Beach and the Falaise d'Aumont* of 1885 (p. 119), which is of a superficially similar subject—a beach scene—is particularly instructive, revealing Gauguin's dramatic departure from the Impressionism that had first formed him. Besides the obvious differences in topography between the two scenes, there is a radical difference in approach. While Monet focused on the drama of light as it bathed vast expanses of sky, land, and sea, Gauguin was concerned with suggesting a state of mind and feeling. Monet joyously reveled in the natural spectacle before him, straining to convey with exquisite subtleness the atmospheric nuances of the scene. Gauguin instead filtered his subject through his own brooding temperament and indeed believed that a concern with precisely rendered naturalistic effects robbed the world of its essential mystery, its capacity to resonate with meaning.

ODILON REDON (French, 1840–1916)

Sita, c. 1893

Pastel over charcoals on paper; 53.6 x 37.7 cm

Signed, lower left: *ODILON REDON*

Joseph Winterbotham Collection, 1954.320

Odilon Redon's gift for poetically evocative images and his exceptional eye for color are superbly illustrated in this work. Associated in his own lifetime with a group of artists, poets, and writers known as Symbolists (he was a particularly close friend of the poet Stéphane Mallarmé), Redon occupies a major place in the history of modern art, not only for the intrinsic beauty of his works, but also and perhaps most importantly for the daring quality of his imagination. Well before the Surrealists, Redon focused on his inner world, on the fantastic, sometimes frightening, and always mysterious creatures of his imagination, to evoke a realm of dreams, distant memories, and indefinable emotions. As illustrated by this pastel, Redon drew inspiration from a wide range of sources, reflecting the fascination of many of his contemporaries with exotic and occult forms of spirituality.

Until recently, this work bore the generic title *Evocation*. Based on Redon's own records, we now know that this pastel was originally entitled *Sita*, after the loyal and noble wife of Rama, hero of the Indian epic *The Ramayana*. According to this ancient text, Rama faced and ultimately prevailed over numerous misfortunes, among them the abduction of his wife by Ravana, the demonic ruler of Lanka. As she was transported through the sky, Sita tore off and threw down to earth jewels and other pieces of her attire to give Rama clues to her location. This pastel can be interpreted as a very free rendering of this story. While clearly inspired by this exotic tale, the artist alludes to its details only in the vaguest terms, as in the sparkling objects that indeed appear to be falling from Sita's image, in shimmering bursts of color, at lower right. Redon's own brief description, given in the record he kept of his works, emphasizes the image's composition and striking color scheme: "Her head in profile, surrounded by a golden-green radiance, against a blue sky, stardust falling, a shower of gold, a sort of undersea mountain below."

Sita's profile dominates the composition, hovering on a feathery pink cloud and surrounded by a luminous green halo in a manner that recalls Christian conventions for representing saints. Sita's exemplary life does in fact suggest saintly associations and perhaps inspired Redon to adapt a Christian tradition to his representation of her. Her profile is delicate, firm, and somber, with an androgynous quality that heightens the appealing mystery of her face and that has sometimes led writers, unaware of the pastel's original title, to identify the figure as male. Her gaze is steadfast, almost trancelike, and seems focused on the oval form hovering in the night sky. This may allude to the golden egg or embryo that embodied the essence of life and the source of cosmic light in the ancient Hindu text known as the Veda. Sita's skin is a richly toned brown and on her head she wears a bejeweled diadem, whose most distinctive feature is a decorative element echoing a nautilus shell in its spiraling shape. The mood is one of wonder tinged with melancholy before the beauty of this visionary landscape, which seems to evoke both the spectacle of a star-studded sky and, as suggested by Redon's own description, the silence and depth of an undersea world. As we gaze at this image, we are increasingly drawn under the spell of its luminous colors, its velvety textures, and the figure's unfathomable, almost sphinxlike expression, which seems to hint at a world of spiritual awareness and knowledge barely accessible to us.

HENRI MATISSE (French, 1869–1954)

The Geranium (Le Géranium), summer 1906

Oil on canvas; 101.3 x 82.6 cm

Signed, lower left: *Henri Matisse*

Joseph Winterbotham Collection, 1932.1342

When Henri Matisse painted this picture, he was the central figure of a group of artists labeled Fauves (wild beasts) because of their seemingly violent way of painting. During the first decade of this century, these artists (including André Derain, Georges Braque, and Maurice de Vlaminck) produced some of the most influential and advanced painting in Europe. They used color with an unprecedented freedom and freshness, with what appeared at the time as a reckless disregard for its descriptive function, applying the paint with a vigor and impulsiveness that far surpassed that of their Impressionist and Post-Impressionist predecessors. *The Geranium* illustrates especially well the highly experimental nature of this period in Matisse's career by touching upon his struggles at the time not only with issues of color, but also with facture, structure, and the human figure, and his intermittent ventures into an entirely different medium, sculpture.

Matisse organized the different elements of the picture around the geranium plant. The stick that supports its arching stem establishes a strong vertical axis around which the rest of the composition revolves—the explosion of leafy greenery that occupies the upper half of the painting and the constellation of objects on the table arranged in a circle around the plant. Matisse employed here many of the same colors (pink, green, orange, blue) used to dazzling effect in such quintessentially Fauvist paintings as his *Open Window* of the previous year (Collection of Mr. and Mrs. John Hay Whitney, New York), but somewhat tempered and muted by a thinner application of paint and a greater use of black contours and dark areas. The brushwork is unusually varied in density, length, and direction, exhibiting a nervous intensity that differs markedly from the broad, confident strokes that characterize some of Matisse's earlier Fauvist paintings. The four reddish, round forms, arranged in a row in the foreground, are apparently pink onions. Behind the pot and to the right is a Biskra jug (Biskra is a town in Algeria), a souvenir of Matisse's travels to North Africa earlier that year, which hints at the richly patterned props favored in so many of the artist's paintings from then on. Finally, two of the statuettes Matisse modeled at this time are depicted to the left and right of the geranium, reminding us of Matisse's intense interest in the human figure, which he portrayed in such large decorative works as *The Joy of Life* (The Barnes Foundation, Merion, Pennsylvania) completed earlier in the same year. The sculpture on the right is *Woman Leaning on Her Hands* of 1905, a 1907 cast of which is in the collection of the Art Institute (fig. 1), while the one on the left can be identified as Matisse's *Thorn Extractor* of 1906.

FIGURE 1.

Henri Matisse. *Woman Leaning on Her Hands,* 1907 cast of 1905 work. Bronze (from edition of ten); 15.2 x 27.9 x 17.1 cm. The Art Institute of Chicago, through prior acquisitions of the George F. Harding Collection, 1992.654.

OSKAR KOKOSCHKA (British [born Austria], 1886–1980)

Commerce Counselor Ebenstein, 1908

Oil on canvas; 101.8 x 81.1 cm

Signed, lower right: *O K*

Joseph Winterbotham Collection, 1956.364

Despite its early date (Oskar Kokoschka described it as his second finished painting), this portrait already reveals the artist's great gifts as a portraitist and the hallmarks of his highly personal form of Expressionism. Like Max Beckmann (see p. 163) and Chaim Soutine (see p. 161), Kokoschka used calculated distortions of line and color in a highly individual manner to give emotional force to his paintings. As a student in Vienna, he was influenced not only by the German Expressionist artists of *Die Brücke* (The Bridge), but also by Gustav Klimt and by Jugendstijl art, as shown by the sensitive, nervous line and the touch of melancholy that came to characterize his work.

Kokoschka met his sitter through the avant-garde architect Adolf Loos, who introduced him to Vienna's high society and thus provided him with subjects for a penetrating series of portraits. As tailor to the Austrian imperial court, Ernst Ebenstein was one of the most accomplished and admired members in the world of Viennese high fashion. During a visit to the Art Institute in 1958, Kokoschka remembered him as kind and generous. Ebenstein had offered to make the artist some clothes and had taught him a great deal about anatomy based on his sartorial experience as a perceptive observer of the human body. Kokoschka's affection for his sitter seems to be reflected in the compassionate yet unflinching honesty with which he recorded the signs of age on his face and hands. The sitter has been caught in a moment of relaxed introspection, his gaze averted from the viewer, his social persona momentarily laid aside to reveal his inner self. Even the sitter's impeccable black attire has a crumpled, weathered quality that bespeaks human vulnerability and frailty. As in other portraits by Kokoschka, the hands constitute a psychological focus as strong as that of the face. The artist's expressive distortions are especially evident here. Painted in a vivid orange, these gnarled and bony hands seem to express the man's very essence and become the locus of his professional and psychological identity.

PABLO PICASSO (Spanish, 1881–1973)

Fernande Olivier, summer 1909

Oil on canvas; 60. 6 x 51.3 cm

Joseph Winterbotham Collection, 1940.5

This painting dates to one of the most productive and inventive periods of Pablo Picasso's career, a summer stay in the town of Horta de Ebro (now Horta de San Juan) in Spain, which lasted, with minor interruptions, from May to September of 1909. During these months, Picasso produced a series of landscapes, heads, and still lifes that are among the most highly acclaimed achievements of early Cubism. Fernande Olivier, Picasso's mistress, was the model for the series of heads that the artist produced at this time.

In this painting, the contrast between the naturalistic still life in the background and the boldly faceted figure in the foreground illustrates an important stage in Picasso's evolution at the time. A series of still lifes by Picasso that were inspired by the art of Paul Cézanne preceded Picasso's powerful probing into the nature of solid form, which is exemplified here by the treatment of the head. By vigorously modeling the form in a manner that blatantly disregards the rules of illusionistic painting, Picasso conveyed information about the subject's underlying structure, about its development in the round (Olivier's bun, for example, which would normally not be visible from the front, is brought into full view), and a remarkably tactile sense of its projections and recessions. Not surprisingly, these highly sculptural portraits led Picasso to turn, as he did intermittently throughout his career, to actual sculpture upon his return to Paris in the autumn of 1909. The result was the head of Fernande Olivier, an early bronze cast of which is in the Art Institute (fig. 1). In this sculpture, Picasso combined the faceting of the face seen in our painting with the scalloped treatment of the hair found in a drawing from this same period, which is also in the collection of the Art Institute (fig. 2). The artist then energized the head through a dynamic torsion of the neck, replacing the relaxed, fleshy folds in the painting with an emphasis on the taut curve of the back of the neck, as the head

bends and twists in space. Although Cubism was to exert an enormous influence on the move toward abstraction among many artists in the early part of this century, *Fernande Olivier* reminds us that Cubism itself was firmly rooted in an intense study of material reality.

This painting was once in the famed collection of expatriates Leo and Gertrude Stein in Paris, and can in fact be seen hanging on the wall of Gertrude Stein's study in a photograph of 1914/15.

FIGURE 1.
Pablo Picasso. *Head of Fernande Olivier,* autumn 1909. Bronze; h. 41.3 cm. The Art Institute of Chicago, Alfred Stieglitz Collection, 1949.584.

FIGURE 2.
Pablo Picasso, *Head of Fernande Olivier,* summer 1909, brush and ink and watercolor on paper; 33.3 x 25.5 cm. The Art Institute of Chicago, Alfred Stieglitz Collection, 1949.578.

JEAN LOUIS FORAIN (French, 1852–1931)

Sentenced for Life (A Perpétuité), c. 1910

Oil on canvas; 65.4 x 81 cm

Signed, lower right: *forain*

Joseph Winterbotham Collection, 1923.6

Jean Louis Forain is best known as a prodigious draftsman and graphic artist, who regularly contributed illustrations to the satirical papers in Paris from the 1870s on. He also produced a small but substantial body of paintings. Until 1900, these were closely related in style and subject matter to the art of the Impressionists, with whom Forain exhibited repeatedly between 1879 and 1886. After 1900, the artist's work changed considerably as a result of an intense renewal of his religious faith and an accompanying desire to imbue his work with greater seriousness. Forain abandoned the bright palette of the Impressionists in favor of a somber, dramatic style of painting, reflecting the influence of Rembrandt van Rijn, Francisco Goya, and Honoré Daumier. At the same time, he turned increasingly for his subjects to Biblical themes, as in his many versions of *The Prodigal Son,* and to courtroom scenes, which focus on the plight of ordinary people caught in the web of the French legal system.

In this fine painting, Forain deftly sketched the last scene in a trial, using a palette largely limited to black, brown, and a few strategically placed touches of white. At center, the defendant, who has just escaped the death penalty by being sentenced to life imprisonment, bends in a gesture of abject gratitude to kiss the hand of his lawyer. The lawyer, who is the focus of Forain's satire, is shown swelling with self-importance and pride, completely oblivious to the tragedy that has befallen his client and his family. Raising his head high with a smug, self-satisfied expression, he is juxtaposed to the figure on the far right, who, barely visible both to us and to the justice system, buries her head as she weeps into a handkerchief. Presumably a relative or perhaps even the wife of the condemned man, she stands for the many unsung victims of so-called justice. In contrast to the lawyer, the guard seems to show some sympathy for the condemned man, perhaps because he is also an ordinary man without the self-serving pretensions often associated with the administrators of justice. As the guard hovers above the accused, he extends his arm over his shoulders in a complex gesture that is both a reminder that the man must follow him soon to prison and an expression of comfort and human solidarity. In this incisive piece of social commentary, Forain revealed all the ironies and hollowness of a system that dispenses justice without compassion.

ROBERT DELAUNAY (French, 1885–1941)

Champs de Mars: The Red Tower, begun in 1911, reworked sometime before 1923

Oil on canvas; 160.7 x 128.6 cm

Signed and dated, lower right: *r. d. 1911*

Titled, dated, and signed on back: *Champs de Mars /*

LA Tour rouge / 1911 / r. delaunay / (époque destructive)

Joseph Winterbotham Collection, 1959.1

This is one of the most imposing of a series of about eleven paintings that Robert Delaunay devoted to the Eiffel Tower between 1909 and 1911. Erected for the 1889 World's Fair on the Champs de Mars, a military parade ground, the Eiffel Tower had become a widely recognized symbol of modernity. It was originally painted a brilliant red, a color that, together with its steel-girded construction and size (it was the tallest structure in the world, reaching a height of 984 feet), set it apart from the prevalent grayness of the surrounding city, as Delaunay emphasized so effectively in his painting. The imposing size of this canvas further enhances the visionary impact of the tower caught in a blaze of light as shafts of sunlight emanate from it in all directions and yellow sun disks dance around its top. Like an apparition, the tower rises above the surrounding houses, metaphorically shaking the very foundations of the old order.

Unlike his Cubist colleagues, who limited themselves to muted colors and a restricted range of traditional subjects (mostly still lifes, landscapes, and portraits), Delaunay combined a Cubist treatment of form with an interest in color theory and a fascination with contemporary subjects. In this painting, Delaunay brilliantly adapted the Cubist vocabulary of faceted and fragmented forms to render the transparent and seemingly weightless structure of the tower, as well as to evoke the extraordinary sense of excitement many experienced at the dawn of a great, new age of technological marvels. Delaunay's painting conveys this feeling of boundless optimism, the innocence and freshness of a time that had not yet witnessed the two world wars and the destructive potential of this same technology.

A 1912 exhibition photograph of this painting shows that Delaunay elaborated it at a later date.

LYONEL FEININGER (American, 1871–1956)

Carnival in Arcueil, 1911

Oil on canvas; 104.8 x 95.9 cm

Signed and dated, upper left: *Feininger / 1911*

Joseph Winterbotham Collection, 1990.119

This is one of a group of recently rediscovered early masterpieces by Lyonel Feininger that had been left behind when the artist and his family were forced to leave Nazi Germany in 1937 for the United States. For over forty years, this group of roughly fifty pictures remained unknown and inaccessible in the East German home of the friend in whose custody Feininger had left them. Only after a prolonged legal battle were all but three of the pictures finally returned to the artist's heirs in 1984 and exhibited as a group in 1985.

This picture reveals an artist of remarkable maturity and vision, despite the fact that Feininger had not turned seriously to painting until 1907. It was only then that improved financial circumstances allowed him to give up his successful career as a cartoonist. The setting for this painting is the town of Arcueil, south of Paris, where Feininger spent several months a year from 1906 to 1912. Its majestic viaduct became a frequent subject in the artist's drawings starting as early as 1908. His intense interest in architecture, which was to remain constant in Feininger's work, is apparent here not only in the use of the viaduct but also in the brilliantly colored block of houses in the middle ground. It may have been reinforced at this time by his interest in Robert Delaunay's work (see p. 143), in which architectural subjects likewise plays a primary role.

Feininger's early admiration for Vincent van Gogh (see pp. 123 and 127) seems evident in the heavily impastoed surface and in the use of highly saturated colors, especially yellow, which in the row of houses is beautifully modulated by touches of pink, green, and orange. Also reminiscent of van Gogh are the animated, billowing contours of the houses' rooftops, which in turn echo the sweeping movement of

the clouds. Against this dramatic backdrop, Feininger deployed a motley crew of grotesque and vaguely sinister characters, some of whom recall Feininger's earlier cartoons (see fig. 1). With their vividly colored costumes, these figures create a striking counterpoint to the dominant yellow of the background. But the ultimate impression is one of dissonance between the grandeur and beauty of the town's architecture and the bombastic artificiality of its inhabitants.

FIGURE 1.
Cartoon characters by Lyonel Feininger reproduced in the *Chicago Sunday Tribune*, April 29, 1906.

GIORGIO DE CHIRICO (Italian, 1888–1978)

The Philosopher's Conquest (*La Conquête du philosophe*), 1914

Oil on canvas; 125.1 x 99.1 cm

Signed, lower right: *G. de Chirico*

Joseph Winterbotham Collection, 1939.405

Giorgio de Chirico created his greatest and most influential works during a span of a few years, from 1911 to 1917. This large painting is one of his masterpieces. He was one of the first artists to concentrate on evoking a psychic rather than material reality through incongruous juxtapositions of objects, thus foreshadowing the central goal and one of the principal techniques of Surrealism.

In this painting, de Chirico deployed a repertoire of images that he was to combine and recombine in many other paintings of the period: the vast, empty spaces, the mysterious archways, the long, eerie shadows, the train, clock, and factory chimneys. An aching melancholy pervades the scene. The warmth and bustle of human activity seem to have receded from this place. This is the stillness and silence of a Mediterranean city under the midday sun, but heightened and transformed. Only distant or menacing traces of human activity remain: the train and ship far in the background, dwarfed by the factory chimneys; the shadows of two unseen figures; the cannon jutting out of the left edge of the picture, with its two cannon balls awkwardly and provocatively stacked above it; and, in the immediate foreground, two huge artichokes, which, in their spikiness and size, discourage the viewer's approach, keeping the spell of the scene behind them unbroken.

The formal features of de Chirico's paintings, although generally overlooked in favor of the subject, are also significant. While the individual objects are rendered realistically, there is no bravura in de Chirico's approach. The forms are depicted in a flat, simplified, almost crude manner, and are either starkly silhouetted, as is the train and clock, or heavily outlined in black, with a self-conscious lack of sophistication (for example, every brick is outlined in the factory chimney in the left background). The perspective and surfaces are also often skewed and tipped in ways that have been attributed to the influence of Cubism. The artist's skill clearly does not reside in a traditional display of realistic painting, but rather in the strong structure of his compositions and in the telling choice of and relations among objects.

A related drawing (fig. 1), dated no earlier than fall 1913, shows many of the principal features of this painting. The main differences in the drawing are a palm tree in the background, to the far left, which has been replaced in the painting by the belching factory chimney, and a group of bananas in the foreground, where the artist later placed the two oversized artichokes. Interestingly, in his choice and treatment of the artichokes, de Chirico has preserved the emphasis on a profusion of pointed shapes found in the bananas, while heightening with his new choice the incongruity of the objects placed in the picture's foreground. De Chirico also later added the two cannon balls poised above the cannon. The drawing is entitled *Le vainqueur* (*The Conqueror*). The title that the picture bears today, *The Philosopher's Conquest*, suggests that the picture represents a triumph of the inner world, the painter's conquest of the human psyche.

FIGURE 1.
Giorgio de Chirico.
Le vainqueur (*The Conqueror*), 1913–14.
Crayon on cardboard;
13.7 x 10.5 cm. Inscribed
Le vainqueur. Paris,
Musée Picasso.

MARC CHAGALL (French [born Russia], 1887–1985)

The Praying Jew, 1923 copy of a 1914 work

Oil on canvas; 116.8 x 89.4 cm

Signed, lower right: *Marc / Chagall*

Joseph Winterbotham Collection, 1937.188

Together with *Birth* of 1911 and *White Crucifixion* of 1938, this painting forms the nucleus of The Art Institute of Chicago's outstanding group of works by Marc Chagall. This masterful portrait shows that Chagall, although best known for works of a lyrical exuberance and color as in the Art Institute's *Juggler* of 1943, could excel with a much more limited palette and invest his images with great dignity and power.

This painting is one of two copies the artist made in 1923 before parting with the original, which had been painted in 1914 during a visit to his home town of Vitebsk (in present-day Belarus). The original is now in a private collection in Switzerland and the other copy is in the Museo d'arte moderna in Venice.

As Chagall explained in his autobiography, the model for *The Praying Jew* was an old beggar whom the artist invited to sit for the painting, wearing his father's prayer clothes. These consist of a tallis—a fringed shawl with black bands—and phylacteries—two small square leather boxes containing passages from the scriptures, which were bound with leather straps to the head and left arm of Jewish men during prayer. Chagall used the white-and-black color scheme and geometric patterns characterizing this ritual garb as the basis for a dazzling composition of highly abstracted shapes bearing witness to his assimilation of early modernist movements (such as Cubism, Orphism, and Expressionism). What is remarkable is that the artist did so without sacrificing any of the portrait's emotional impact. The abstract shapes that swirl around the figure contribute to transforming this portrait into an icon or symbol for an entire world, the Jewish world of Chagall's youth. In painting this and other pictures of Jewish life, the artist was clearly motivated by a desire to preserve a tie to a past that was threatened for him both by the passage of time and by geographical distance (Chagall had intended to return to Paris after his 1914 visit to Vitebsk, but was detained in Russia until 1923 by the outbreak of World War I and events connected with the Russian Revolution). From the perspective of the late twentieth century, this image is all the more moving, since we know that this world and its people were to face a far greater threat than Chagall could have possibly imagined in 1914.

AMEDEO MODIGLIANI (Italian, 1884–1920)

Madame Pompadour, 1915

Oil on canvas; 61.1 x 50.2 cm

Signed, lower right: *modigliani*

Titled and dated, upper left: *Madam / Pompadour / 1915*

Joseph Winterbotham Collection, 1938.217

Born of Jewish parents in the Italian coastal town of Leghorn, Amedeo Modigliani settled in Paris in 1906, where he developed friendships with Pablo Picasso, the poet Max Jacob, the sculptor Constantin Brancusi, and other members of the literary and artistic avant-garde, many of whom appear in his portraits. He led a notoriously bohemian life, shortened by a self-destructive use of alcohol and drugs. Modigliani produced his finest paintings between 1914 and his premature death in 1920. Within a limited range of subjects, mainly portraits and nudes, he developed a highly distinctive style of sensitively elongated forms.

In this portrait, Modigliani's emphasis is on a strong formal structure dominated by the grid in the background and the echoing curves of the sitter's hat, shoulders, and features. There is none of the pathos often associated with his work. The artist seems instead to have invested this portrait with a note of ironic detachment, even humor, reflected in both the title of the painting (which refers to Madame de Pompadour, mistress of King Louis XV of France) and the expression of amused inscrutability worn by the sitter. Were painter and sitter perhaps both amused by the flamboyant hat? Modigliani's skill in rhyming forms, while at the same time keeping us visually interested and slightly off-balance, is evident throughout the picture, which resonates with the lessons of Paul Cézanne, Cubism, and African sculpture.

The sitter for this portrait may well have been Beatrice Hastings, an English poetess who was Modigliani's mistress at the time. Because of the artist's tendency to generalize his sitter's features, however, a comparison of this portrait with others of Hastings is inconclusive.

JOAN MIRÓ (Spanish, 1893–1983)
Portrait of Juanita Obrador, 1918

Oil on canvas; 69.5 x 62 cm

Signed, lower left: *Miró/1918*

Joseph Winterbotham Collection, 1957.78

This painting belongs to a group of fascinating and highly individual works by Joan Miró that document his early efforts to grapple with revolutionary developments in modern art (such as Fauvism and Cubism) and to forge his own direction. These efforts culminated in the early 1920s in the artist's breakthrough to a style of fantastic, simplified forms, freely and loosely scattered across the surface of his pictures with an exuberant abandon that is hard to imagine based on this tightly constructed portrait. And yet, something of this exuberance—of the vitality and poetic intensity of Miró's later works—seems indeed to underly this strangely powerful portrait, manifesting itself, for example, in the unrestrained rhythms of the dress, barely held in check by the diamond grid in the background, or in the lyrical note introduced by the small flower on the front of the dress.

Different and often contrasting impulses are brought here into uneasy balance through the sheer force of Miró's talent for creating compelling simplifications of the forms before him. The strong rhythms established by the dress, wallpaper, and face all vie for attention, as do the artist's various sources of inspiration: the influence of the Fauves and especially of Henri Matisse (see p. 135) in the bold use of color, dense application of paint, and flat patterning of the dress and background; the effect of Cubism in the far more sculptural, angular treatment of the face; and the impact of the Romanesque frescoes of Miró's native Catalonia (which the artist himself acknowledged as a major inspiration) in the linear rhythms of the dress, hair, and background, in the frontal pose, and in the large, staring eyes. This is a painting of dramatic contrasts, between the insistent flatness of the dress and background and the Cubist modeling of the face, between the startling pink of the wallpaper and the restrained black-and-white color scheme of the dress, between the human presence of the sitter and the strong linear patterns that threaten to engulf it. It does not seem surprising, given the impact this portrait still has today, that the young woman who initially agreed to sit for it became frightened both by Miró's intensity and his strange style of painting, forcing him to finish the portrait from memory.

GEORGES BRAQUE (French, 1882–1963)

Still Life, 1919

Oil on canvas; 50.2 x 92.2 cm

Signed, lower right: *G. Braque*

Joseph Winterbotham Collection, 1929.764

Together with Pablo Picasso (see p. 139), Georges Braque was responsible for developing the revolutionary approach to painting known as Cubism (c. 1907–14). Starting with their meeting in 1907, Picasso and Braque moved together through the successive phases of this radically new style: the early phase (c. 1907–09), which was strongly influenced by the study of African art and Cézanne; the so-called Analytical phase (c. 1910–12), in which the rhythm of the picture becomes dense and broken, at times making the subject almost unreadable; and the so-called Synthetic phase (c. 1912–14), which is marked by a loosening of the picture's structure, partly under the influence of collage, in favor of broader planes, brighter color, and more decorative effects.

In this painting, we see Braque emerging after World War I (he was seriously wounded in 1915 and did not resume painting until 1917) with a style clearly indebted to his earlier Cubist works, but tempered by a mood of quiet reflection. There is a fluidity and looseness in the way Braque applied traditional Cubist devices here that bespeaks an easy familiarity without the urgency and edge of the earlier experimental work. The artist handled this favorite Cubist subject here with a fuguelike sense of visual counterpoint that seems indeed to illustrate the analogy between painting and music so widespread in the early part of this century. The broad planes and patterned surfaces of Synthetic Cubism are evident in the treatment of the objects, which are defined by large, overlapping areas of color. The decorative pointillism used to distinguish certain planes and the simulated wood grain used for the guitar's neck recall the Cubists' earlier radical experiments with collage. Cubism's legacy is, however, best exemplified here by the startling liberty Braque took with the guitar's body, its customary curvature broken at left by a gaping, angular opening, which finds its primary justification not in resemblance to an outside model but in the painting's inner logic.

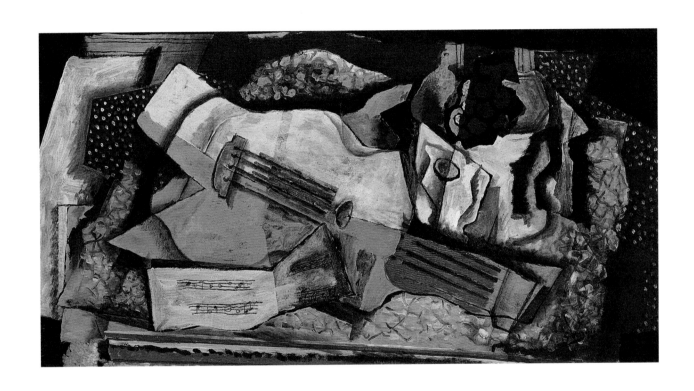

FERNAND LÉGER (French, 1881–1955)

The Railway Crossing (Preliminary Version), 1919

Oil on canvas; 54.1 x 65.7 cm

Signed and dated on back: *Le Passage à niveau, esquisse F. Léger/19*

Joseph Winterbotham Collection, gift of Mrs. Patrick Hill in memory of Rue Winterbotham Carpenter, 1953.341

Like Robert Delaunay's *Champs de Mars: The Red Tower* of 1911 (p. 143), Fernand Léger's *The Railway Crossing* (Preliminary Version) is a paean to modernity, its dynamism, energy, and movement. Unlike Delaunay's earlier work, however, this painting contains no specifically recognizable objects, except the directional sign with the arrow. Rather than a representation of a railroad crossing, Léger created a new kind of visual poetry from the fragments, colors, and shapes of his environment, evoking the rich sensations elicited by modern industrialized life. Tubular beams appear to intersect the surface, evoking both the pistons of a machine and the open, metal structures used in modern construction. Other forms, such as the circular, targetlike shape on the left, the stripes that proliferate throughout the painting, and most obviously the directional sign with the arrow, seem to have been inspired by the colorful, simplified geometry of road signs or the loud, attention-getting designs of billboards and posters. In this respect, Léger prefigured the later fascination of Pop artists with these elements of modern life.

The railroad crossing, a subject epitomizing the noisy mechanical world that Léger loved, had first been painted by the artist as early as 1912. In 1919, he resumed portraying this subject, making a number of drawings and oil sketches, including our own, in preparation for a much larger, finished painting (fig. 1). The Art Institute version already contains the major compositional elements found in the final work. There is, however, one dramatic difference: for the final painting, Léger decided to turn the entire composition upside down, in what amounts to a declaration of the painting's complete autonomy from representation.

FIGURE 1.
Fernand Léger. *The Railroad Crossing*, 1919. Oil on canvas; 97 x 130 cm. Collection of Raoul Laroche.

MAX ERNST (French [born Germany], 1891–1976)

The Blue Forest, 1925

Oil on canvas; 116.2 x 73 cm

Signed and dated, lower left: *max ernst/25*

Joseph Winterbotham Collection, 1988.221

Max Ernst was one of the most gifted artists associated with Surrealism, exhibiting a protean imagination that led him to produce work in an unusually wide range of styles and techniques. This painting belongs to a period, from 1925 to 1928, that was perhaps the most productive and creative of his long career. Most of the artist's extraordinarily rich work of these years depended, directly or indirectly, on a technique referred to as *frottage* (rubbing), which Ernst used to stimulate his imagination, encouraged in this by Surrealist theories about the processes of inspiration. This technique consisted in placing a piece of paper over a textured object or surface and then rubbing it with a pencil or other tool to obtain an image. Using this method as his point of departure, Ernst produced in 1925 a series of exceptionally beautiful drawings, thirty-four of which were published the following year under the title *Histoire naturelle* (*Natural History*). This painting shares with these drawings a stark and delicate beauty. Like many other works of this period, it was produced by adapting *frottage* to oil painting. The techniques used included scraping paint off the canvas, a procedure Ernst called *grattage* (scraping), or rubbing a cloth dipped in paint over the canvas, as it lay on a variety of textured surfaces from wood planks and wire mesh, as in this case, to string, chair caning, shells, and many other materials. As the title of Ernst's portfolio of drawings indicates, many of his works of these years allude to the natural world. The "Forest" series, exemplified by this painting, resumed a popular Romantic theme that continued to fascinate Surrealist artists (compare, for example, the work of Ernst's close friend Jean Arp) as a repository of mysterious, primeval forces.

Here the chance patterns produced by the wood grain of several wood planks have been transformed into a cluster of towering forms, outlined against a pale sky flecked with blue, yellow, and green. The forest's floor presents a honeycomb pattern seemingly produced by means of a wire mesh, a pattern that is echoed in the sky in scattered bursts of color. The spare simplicity of this image enhances its associative powers, as we are drawn into our own cosmic reverie about a primordial world, encompassing far more than the forest mentioned in the title. Ernst's works thus become, in his own words, a kind of "hypnotic language [that] takes us back to a lost paradise, to cosmic secrets, and teaches us to understand the language of the universe."

CHAIM SOUTINE (Lithuanian, 1893–1943)

Dead Fowl, c. 1926

Oil on canvas; 95.9 x 61.6 cm

Signed, lower left: *Soutine*

Joseph Winterbotham Collection, 1937.167

Like Marc Chagall (see p. 149), Chaim Soutine was a Russian Jew, who made his way to Paris in 1913 in pursuit of his passion for painting. In Paris he became friends with other Jewish artists, such as Chagall, Jacques Lipchitz, and especially Amedeo Modigliani (see p. 151), who painted several portraits of him. Like Modigliani and Chagall, he forged a personal idiom that did not fit neatly into a group movement, though it shows the influence of Vincent van Gogh (see pp. 123 and 127), the Fauves, and particularly Expressionism. The highly expressive work of earlier artists, such as El Greco and Rembrandt van Rijn, was also a major inspiration, as Soutine developed his feverishly intense vision of reality.

One of more than twenty pictures of dead birds painted by the artist in the mid-1920s, this powerful work demonstrates Soutine's talent at extracting the last ounce of tragic meaning from his otherwise ordinary subjects. In typical fashion, the painter has invested this still life with a frenzied vitality, which contrasts markedly with the lifeless condition of the bird. Rather than the limp surrender of death, Soutine seems to have been portraying the bird's writhing battle against death, its fierce resistance to its fate. This is reflected in the savage application of paint, in the flickering color, and in the highly unstable composition. The front of a table or chair emerges from the dark ground, but rather than supporting the dead bird, it is skewed at a dizzying angle, thus emphasizing the turbulent drama of the scene.

MAX BECKMANN (German, 1884–1950)

Reclining Nude, 1927

Oil on canvas; 83.4 x 119 cm

Joseph Winterbotham Collection, 1988.220

World War I was the decisive event in Max Beckmann's career. The slaughter and suffering that he witnessed at the front, where he served as a medical orderly, and his subsequent nervous breakdown drastically changed his outlook and, by extension, his work. Discharged from the army, Beckmann soon started to produce a series of shockingly new paintings reflecting what he described in a letter from the front as "life's unspeakable contradictions." Unflinching and brutally direct, works such as the barbaric *Night* of 1918–19 (Düsseldorf, Kunstsammlung Nordrhein-Westfalen), which depicts a band of thugs torturing a man and woman, set the tone for the rest of Beckmann's career. As shown by the sinister *Self-Portrait with Red Scarf* of 1917 (Staatsgalerie Stuttgart), and the many other self-portraits that were to follow (such as his *Self-Portrait* of 1937 in the collection of the Art Institute), Beckmann spared no one, not even himself, from his merciless scrutiny.

Within this context, it comes as no surprise that the theme of the nude is fairly rare in Beckmann's work, harking back as it does to a tradition that often treated the female body as an exercise in the representation of ideal beauty. Masterfully painted, this work shows Beckmann's vehement handling of pigment laid down in broad slabs of color and in dark, chiseling contours. Although the picture's theme is related to the countless reclining female nudes of art history, from Titian's *Venus of Urbino* (1538; Galleria degli Uffizi, Florence) to Francisco Goya's *Naked Maja* (c. 1798–1805; Museo del Prado, Madrid) to Edouard Manet's *Olympia* (1863; Musée du Louvre, Paris), Beckmann has injected it with something of the unsettling quality so pronounced in his more well-known works. This is the nude stripped of its idealizing veneer and depicted as the object of blatant and disquieting erotic impulses. The woman's body is shown through the distorting lens of the viewer's intense desire. The torso is unnaturally compressed and reduced to a pair of huge, bulging breasts. So dominant is this feature, in fact, that the woman's head seems overshadowed, no more than a perfunctory afterthought, and oddly discontinuous with the rest of the figure. From the abbreviated torso, the figure's limbs—the thighs and arms inordinately long—sprawl in different directions. Despite the lush handling of paint and the beautifully sketched still life on the lower right, there seems to be more than a hint of aggression in the unabashed emphasis on the woman's breasts and in the ostentatious splaying of the figure.

RAOUL DUFY (French, 1877–1953)

Open Window, Nice, 1928

Oil on canvas; 65.1 x 53.7 cm

Signed, lower right: *Raoul Dufy*

Joseph Winterbotham Collection, 1937.166

Raoul Dufy's work often draws comparison with
that of Henri Matisse, and the two artists indeed
had a number of things in common: they both worked
on the Riviera, a circumstance that led them at times to
treat very similar subjects (compare, for example,
Matisse's *Woman Standing at the Window* of 1919, formerly in the Winterbotham Collection [see p. 106, fig.
4]); they both went through a Fauvist phase and continued to give primacy to color in their subsequent work;
and they both traveled to North Africa and were seduced
by the lush, exotic patterns of that region. But in Dufy's
work, an extraordinary facility often masks the traces of
intellectual effort and intense experimentation so apparent in the art of Matisse (see p. 135). The mood in Dufy's
paintings is one of unalloyed pleasure, and so unwaver-
ingly is this mood sustained throughout his work that it
has been said that "Dufy never painted a sad picture."

At his best, as in this superb example, Dufy displayed an unrivaled decorative sense, juggling with con-
summate skill broad areas of bold, saturated color (blue,
red, green, yellow), a calligraphic line of great verve and
fluidity, and an assured if carefree appreciation for the
compositional liberties of modern painting. Dufy here
brilliantly transformed the common modernist motif of
the slanted, upturned tabletop (see, for example, Georges
Braque's *Still Life*, p. 155) into an abstract circular shape
that hovers magically at the joyous center of his composition. Its quiet, undisturbed surface contrasts markedly
with the richly patterned areas that surround it, while its
perfectly self-contained shape becomes a symbol for the
state of sensual fulfillment embodied in this picture.

YVES TANGUY (American [born France], 1900–1955)

Title Unknown, 1928

Oil on wood, hinged folding screen in eight panels,

each panel 200 x 59.7 cm

Signed, lower right: *YVES TANGUY 28*

Joseph Winterbotham Collection, 1988.434

In 1923, Yves Tanguy saw a painting by Giorgio de Chirico (see p. 147) in an art dealer's window and, like Max Ernst, René Magritte, and Paul Delvaux (see pp. 159, 171, and 173), was profoundly affected by his encounter with Metaphysical art. As a result, Tanguy resolved to make painting his life work and, despite his lack of formal artistic training, soon developed his own distinctive brand of Surrealist painting, which consists of vast, imaginary landscapes populated by oddly amorphous creatures.

Surprisingly, nothing is known of the circumstances surrounding the creation of this extraordinary and unique screen, which is certainly one of Tanguy's masterpieces. Given its size and ambition, this work was likely created for a specific patron. It shares many of the characteristics of Tanguy's other works of this period, but because of its almost environmental scale, the haunting grandeur of Tanguy's infinitely expanding vistas reaches here an unprecedented intensity.

As usual, Tanguy painted this work with great care and a profusion of subtle details, which reward close inspection and gently but inexorably draw us under the spell of his strange and marvelous world. For example, the horizon line, which appears almost flat in a reproduction, due to the enormous reduction in size, actually presents numerous hilly modulations. And the color scheme, although muted, reveals an infinite range of gradations, from white to gray to black or brown, punctuated by touches of vivid color—orange-red, blue, green. Similarly, the surface treatment is more varied than would initially appear—smooth and lush in the expanse of the sky, roughly textured through heavy scratching in the dark area below the horizon line. A number of bulbous creatures, uncertainly bridging the animate and the inanimate worlds, are scattered throughout the landscape and are sometimes paired in almost human ways (see the two forms in the lower right corner of the fourth panel from the left). Vaporous, cloudlike entities and plumed, linear structures are interspersed among them. This seems to be a lunar or undersea landscape, in which the pull of gravity is either absent or gentler than in our own world, since these creatures at times rest lightly on the ground, and at other times hover buoyantly above it. As we gaze into this aquariumlike world, Tanguy's forms tenuously join and separate as if engaged in a slow dance. This is a parallel universe, which seems to unveil the deepest secrets and mysteries of our own.

detail

SALVADOR DALI (Spanish, 1904–1989)

Inventions of the Monsters (Les Inventions des monstres), 1937

Oil on canvas; 125.1 x 99.1 cm

Signed and dated on back: *Salvador Dali 1937*

Joseph Winterbotham Collection, 1943.798

While Surrealists such as Giorgio de Chirico (see p. 147) and René Magritte (see p. 171) generally focused on unlocking the mystery of everyday objects, Salvador Dali populated his visionary landscapes with the often monstrous creatures of his imagination. Dali also favored dazzling displays of painterly skill, rather than the deadpan realism of de Chirico and Magritte, in giving his scenes a dramatic and hallucinatory intensity.

When this painting was acquired by the Art Institute in 1943, Dali sent the following telegram commenting on the circumstances of the work's creation and its symbolism:

Am pleased and honored by your acquisition. According to Nostradamus [sixteenth-century French physician and astrologer] the apparition of monsters presages the outbreak of war. This canvas was painted in the Semmering mountains near Vienna a few months before the Anschluss [the annexation of Austria by Nazi Germany in March 1938] and has a prophetic character. Horse women equal maternal river monsters. Flaming giraffe equals masculine apocalyptic monster. Cat angel equals divine heterosexual monster. Hourglass equals metaphysical monster. Gala [Dali's wife] and Dali equal sentimental monster. The little blue dog alone is not a true monster.

As Dali's comments suggest, there is an ominous mood to the painting. A hand mysteriously emerges from the lower left corner of the picture and points admonishingly to the scene before us. Here a sibylline figure gazes from black sockets at the butterfly and hourglass she holds in her hands, both of which may be interpreted as *memento mori*, reminders of death. Behind her emerge the heads of Gala and Dali, which are vividly caught in a happily shared moment, as they gaze with apparent amusement and fascination at the varied objects (a hand holding a ball, a long loaf of bread, and what seems to be a small portrait bust) on the long table before them. In the center of the picture, a kind of altar supports a female bust, her nakedness painted with the lush eroticism that so appealed to the Surrealists. The

woman's head merges with that of a horse, associating her with the horse-women shown bathing at left. What Dali refers to above as a "cat angel" leans against the altar, seemingly in conversation with the horse-woman. In what is now the empty right-hand corner of the picture, a dog was once visible (painted in a chemically unstable pigment, it has now faded almost completely). The populated areas of the picture in the foreground and middleground seemed to be threatened by some kind of conflagration in the far right corner, a danger epitomized by the "flaming giraffe." As Dali's comments make clear, the artist understood this to refer to the approaching threat of World War II.

A number of preparatory drawings exist for this painting. One of these is presently on loan to the Art Institute (fig. 1) and shows Dali working to define the painting's double-headed woman by combining a profile and frontal view. The deep, receding perspective found in the painting is already suggested here by the small figure and hill sketched in the far distance.

FIGURE 1.
Salvador Dali. *Formation of the Monsters (Formation des monstres)*, 1937. Black ink on pink paper; 23.8 x 15.9 cm. The Art Institute of Chicago, Lindy and Edwin Bergman Collection, 110.1991.

RENÉ MAGRITTE (Belgian, 1898–1967)

Time Transfixed (La Durée poignardée), 1938

Oil on canvas; 137 x 98.7 cm

Signed, lower right: *Magritte*

Titled, signed, and dated on back: "*LA DURÉE / POIGNARDÉE*" / *80P* / *MAGRITTE* / *1938*

Joseph Winterbotham Collection, 1970.426

René Magritte owed a direct debt to Giorgio de Chirico, whose work he first saw in 1922. This painting is one of Magritte's most compelling images. In it, the influence of de Chirico is apparent in a shared approach to the creation of mysterious and enigmatic images through incongruous juxtapositions of familiar objects; it is also evident in Magritte's adoption of some of de Chirico's motifs (the clock, the locomotive), as a comparison with de Chirico's *The Philosopher's Conquest* (p. 147) makes clear. Magritte has, however, given his own imprint to the ideas implicit in de Chirico's early paintings. His images are less complicated and more immediately comprehensible than de Chirico's. His brand of realism is more meticulous in both technique and composition. Magritte's emphasis on order is apparent in the uncluttered and precisely rendered surfaces, in the grid of moldings and frames that controls the composition, and in details such as the smoke of the locomotive, which tidily disappears under the mantelpiece. There is an engaging coarseness and naiveté to de Chirico's images that Magritte exchanged in this painting for clarity and immediacy. There is, nevertheless, nothing slavish about Magritte's realism, as illustrated by his deliberate omission, in his final composition, of the shadow of the candlestick on the right. A comparison of the painting with a preparatory sketch (fig. 1) shows this and other small but significant changes, such as the enlargement of both the clock's face and the locomotive. In typically compulsive fashion, these two circular forms are made to share the same diameter.

In a letter of 1959, Magritte commented at length on this painting, emphasizing that his goal was to unveil or evoke "the mystery" of things "that seem familiar to us [out of error or habit]." Having decided on a locomotive as his subject,

"the problem," he explained, was "how to paint this image so that it would evoke mystery." Magritte added, "The image of a locomotive is immediately familiar: its mystery is not perceived. In order for its mystery to be evoked, another *immediately* familiar image without mystery—the image of a dining room fireplace—was joined with the image of the locomotive." He also remarked that "the title *La durée poignardée* is itself an image (in words) joined to a painted image" and that *Time Transfixed* did not seem to him "a very accurate translation." Indeed, although the English title has the memorable quality that Magritte often sought, it is both more catchy and less forceful than the original French. It does not convey the sense of duration and passage through time in the word "durée" (duration) or the violent impact of something stabbed with a dagger in the word "poignardée" (stabbed).

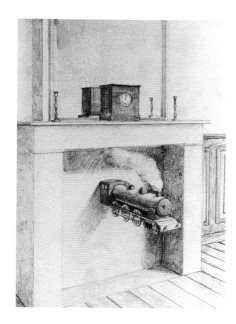

FIGURE 1.

René Magritte. Study for *Time Transfixed* of 1938. Pencil on paper; 30 x 25 cm. Private collection, Brussels.

PAUL DELVAUX (Belgian, 1897–1994)

The Awakening of the Forest (L'Eveil de la forêt), August 1939

Oil on canvas; 170.2 x 225.4 cm

Signed and dated on rock at lower right:

P. DELVAUX / 8–39

Joseph Winterbotham Collection, 1991.290

This is one of the most ambitious paintings that Paul Delvaux produced during the late 1930s, when, under the influence of Surrealism, he made a dramatic and lasting change in his work. Like so many of his Surrealist predecessors, he was particularly affected by the early paintings of Giorgio de Chirico (see p. 147), whom Delvaux dubbed "the poet of emptiness" and whose work he admired for giving pictorial form to "a poetry of silence and absence." In de Chirico's work and in that of Salvador Dali (see p. 169) and René Magritte (see p. 171), Delvaux discovered new possibilities for giving visual form to his complex inner world, a world populated with childhood memories and dominated by the obsessive recurrence of the same mysterious female type.

In *The Awakening of the Forest,* it is the artist's childhood passion for the novels of Jules Verne that inspired this elaborate recasting of a traditional, bucolic subject. The artist has freely rendered here an episode from Jules Verne's novel *Journey to the Center of the Earth* (1864), in which Professor Otto Lidenbrock and his nephew Axel discover deep inside the earth a prehistoric forest, beautifully preserved with its profusion of now-extinct vegetation. As Delvaux explained, he was drawn to the figure of the professor by "the somewhat comic, very picturesque side of his personality." In the painting, the professor is shown at left, immersed in the examination of a rock or fossil, apparently oblivious to the scene unfolding before him. Behind him, the artist has portrayed himself in the role of Axel, gazing away from the scene with the same wide-eyed, trancelike, self-absorbed expression shared by the other figures in the painting. In the background, under the gray light of a full moon, a group of women, as pristine in their nakedness as the forest is geologically, advance like automatons, as if moved or drawn by some invisible force. In the foreground, several figures combine elements from different realms, the human and the vegetal in the case of the two

women who have sprouted leaves in the place of hair, the male and the female in the case of the two hermaphrodites (the adolescent languidly resting on a huge leaf at center and the flutist standing at right). In their ambiguity, these figures seem to belong to a primordial, not yet completely differentiated state. On either side, a female figure in long Victorian dress advances holding an oil lamp, vainly attempting to shed light on the unyielding mystery of the scene.

There is in fact a sense of emotional estrangement, an oppressive silence at the very heart of the picture, that will not be denied, despite the languid eroticism evoked by the proliferation of naked forms and the artist's fussy preoccupation with details. There seems to be no genuine connection between the many figures populating the scene, all of whom seem ultimately isolated in their own world. Even when engaging in some action, as are the two women embracing in the far center of the picture, there is an automatic, passive, unfulfilling quality to their gestures that seems to defy real communication. This is a world of suspended and unrequited desires, in which all but the comically oblivious professor, who may well function in some respects as an alter ego for the artist obsessed with his work, seem to express a melancholy awareness of the unbridgeable distance between desire and its fulfillment.

BALTHUS (COUNT BALTHASAR KLOSSOWSKI DE ROLA) (French, born 1908)

Solitaire (Patience), 1943

Oil on canvas; 161.3 x 161.5 cm

Signed and dated, lower left: *Balthus 1943*

Joseph Winterbotham Collection, 1964.177

Balthus is a master of vague menace and unease. As in many of his other paintings, the artist focused here on the unself-consciously provocative pose of a pubescent girl, thereby injecting something unsettling into an otherwise banal scene. The girl's taut, arching pose indicates a physical restlessness, an impulsive and unrestrained quality, that seems to threaten the normality and predictability of this bourgeois interior. Against the insistent regularity of the back wall, which is covered with striped wall paper and is perfectly aligned with the picture's rectangular frame, the artist has placed every object slightly askew, as if to suggest the disruptive effect of the girl's presence. Many of these objects, especially the open book and box on the chair, seem to reflect, in their disordered state the girl's distracted, bored handling of them. In her restlessness, she seems to have carelessly moved many of the objects from their customary position: the cluster of containers and books stacked on the lower left, the open book and box dumped on the chair, the silver candlestick and cup pushed to the edge of the table. Even the furniture and rug seem to have been disturbed. The activity in which the girl is engaged, a game of solitaire, seems insufficient to contain her pent-up energy. A sense of frustration, of a force and impulse vainly seeking an appropriate channel, pervades the picture.

The muted colors and simplified volumes of Balthus's style of painting hark back to the figurative tradition of artists such as Piero della Francesca, whom he greatly admired. In its tight execution and controlled contours, this style confers to the scene a still, frozen quality that further heightens the feeling of repressed sexual energy expressed by the girl's pose. Painted in Switzerland, where Balthus took refuge during World War II, this picture has, not surprisingly, been interpreted as a metaphor for the restless waiting game of the émigré.

YVES TANGUY (American [born France], 1900–1955)

The Rapidity of Sleep (*La Rapidité des sommeils*), 1945

Oil on canvas; 127 x 101.6 cm

Signed, lower right: *YVES TANGUY 45*

Titled on back: *La Rapidité des sommeils*

Joseph Winterbotham Collection, 1946.46

This painting exemplifies Yves Tanguy's late style, especially as he practiced it after his move to the United States in 1939, where he married the American painter Kay Sage. The forms have become harder and more sculptural, resembling strangely shaped stones, rather than the amorphous creatures of his earlier paintings, and echoing more clearly the prehistoric stones—the dolmens and menhirs—of Tanguy's native Brittany. Color is also intensified, as the artist makes more generous use of the orange-red and blue found only spottily in earlier works, such as his 1928 screen (p. 167). The arrangement, size, and shape of these forms has become more varied, from the regimented clustering of forms on the right to the horizontal scattering of forms on the left and in the background. The viewer is also brought visually closer to the scene through the cropping of forms in the foreground.

The title of the painting (inscribed on the back as *La Rapidité des sommeils*) works in conjunction with the image to heighten its enigma and mystery, as in the works of Giorgio de Chirico and René Magritte (see pp. 147 and 171). Perhaps the title refers to the onset of sleep, or to the different stages of sleep, as the French use of the plural "sommeils" seems to suggest. This interpretation seems to find a visual equivalent in the progression from congested, active foreground to sparse, quiet background, from the thicket of vertical forms on the right to the more relaxed rhythm of horizontal forms extending into the distance. In the middle ground, at left, is an unusual configuration that seems particularly evocative in relation to the title. A horizontal form reminiscent of a sleeping figure lies, as in a bed or coffin, within the rectangular space defined by a rocklike border. Is Tanguy referring to the sleep that ushers in the dream-world of his landscapes or to the ultimate sleep, the sleep of death? The mood of the picture hovers uncertainly between the ominous and the contemplative, between lower and upper halves, engendering a desire to traverse the inhospitable foreground to reach the soothing, misty reaches of the background. Given the date of the work, at the end of World War II, one also wonders whether there is embedded in this work something of the emotional tenor of the times, a yearning for a peace that would transcend recent history.

JEAN DUBUFFET (French, 1901–1985)

Genuflection of the Bishop (L'Agenouillement de l'évêque), 1963

Oil on canvas; 217.8 x 298.5 cm

Signed and dated, lower left: *J. Dubuffet 63*

Titled, signed, and dated on back: *L'agenouillement /
de l'évêque / J. Dubuffet / octobre 63*

Joseph Winterbotham Collection, 1964.1087

In 1942, Jean Dubuffet gave up a successful career as a wine merchant to become a full-time artist. His goal was to create art outside the boundaries of tradition and received notions of beauty and ugliness. In the pursuit of this goal, Dubuffet turned for inspiration to so-called "outsider" art—the art of children, the insane, prison inmates, naive artists, and the "primitives," whose work he described as *art brut* ("raw art").

This painting belongs to a long series of works that occupied Dubuffet from 1962 to 1974, and for which he coined the term *Hourloupe*. As the artist himself explained, "L'Hourloupe [in French] calls to mind some object or personage of fairytale-like and grotesque character and at the same time something tragically growling and menacing." A quality both whimsical and disturbing indeed characterizes this painting. Following his resolve to make art from the raw stuff of "daily life," stripped of the veneer of culture, which he regarded as "a dead language" or as "a coat that . . . no longer fits us," Dubuffet took his inspiration for the *Hourloupe* series from his own ballpoint doodles. These soon took on a life of their own, expanding, as in this case, to huge proportions and eventually encompassing not only painting, but sculpture and architecture as well. One of the sculptures to emerge from this series, *Monument to the Standing Beast* of 1969, has since become a Chicago landmark in its position in front of Helmut Jahn's equally unorthodox State of Illinois Building (now the James R. Thompson Center).

This painting initially overwhelms the viewer with a dizzying proliferation of forms, all of which fit together with the unyielding flatness of a jigsaw puzzle. On closer scrutiny, five indeterminate figures or personages emerge from the background, including, at center, the kneeling "bishop" of the title. There is an unsettling tension between the painting's insistently repetitive design and its figurative and possibly narrative content, which makes us constantly waver between abstraction and figuration in our reading of the surface. Similarly disturbing is the tension between the endearingly grotesque figures conjured from the artist's imagination and the feeling of their suffocating spatial confinement within the painting. At any moment, the figures seem in danger of being swallowed up by the obsessive patterning of the picture's surface.

GERHARD RICHTER (German, born 1932)
Christa and Wolfi (Christa und Wolfi), 1964

Oil on canvas; 150 x 130 cm

Titled on back: *Christa u. Wolfi*

Joseph Winterbotham Collection, 1987.276

Considered in its entirety, Gerhard Richter's work seems to defy traditional notions of cohesion, for he has worked, often simultaneously, in diametrically different modes. In addition to the so-called Photo Paintings of the 1960s, of which this is a major example, his work includes austere grids of colored rectangles, based on color charts, and, most recently, a series of colorful, exuberant, and highly gestural abstractions. At first, it would seem that the only common element among these is a surprisingly single-minded devotion to the traditional medium of oil painting. It is only on closer inspection that one begins to appreciate the questioning, exploratory attitude that underlies Richter's work, an attitude that leads him to focus, in a quintessentially modern manner, on the different and even contradictory ways in which we record reality. In his Photo Paintings, he concentrated on photography, especially family snapshots and journalistic photographs; in his impersonal, gridlike works, he focused on the symbolic language of maps and charts; and in his most recent paintings, he has self-consciously adopted the style of Abstract Expressionism. Richter thus increases our awareness not only of the different ways in which we are accustomed to perceiving or constructing reality, but also of the incompleteness and inadequacy of any single mode of representation before a reality that is irreducibly elusive and complex. "My own relation to reality," Richter has said, "has always to do with haziness, insecurity, inconsistency."

In this painting, which appears to be based on a family photograph, Richter gave to the image a blurred, liquid quality, as if it were no more than an unsteady, fleeting reflection, like a reflection on water. In some instances, parts of the picture are entirely obscured, as in the case of the hand of the figure on the left, which is reduced to a hazy stump. The title of the painting, which is inscribed on the back of the canvas, further enhances the sense of incompleteness and mystery evoked by the image, since only one of the two women is identified by name (Wolfi presumably refers to the dog). All of these factors heighten our awareness of time's inevitable blurring of the past and the nostalgia—a word used by Richter—associated with this kind of family snapshot.

Checklist of the
Joseph Winterbotham Collection, 1921–1994

SOPHIA SHAW PETTUS

Department of Twentieth-Century

Painting and Sculpture

The Art Institute of Chicago

ROBERT DELAUNAY. *Champs de Mars: The Red Tower,* begun in 1911, reworked sometime before 1923 (pp. 142-43).

The checklist below includes every painting that is currently in the Winterbotham Collection or that was formerly in the collection. The year above each work or group of works indicates the date that a work was added to the collection. The symbol † indicates that a painting is currently in the collection, and a page number indicates where the painting is reproduced in color in this issue. Every painting, regardless of its current status, is listed with its accession number.

An asterisk (*) indicates that a painting has been removed from the Winterbotham Collection but remains in the permanent collection of the Art Institute.

Whenever possible, photographs of works that are no longer in the Winterbotham Collection have been provided below.

1921

HENRI MATISSE
(French, 1869–1954)
Woman Standing at the Window, 1918
1921.93
SOLD IN 1958

1922

MAX CLARENBACH
(German, 1880–1952)
The Garden, c. 1914
1922.6
SOLD IN 1948

1922

JULIUS PAUL JUNGHANNS
(Austrian, 1876–1953)
Memories from the Tyrol, c. 1914
1922.7
WITHDRAWN IN 1955; SOLD IN 1957

1923

† JEAN LOUIS FORAIN
(French, 1852–1931)
Sentenced for Life, c. 1910
1923.6
(P. 141)

† PAUL GAUGUIN
(French, 1848–1903)
The Burao Tree (Te Burao), 1892
1923.308
(P. 131)

LEO PUTZ
(Austrian, 1869–1940)
On the Shore, 1909
1923.323
WITHDRAWN IN 1955; SOLD IN 1957

1924

* ALBERT BESNARD
(French, 1849–1934)
By the Lake, 1923
1924.221
REPLACED WITH GAUGUIN'S *Portrait of a Woman* IN 1925

1925

† PAUL GAUGUIN
(French, 1848–1903)
Portrait of a Woman in front of a Still Life by Cézanne, 1890
1925.753
(P. 129)

† HENRI DE
TOULOUSE-LAUTREC
(French, 1864–1901)
*Equestrienne (At the Circus
Fernando)*, 1887–88
1925.523
(P. 125)

1928

EMILE OTHON FRIESZ
(French, 1879–1949)
Port of Toulon, late 1920s
1928.258
REPLACED WITH MANET'S *Young Woman*
IN 1963; SOLD IN 1971

1929

JEAN HIPPOLYTE
MARCHAND
(French, 1883–1941)
The Garden, 1920
1929.766
WITHDRAWN IN 1956; SOLD IN 1971

† GEORGES BRAQUE
(French, 1882–1963)
Still Life, 1919
1929.764
(P. 155)

1929

CHARLES GEORGES
DUFRESNE
(French, 1876–1938)
Still Life with Compote, 1927–29
1929.767
WITHDRAWN IN 1959; SOLD IN 1971

* EDOUARD GOERG
(French [born Australia], 1893–1969)
The Epicure, 1923
1929.765
REPLACED WITH ORDINAIRE'S *Landscape*
IN 1963

JEAN LURÇAT
(French, 1892–1966)
Delphi, c.1928
1929.768
DEACCESSIONED IN 1959; SOLD IN 1971

ANDRÉ DUNOYER
DE SEGONZAC
(French, 1884–1974)
*Summer Garden (The Hat with
the Scottish Ribbon)*, 1926
1929.184
SOLD IN 1992

1931

RAOUL DUFY
(French, 1877–1953)
Villerville, 1928
1931.708
SOLD IN 1987

CHAIM SOUTINE
(Lithuanian, 1893–1943)
Small Town Square, Vence, 1929
1931.709
SOLD IN 1989

1932

† HENRI MATISSE
(French, 1869–1954)
The Geranium, 1906
1932.1342
(P. 135)

1936

ANDRÉ DERAIN
(French, 1880–1954)
Mme Catherine Hessling, 1921
1936.119
TRADED FOR KOKOSCHKA'S *Commerce
Counselor Ebenstein* IN 1956

* KARL HOFER
(German, 1878–1955)
Girls Throwing Flowers, 1934
1936.221
REPLACED BY DUBUFFET'S *Genuflection of the Bishop* IN 1964

DIETZ EDZARD
(German, 1893–1963)
The Opera Box/At the Theater, 1934
1936.90
SOLD IN 1955

1937

EDOUARD GOERG
(French [born Australia], 1893–1969)
Maria Lani, c.1930
1937.1102
WITHDRAWN IN 1956; SOLD IN 1971

SALVADOR DALI
(Spanish, 1904–1989)
Shades of Night Descending, 1931
1937.1101
TRADED FOR DALI'S *Inventions of the Monsters* IN 1943

† CHAIM SOUTINE
(Lithuanian, 1893–1943)
Dead Fowl, c. 1926
1937.167
(P. 161)

† MARC CHAGALL
(French [born Russia], 1887–1985)
The Praying Jew, 1923
copy of a 1914 work
1937.188
(P. 149)

1937

† RAOUL DUFY
(French, 1877–1953)
Open Window, Nice, 1928
1937.166
(P. 165)

1938

ANDRÉ DERAIN
(French, 1880–1954)
Stag Hunt, 1938
1938.1325
SOLD IN 1957

† AMEDEO MODIGLIANI
(Italian, 1884–1920)
Madame Pompadour, 1915
1938.217
(P. 151)

1939

† GIORGIO DE CHIRICO
(Italian, 1888–1978)
The Philosopher's Conquest, 1914
1939.405
(P. 147)

OSKAR KOKOSCHKA
(Austrian, 1886–1980)
Elbe River near Dresden, 1919
1939.2244
SOLD IN 1989

1940

† PABLO PICASSO
(Spanish, 1881–1973)
Fernande Olivier, 1909
1940.5
(P. 139)

1941

* JOSÉ CLEMENTE
OROZCO
(Mexican, 1883–1949)
Zapata, 1930
1941.35
REPLACED WITH BALTHUS'S *Solitaire* IN
1964

1942

* RUFINO TAMAYO
(Mexican, 1899–1991)
Woman with Bird Cage, 1941
1942.57
REPLACED WITH MONET'S *Etretat* IN 1973

1943

† SALVADOR DALI
(Spanish, 1904–1989)
Inventions of the Monsters, 1937
1943.798
(P. 169)

1945

DIEGO RIVERA
(Mexican, 1886–1957)
Mother Mexico, 1935
1945.360
SOLD IN 1958

1946

† YVES TANGUY
(American [born France], 1900–1955)
The Rapidity of Sleep, 1945
1946.46
(P. 177)

1949

* EL GRECO (DOMENICO
THEOTOKÓPOULOS)
(Spanish, 1541–1614)
The Feast in the House of Simon,
c. 1610–14
1949.397
TRANSFERRED OUT OF WINTERBOTHAM
COLLECTION IN 1994

1953

† FERNAND LÉGER
(French, 1881–1955)
*The Railroad Crossing
(Preliminary Version),* 1919
1953.341
(P. 157)

† VINCENT VAN GOGH
(Dutch, 1853–1890)
The Drinkers (after Daumier), 1890
1953.178
(P. 127)

PAUL CÉZANNE
(French, 1839–1906)
Apples on a Tablecloth, c. 1886–90
1953.333
SOLD IN 1987

1954

† PAUL CÉZANNE
(French, 1839–1906)
House on the River, 1885/90
1954.304
(P. 121)

ATTRIBUTED TO
PAUL GAUGUIN
(French, 1848–1903)
Of Human Misery/Brittany, 1889
1954.304
REPLACED WITH DEGAS'S *Portrait after
a Costume Ball* AND SOLD IN 1961

MAURICE UTRILLO
(French, 1883–1955)
Argentan, Orne, 1922
1954.323
SOLD IN 1986

1956

† VINCENT VAN GOGH
(Dutch, 1853–1890)
Self-Portrait, 1886/87
1954.326
(P. 123)

1956

† ODILON REDON
(French, 1840–1916)
Sita, c. 1893
1954.320
(P. 133)

† OSKAR KOKOSCHKA
(Austrian, 1886–1980)
Commerce Counselor Ebenstein,
1908
1956.364
(P. 137)

1957

† JOAN MIRÓ
(Spanish, 1893–1983)
Portrait of Juanita Obrador, 1918
1957.78
(P. 153)

1959

HENRI MATISSE
(French, 1869–1954)
Dancer in Red, date unknown
1954.315
TRADED FOR DELAUNAY'S *Champ de Mars:*
The Red Tower IN 1959

† ROBERT DELAUNAY
(French, 1885–1941)
Champs de Mars: The Red Tower,
begun in 1911, reworked sometime
after 1923
1959.1
(P. 143)

1961

† EDGAR DEGAS
(French, 1834–1917)
*Portrait after a Costume Ball
(Portrait of Mme Dietz-Monin),*
1877/79
1954.325
(P. 115)

1961

BEN NICHOLSON
(British, 1894–1982)
November 1956 (Pistoia), 1956
1962.667
SOLD IN 1992

1963

* MARCEL ORDINAIRE
(French, 1848–1896)
Landscape, 1867
1954.306
ACCESSIONED AS A COURBET AND
REPLACED WITH MAGRITTE'S
Time Transfixed IN 1970

EDOUARD MANET
(French, 1832–1896)
Young Woman, 1879
1954.314
SOLD IN 1987

1964

† BALTHUS (COUNT
BALTHASAR KLOSSOWSKI
DE ROLA)
(French, born 1908)
Solitaire, 1943
1964.177
(P. 175)

† JEAN DUBUFFET
(French, 1901–1985)
Genuflection of the Bishop, 1963
1964.1087
(P. 179)

1970

† RENÉ MAGRITTE
(Belgian, 1898–1967)
Time Transfixed, 1938
1970.426
(P. 171)

1973

† CLAUDE MONET
(French, 1840–1926)
*Etretat: The Beach and the
Falaise d'Amont,* 1885
1964.204
(P. 119)

1987

† GUSTAVE COURBET
(French, 1819–1877)
*Reverie (Portrait of
Gabrielle Bourreau),* 1862
1987.259
(P. 113)

† GERHARD RICHTER
(German, born 1932)
Christa and Wolfi, 1964
1987.276
(P. 181)

1988

† MAX BECKMANN
(German, 1884–1950)
Reclining Nude, 1927
1988.220
(P. 163)

† MAX ERNST
(French [born Germany], 1891–1976)
The Blue Forest, 1925
1988.221
(P. 159)

1988

† YVES TANGUY
(American [born France], 1900–1955)
Title Unknown, 1928
1988.434
(P. 167)

1990

† LYONEL FEININGER
(American, 1871–1956)
Carnival in Arcueil, 1911
1990.119
(P. 145)

† ARNOLD BÖCKLIN
(Swiss, 1827–1901)
In the Sea, 1883
1990.443
(P. 117)

1991

† PAUL DELVAUX
(Belgian, 1897–1994)
The Awakening of the Forest,
August 1939
1991.290
(P. 173)

Selected References and Index

Pages cited in bibliographical sources refer specifically to works in the Winterbotham Collection.

BALTHUS (COUNT BALTHASAR KLOSSOWSKI DE ROLA), *Solitaire*, pp. 174-75

London, Tate Gallery. *Balthus: A Retrospective Exhibition*, exh. cat. Intro. by John Russell. London: Arts Council of Great Britain, 1968. Pp. 20, 60 (ill.); cat. no. 20.
Paris, Centre Georges Pompidou. *Balthus*, exh. cat. Paris: Musée National d'Art Moderne, 1983. Pp. 59, 69, 160–61 (pl. 28), 290, 351 (ill.); cat. no. 66.
Rewald, Sabine. *Balthus*, exh. cat. New York: Harry N. Abrams, 1984. P. 108 (ill.); cat. no. 27.

BECKMANN, MAX, *Reclining Nude*, pp. 162-63

Göpel, Erhard, and Barbara Göpel. *Max Beckmann: Katalog der Gemälde*. Bern: Verlag Kornfeld und Cie, 1976. Pp. 222–23 (pl. 108); cat. no. 308.
Schulz-Hoffmann, Carla, and Judith C. Weiss, eds. *Max Beckmann Retrospective*, exh. cat. St. Louis, Mo.: St. Louis Art Museum, 1984. Cat. no. 59.
Wiesbaden, Museum Wiesbaden. *Schwerpunkte: 30 Neuerwerbungen aus der Sammlung Hanna Bekker vom Rath*, exh. cat. Wiesbaden, 1988. Pp. 104–05, 114; cat. no. 28.

BÖCKLIN, ARNOLD, *In the Sea*, pp. 116-17

Andree, Rolf. *Arnold Böcklin: Die Gemälde*. Basel: Friedrich Reinhardt Verlag, 1977. P. 449; no. 376 (ill.).
Basel, Kunstmuseum Basel. *Arnold Böcklin, 1827–1901*, exh. cat. Basel, 1977. P. 207 (ill.); cat. no. 169.

BRAQUE, GEORGES, *Still Life*, pp. 154-55

Isarlov, George. "Georges Braque." *Orbes* 3 (Paris, 1932). P. 88; cat. no. 265.
Mangin, Nicole S. *Catalogue de l'oeuvre de Georges Braque: Peintures 1916–1923*, vol. 6. Paris: Maeght Éditeur, 1973. Pp. 50 (ill.), 51.

CÉZANNE, PAUL, *House on the River*, pp. 120-21

Albi, Musée Toulouse-Lautrec. *Trésors impressionnistes du Musée de Chicago*, exh. cat. Albi, 1980. Pp. 49, 69 (ill.); cat. no. 34.
Tokyo, Seibu Museum of Art. *The Impressionist Tradition: Masterpieces from The Art Institute of Chicago*, exh. cat. Tokyo: The Seibu Museum of Art, 1985. Cat. no. 45.

CHAGALL, MARC, *The Praying Jew*, pp. 148-49

Arnason, H. Harvard. *History of Modern Art*, rev. ed. New York: Harry N. Abrams, 1977. Pp. 290–92, fig. 464.
Compton, Susan. *Chagall*, exh. cat. London: Royal Academy of Arts, 1985. Pp. 37, 186 (ill.); cat. no. 43.
Davies, Horton, and Hugh Davies. *Sacred Art in a Secular Century*. Minnesota: Liturgical Press, 1978. P. 21 (pl. 6).
Kamenskii, Aleksandr. *Chagall: The Russian Years, 1907–1922*. New York: Rizzoli, 1989. Pp. 212–13, 216 (ill.) (reproduction and discussion of 1912–13 version).
Meyer, Franz. *Mark Chagall*. London: Thames and Hudson, 1964. Pp. 221, 234 (ill.), 243, 322, 324 n. 607; cat. no. 234.
Venturi, Lionello. *Mark Chagall*. New York: Pierre Matisse Éditions, 1945. P. 30.

CHIRICO, GIORGIO DE, *The Philosopher's Conquest*, pp. 146-47

Ades, Dawn. *Dada and Surrealism*. London: Thames and Hudson, 1974. P. 43 (fig. 27).
Fagiolo dell'Arco, Maurizio. "Giorgio de Chirico à Paris, 1911–1914." *Cahiers du Musée National d'Art Moderne* 13 (1984). Pp. 47–73 (fig. 29).
————. *L'Opera completa di De Chirico*. Milan: Rizzoli, 1984. Pp. 78, 86–87, no. 45 (ill.), pl. xiii.
Rubin, William S. *Dada, Surrealism, and Their Heritage*, exh. cat. New York: The Museum of Modern Art, 1968. Pp. 77–78 (fig. 101), 80.
Rubin, William S., ed. *De Chirico*, exh. cat. New York: The Museum of Modern Art, 1982. Pp. 149 (pl. 24).
Soby, James Thrall. *The Early Chirico*. New York: Dodd, Mead and Co., 1941. Pp. 38–40 (fig. 26).
————. *Giorgio de Chirico*. New York: The Museum of Modern Art, 1955. Pp. 65, 68–69, 188 (ill.).

COURBET, GUSTAVE, *Reverie (Portrait of Gabrielle Borreau)*, pp. 112-13

Bonniot, Roger. *Gustave Courbet en Saintonge, 1962–1863*. Paris: Librairie C. Klincksieck, 1973. Pp. 216, 228–29, 231 (fig. 51), 244–45, 263, 278–79, 337–38.
Fernier, Robert. *La Vie et l'oeuvre de Gustave Courbet: Catalogue raisonné*, vol. 1. Lausanne: Fondation Wildenstein, La Bibliotèque des Arts, 1977. Cat. no. 334.
Lindsay, Jack. *Gustave Courbet: His Life and Art*. New York: Harper and Row, 1973. Pp. 179, 356 n. 48.

DALI, SALVADOR, *Inventions of the Monsters*, pp. 168-69

Arnason, H. Harvard. *History of Modern Art*, rev. ed. New York: Harry N. Abrams, 1977. Pp. 366–69, 379 (pl. 164).

Descharnes, Robert. *Salvador Dali: The Work, the Man.* Trans. by Eleanor R. Morse. New York: Harry N. Abrams, 1984. Pp. 212–13 (ill.).

Rotterdam, Museum Boymans-van Beuningen. *Dali,* exh. cat. Rotterdam, 1970. Cat. no. 56 (ill.).

Soby, James Thrall. *Salvador Dali,* exh. cat. New York: The Museum of Modern Art, 1941. Pp. 26, 62 (ill.); cat. no. 33.

DEGAS, EDGAR, *Portrait after a Costume Ball*
(Portrait of Mme Dietz-Monnin),
pp. 114-15

Brettell, Richard R., and Suzanne Folds McCullagh. *Degas in The Art Institute of Chicago,* exh. cat. Chicago: The Art Institute of Chicago, 1984. Pp. 105 (ill.), 106–09; cat. no. 47.

Guérin, Marcel, ed. *Edgar Germain Hilaire Degas: Letters.* Oxford: Bruno Cassirer, 1947. Pp. 60–61.

Lemoisne, Paul André. *Degas et son oeuvre,* vol. 2. Paris: Paul Brame et C. M. de Hauke, 1946–49. Pp. 302–03 (ill.); cat. no. 534.

Reff, Theodore. "Some Unpublished Letters of Degas." *Art Bulletin* 50 (Mar. 1968). Pp. 90–91.

Werner, Alfred. *Degas Pastels.* New York: Watson-Guptill, 1968. P. 22.

DELAUNAY, ROBERT, *Champs de Mars: The Red Tower,*
pp. 142-43

Buckberrough, Sherry A. *Robert Delaunay: The Discovery of Simultaneity.* Ann Arbor: UMI Research Press, 1982. Pp. 71–73 (pl. 35).

d'Harnoncourt, Anne. *Futurism and the International Avant-Garde,* exh. cat. Philadelphia: Philadelphia Museum of Art, 1980. Cat. no. 84 (ill.).

Düchting, Hajo. *Robert und Sonia Delaunay: Triumph der Farbe.* Köln: Benedikt Taschen Verlag, 1993. Pp. 20–26 (ill.).

Habasque, Guy. *Robert Delaunay: Du Cubisme à l'art abstrait.* Paris: S.E.V.P.E.N., 1957. P. 261; cat. no. 88.

Paris, Orangerie des Tuileries. *Robert Delaunay,* exh. cat. Intro. by Michel Hoog. Paris: Éditions des Musées Nationaux, 1976. Pp. 21 (ill.), 54; cat. no. 29.

Rudenstine, Angelica Zander. *The Guggenheim Museum Collection: Paintings, 1880–1945,* vol. 1. New York: Solomon R. Guggenheim Foundation, 1976. Pp. 104–07.

DELVAUX, PAUL, *The Awakening of the Forest,*
pp. 172-73

Butor, Michel, Jean Clair, and Suzanne Hobart-Wilkin. *Delvaux.* Lausanne: La Bibliotèque des Arts, 1975. Pp. 78–79 (ill.).

Emerson, Barbara. *Delvaux.* Antwerp: Fonds Mercator, 1985. Pp. 43, 57, 80, 98–99 (ill.), 101, 231, 266, 278.

Pacquet, Marcel. *Paul Delvaux et l'essence de la peinture.* Paris: Éditions de la Difference, 1982. Pp. 93–97.

Sojcher, Jacques. *Delvaux ou la passion puérile.* Paris: Éditions Cercle d'Art, 1991. Pp. 164–65 (ill.); no. 24.

DUBUFFET, JEAN, *Genuflection of the Bishop,*
pp. 178-79

Barilli, Renato. *Dubuffet: Le Cycle de l'Hourloupe.* Turin: Edizioni d'Arte Fratelli Pozzo, 1976. Pp. 27, 30–31 (ill.); cat. no. 33.

Loreau, Max. *Catalogue des travaux de Jean Dubuffet: L'Hourloupe I,* vols. 20–21. Paris: Jean Jacques Pauvert, 1966. P. 100 (ill.); cat. no. 183.

Venice, Centro internazionale delle arti e del costume. *L'Hourloupe di Jean Dubuffet,* exh. cat. Venice: Rizzoli, 1964. Cat. no. 33 (ill.).

Washington, D.C., Hirshhorn Museum and Sculpture Garden. *Jean Dubuffet, 1943–1963,* exh. cat. Washington, D.C.: Smithsonian Institution Press, 1993. P. 145; cat. no. 98.

DUFY, RAOUL, *Open Window, Nice,*
pp. 164-65

Laffaille, Maurice. *Raoul Dufy: Catalogue raisonné de l'oeuvre peint,* vol. 3. Geneva: Édition Motte, 1972–77. P. 256 (ill.); cat. no. 1234.

San Francisco Museum of Art. *Raoul Dufy, 1877–1953,* exh. cat. San Francisco, 1954. P. 39; cat. no. 37.

ERNST, MAX, *The Blue Forest,*
pp. 158-59

Camfield, William A. *Max Ernst: Dada and the Dawn of Surrealism,* exh. cat. Houston: The Menil Collection, 1993. P. 157 (pl. 185); cat. no. 196.

Gimferrer, Pere. *Max Ernst Ola Dissolució de la Identitat.* Barcelona: Ediciones Poligrafa, 1977. Pl. 57.

Matthews, J. H. *The Imagery of Surrealism.* Syracuse, N.Y.: Syracuse University Press, 1977. P. 120 (as *La Fôret*).

Quinn, Edward. *Max Ernst.* Boston: New York Graphics Society, 1977. P. 149 (ill.); cat. no. 146 (as *La Fôret*).

Speis, Werner. *Max Ernst: Oeuvre-Katalog,* vol. 2. Houston and Köln: The Menil Foundation and DuMont Buchverlag, 1976. P. 75; cat. no. 936.

—————. *Max Ernst Retrospective,* exh. cat. Munich: Prestel-Verlag, 1979. P. 252; cat. no. 105.

FEININGER, LYONEL, *Carnival in Arcueil,*
pp. 144-45

Hess, Hans. *Lyonel Feininger.* New York: Harry N. Abrams, 1961. P. 253 (ill.); cat. no. 63.

Luckhardt, Ulrich. *Lyonel Feininger.* Munich: Prestel-Verlag, 1989. P. 65 (ill.); cat. no. 8.

New York, Acquavella Galleries. *Lyonel Feininger,* exh. cat. New York, 1985. Cat. no. 28 (ill.).

FORAIN, JEAN LOUIS, *Sentenced for Life,*
pp. 140-41

Faxon, Alicia. *Jean Louis Forain: Artist, Realist, Humanist,* exh. cat. Washington, D.C.: International Exhibitions Foundation, 1982. Pp. 38 (ill.), 39; cat. no. 10.

University of Chicago, David and Alfred Smart Gallery. *Artists View the Law in the 20th Century,* exh. cat. Chicago: University of Chicago, 1977. Pp. 13, 21; cat. no. 5.

GAUGUIN, PAUL, *The Burao Tree (Te Burao),*
pp. 130-31

Rewald, John. *Post-Impressionism from van Gogh to Gauguin,* 3rd ed. New York: The Museum of Modern Art, 1978. P. 472 (ill.).

Wildenstein, Georges. *Gauguin,* vol. 1. Paris: Les Beaux-Arts, 1964. Pp. 196–97 (ill.); cat. no. 486.

GAUGUIN, PAUL, *Portrait of a Woman in front of a Still Life by Cézanne,*
pp. 128-29

Brettell, Richard, et al. *The Art of Paul Gauguin,* exh. cat. Washington, D.C., and Chicago: National Gallery of Art and The Art Institute of Chicago, 1989. Pp. 192–93 (ill.); cat. no. 111.

Cachin, Françoise. *Gauguin.* Paris: Flammarion, 1988. Pp. 119, 123 (ill.).

Goldwater, Robert. *Paul Gauguin.* New York: Harry N. Abrams, [1957]. Pp. 94–95 (ill.).

Krumrine, Mary Louise, ed. *Paul Cézanne: The Bathers.* New York: Harry N. Abrams, 1990. Pp. 285–87.

Roskill, Mark. *Van Gogh, Gauguin, and French Painting of the 1880s: A Catalogue Raisonné of Key Works.* Ann Arbor, Mich.: University Microfilms, 1970. Pp. 196–97.

——————. *Van Gogh, Gauguin, and the Impressionist Circle.* Greenwich, Conn.: New York Graphic Society, 1970. Pp. 46–47, 52 (pl. IV), 54 (fig. 29) (listed as *Portrait of Marie Lagadu*).

Vance, Peggy. *Gauguin.* London: Studio Editions, 1991. Pp. 24, 50, 96, 97, 100.

Wildenstein, Georges. *Gauguin,* vol. 1. Paris: Les Beaux-Arts, 1964. P. 149 (ill.); cat. no. 387.

GOGH, VINCENT VAN, *The Drinkers (after Daumier),*
pp. 126-27

de la Faille, Jacob-Baart. *The Works of Vincent van Gogh: His Paintings and Drawings.* New York: Reynal and Morrow House, 1970. Pp. 637, 684 (ill.); cat. no. F667.

Gogh, Vincent van. *The Letters of Vincent van Gogh to His Brother, 1872–1886,* vol. 2. London and Boston: Constable and Houghton Mifflin, 1927. P. 83.

——————. *Further Letters of Vincent van Gogh to His Brother, 1886–1889.* London and Boston: Constable and Houghton Mifflin, 1929. Pp. 430, 437.

Pickvance, Ronald. *Van Gogh in Saint-Rémy and Auvers,* exh. cat. New York: The Metropolitan Museum of Art, 1986. Pp. 64, 174, 175; cat. no. 47.

Rewald, John. *Post-Impressionism from van Gogh to Gauguin,* 3rd ed. rev. New York: The Museum of Modern Art, 1978. P. 327 (ill.)

Scherjon, W., and Jos. de Gruyter. *Vincent van Gogh's Great Period: Arles, St. Rémy, and Auvers sur Oise.* Amsterdam: De Spieghel, 1937. P. 291 (fig. 667).

Stein, Susan Alyson. *Van Gogh: A Retrospective.* New York: Hugh Lauter Levin Associates, 1986. Pp. 327–28.

GOGH, VINCENT VAN, *Self-Portrait,*
pp. 122-23

The Art Institute of Chicago. *European Portraits 1600–1900 in The Art Institute of Chicago,* exh. cat. Chicago, 1978. Pp. 18, 86–87 (ill.); cat. no. 20.

de la Faille, Jacob-Baart. *The Works of Vincent van Gogh: His Paintings and Drawings.* New York: Reynal and Morrow House, 1970. Pp. 162, 165 (ill.), 624, 677; cat. no. F345.

Erpel, Fritz. *Van Gogh: The Self-Portraits.* Greenwich, Conn.: New York Graphic Society, [1969]. P. 19 (pl. 22).

Hammacher, Abraham Marie. *Genius and Disaster: The Ten Creative Years of Vincent van Gogh.* New York: Harry N. Abrams, [1968]. Pp. 37 (ill.), 183.

Paris. Musée d'Orsay. *Van Gogh à Paris,* exh. cat. Paris: Éditions de la Réunion, 1988. Pp. 112–13; cat. no. 37.

KOKOSCHKA, OSKAR, *Commerce Counselor Ebenstein,*
pp. 136-37

Hoffman, Edith. *Kokoschka: Life and Work.* London: Faber and Faber, 1947. Pp. 47, 82, 89, 290; cat. no. 11.

Kokoschka, Oskar. *My Life.* Trans. by David Britt. New York: Macmillan, 1974. Pp. 42–43.

Schweiger, Werner J. *Der Junge Kokoschka: Leben und Werk, 1904–1914.* Vienna: Christian Brandstätter, 1983. Pp. 118, 187 (ill.), 262.

Wingler, Hans Maria. *Oskar Kokoschka: The Work of the Painter.* Trans. by Frank S. C. Budgen et al. Salzburg: Galerie Welz, 1958. P. 294 (ill.); cat. no. 10.

LÉGER, FERNAND, *The Railway Crossing* (Preliminary Version),
pp. 156-57

Adelaide, Art Gallery of South Australia. *Fernand Léger,* exh. cat. New York: The Museum of Modern Art, 1976. Cat. no. 5 (ill.).

Bauquier, Georges. *Fernand Léger: Catalogue raisonné de l'oeuvre peint 1903–1919.* Paris: Adrien Maeght, 1990. Pp. 318–20 (ill.); cat. no. 181.

Buffalo, Albright-Knox Art Gallery. *Fernand Léger,* exh. cat. New York: Abbeville Press, 1982. Pp. 33, 61, 78 (ill.); cat. no. 15.

——————. *Masterworks on Paper from the Albright-Knox Art Gallery,* exh. cat. Compiled by Cheryl A. Brutvan, Anita Coles Costello, and Helen Raye. New York: Hudson Hills Press, 1987. P. 64 (ill.).

MAGRITTE, RENÉ, *Time Transfixed,*
pp. 170-71

Hammacher, Abraham Marie. *René Magritte.* Trans. by James Brockway. New York: Harry N. Abrams, 1973. Pp. 114–15 (pl. 25).

Soby, James Thrall. *René Magritte,* exh. cat. New York: The Museum of Modern Art, 1965. P. 37 (ill.); cat. no. 38.

Sylvester, David, ed. *René Magritte: Catalogue Raisonné,* vol. 2. Houston: The Menil Foundation, 1993. Pp. 266–67 (ill.); cat. no. 460.

Torczyner, Harry. *Magritte: Ideas and Images.* Trans. by Richard Miller. New York: Harry N. Abrams, 1977. Pp. 81 (ill.), 82–83; cat. no. 114.

Vovelle, José. *Le Surréalisme en Belgique.* Brussels: A. de Rache, 1972. P. 116 (fig. 121).

Whitfield, Sarah. *Magritte,* exh. cat. London: South Bank Centre, 1992. Cat. no. 81.

MATISSE, HENRI, *The Geranium,*
pp. 134-35

Barr, Alfred H., Jr. *Matisse: His Art and His Public.* New York: The Museum of Modern Art, 1951. Pp. 92, 110, 558.

Elderfield, John. *Henri Matisse: A Retrospective,* exh. cat. New York: The Museum of Modern Art, 1992. P. 157 (ill.); cat. no. 79.

Gowing, Lawrence. *Matisse.* New York and Toronto: Oxford University Press, 1979. P. 65 (fig. 45).

London, Hayward Gallery. *Henri Matisse, 1869–1954,* exh. cat. London: Arts Council of Great Britain, 1968. Pp. 81 (ill.), 162; cat. no. 36.

Madoff, Steven Henry. "Matisse: Imagining Paradise." *Art News* (Dec. 1992). Pp. 107–08 (ill.).

Paris, Galeries Nationales du Grand Palais. *Henri Matisse, Exposition du centenaire,* 12th ed. Paris: Éditions des Musées Nationaux, 1970. Pp. 72–73, 156 (ill.).

Zurich, Kunsthaus. *Henri Matisse,* exh. cat. Zurich, 1982. Cat. no. 21 (ill.).

MIRÓ, JOAN, *Portrait of Juanita Obrador,*
pp. 152-53

Barcelona, Fundación Joan Miró. *Joan Miró,* exh. cat. Barcelona, 1993. Pp. 131, 134; (ill.); cat. no. 31.

Dupin, Jacques. *Joan Miró: Life and Work.* Trans. by Norbert Guterman. New York: Harry N. Abrams, 1962. Pp. 80–81, 505 (ill.); cat. no. 53.

—————. *Miró.* Paris: Flammarion, 1993. Pp. 60–61 (ill.).

Lassaigne, Jacques. *Miró.* Trans. by Stuart Gilbert. Geneva: Albert Skira, 1963. Pp. 21, 23 (ill.).

Washington, D.C., Hirshhorn Museum and Sculpture Garden. *Miró: Selected Paintings,* exh. cat. Washington, D.C.: Smithsonian Institution, 1980. Pp. 16 (fig. 5), 56 (ill.); cat. no. 7.

MODIGLIANI, AMEDEO, *Madame Pompadour,*
pp. 150-51

Castieu-Barrielle, Thérèse. *La Vie et l'oeuvre de Amedeo Modigliani.* Paris: ACR Édition Internationale, 1987. Pp. 127, 131 (ill.).

Hall, Douglas. *Modigliani.* London: Phaidon Press Ltd., 1979. Fig. 23.

Lanthemann, J. *Modigliani, 1884–1920: Catalogue raisonné.* Florence: Edition Vallecchi, 1970. Pp. 112, 178 (ill.); cat. no. 74.

Mann, Carol. *Modigliani.* London: Thames and Hudson, 1980. Pp. 109–10 (ill.); cat. no. 75.

Paris, Musée d'Art Moderne. *Amedeo Modigliani, 1884–1920,* exh. cat. Paris, 1981. Pp. 15, 85, 115 (ill.); cat. no. 26.

Parisot, Christian. *Modigliani: Catalogue Raisonné.* Livorno: Editions Graphis Arte, 1988. Pp. 81 (ill.); cat. no. 21/1915.

MONET, CLAUDE, *Etretat: The Beach and the Falaise d'Amont,*
pp. 118-19

The Art Institute of Chicago. *Paintings by Monet,* exh. cat. Chicago, 1975. Pp. 31, 112 (ill.); cat. no. 58.

Los Angeles County Museum of Art. *A Day in the Country: Impressionism and the French Landscape,* exh. cat. New York: Harry N. Abrams, 1984. Pp. 276–77, 288.

Wildenstein, Daniel. *Claude Monet: Biographie et catalogue raisonné,* vol. 2. Lausanne: Bibliothèque des Arts, 1979. Pp. 168–69 (ill.); cat. no. 1012.

PICASSO, PABLO, *Fernande Olivier,*
pp. 138-39

Burns, Edward, ed. *Gertrude Stein on Picasso.* New York: Liveright, 1970. P. 80 (ill.).

Daix, Pierre, and Joan Rosselet. *Picasso: The Cubist Years, 1907–1916.* Boston: New York Graphic Society, 1979. P. 244 (ill.); cat. no. 287.

New York, The Museum of Modern Art. *Four Americans in Paris: The Collections of Gertrude Stein and Her Family,* exh. cat. New York, 1970. Pp. 95 (ill.), 171.

Zervos, Christian. *Picasso, 1906–1912,* vol. 2. Paris: Éditions Cahier d'Art, 1942. P. 83 (ill.); cat. no. 167.

REDON, ODILON, *Sita,*
pp. 132-33

Berger, Klaus. *Odilon Redon: Fantasy and Colour.* Trans. by Michael Bullock. New York: McGraw-Hill, 1965. P. 213; cat. no. 423.

Druick, Douglas W., et al. *Odilon Redon: Prince of Dreams, 1840–1916,* exh. cat. Chicago: The Art Institute of Chicago, 1994. Pp. 200, 230–31 (fig. 44), 254, 283, 286, 371–72; cat. no. 114.

New York, The Museum of Modern Art. *Odilon Redon, Gustave Moreau, Rodolphe Bresdin,* exh. cat. New York, 1961. P. 174; cat. no. 35.

RICHTER, GERHARD, *Christa and Wolfi,*
pp. 180-81

de Mèredieu, Florence. "La Photographie et ses Prothèses." *Parachute* 34 (Mar./Apr./May 1984). Pp. 25–32 (ill. p. 30).

Harten, Jürgen, ed. *Gerhard Richter: Paintings, 1962–1985,* exh. cat. Köln: Dumont Buchverlag, 1986. P. 13 (ill.); cat. no. 24.

Venice, German Pavilion, Thirty-Sixth Biennale. *Gerhard Richter,* exh. cat. Venice, 1972. P. 51 (ill.); cat. no. 24.

SOUTINE, CHAIM, *Dead Fowl,*
pp. 160-61

Courthion, Pierre. *Soutine: Peintre de déchirant.* Lausanne: Edita, 1972. P. 79 (ill.), 249 (ill.).

Munster, Westfälisches Landesmuseum. *Chaim Soutine, 1893–1943,* exh. cat. Stuttgart: Verlag Gerd Hatje, 1982. Pp. 208 (ill.), 246; cat. no. 65.

Paris, Orangerie des Tuileries. *Soutine,* exh. cat. Paris: Éditions des Musées Nationaux, 1973. Pp. 29 (ill.), 81; cat. no. 24 (listed as *Le Dindon*).

Werner, Alfred. *Chaim Soutine.* New York: Harry N. Abrams, 1977. P. 59 (fig. 70).

TANGUY, YVES, *The Rapidity of Sleep,*
pp. 176-77

Hartford, Conn., Wadsworth Atheneum. *Yves Tanguy, Kay Sage,* exh. cat. Hartford, Conn., 1954. Fig. 3; cat. no. 22.

Soby, James Thrall. *Yves Tanguy,* exh. cat. New York: The Museum of Modern Art, 1955. Pp. 19, 52 (ill.).

Yves Tanguy: Un Recueil de ses oeuvres/A Summary of His Works. New York: Pierre Matisse, 1963. P. 156 (ill.); cat. no. 343.

TANGUY, YVES, *Title Unknown,*
pp. 166-67

Komanecky, Michael, and Virginia Fabbri Butera. *The Folding Image: Screens by Western Artists of the Nineteenth and Twentieth Centuries,* exh. cat. New Haven, Conn.: Yale University Art Gallery, 1984. Pp. 250–53.

Paris, Centre Georges Pompidou, Musée National d'Art Moderne. *Yves Tanguy Retrospective, 1925–1955,* exh. cat. Paris, 1982. P. 49 (ill.).

TOULOUSE-LAUTREC, HENRI DE, *Equestrienne (At the Circus Fernando),*
pp. 124-25

Albi, Musée Toulouse-Laurec. *Trésors impressionnistes du Musée de Chicago,* exh. cat. Albi, 1980. Pp. 20 (ill.), 69; cat. no. 38.

Brettell, Richard R. *Post-Impressionists.* Chicago: The Art Institute of Chicago, 1987. Pp. 24–26 (ill.).

Dortu, M. G. *Toulouse-Lautrec et son oeuvre,* vol. 2. New York: Paul Brame et C. M. de Hauke, 1971. P. 146 (ill.); cat. no. P312.

London, Hayward Gallery, and Paris, Galeries Nationales du Grand Palais. *Toulouse Lautrec,* exh. cat. London and Paris, 1992. Pp. 234–37 (ill.).

Milner, John. *The Studios of Paris.* New Haven, Conn.: Yale University Press, 1988. Pp. 146–47.

Perruchot, Henri. *La Vie de Toulouse-Lautrec.* Paris: Hachette, 1958. Pp. 145, 152, 157, 161.

Stevenson, Lesley. *H. de Toulouse-Lautrec.* London: Weidenfeld and Nicolson, 1991. Pp. 50, 51, 63, 65, 69, 71, 73, 164.

Stuckey, Charles F. *Toulouse-Lautrec: Paintings,* exh. cat. Chicago: The Art Institute of Chicago, 1979. Pp. 124 (ill.), 125–29 (ill.); cat. no. 32.

Guide to
Great
Wine
Values

Wine Spectator Magazine's

Guide to
Great
Wine
Values

$10 and under

WINE SPECTATOR PRESS
A DIVISION OF M. SHANKEN COMMUNICATIONS, INC.

Published by Wine Spectator Press
A division of M. Shanken Communications, Inc.
387 Park Avenue South
New York, New York 10016

ISBN 1-881659-24-0

Foreword

This is *Wine Spectator's* first book devoted exclusively to great wine values. It draws on the accumulated knowledge of our editorial board and the most up-to-date wine ratings possible to bring you informed buying advice on the best wines you can find for $10 and under.

The heart of this book is a collection of more than 1,000 tasting notes, with retail prices and wine ratings on our 100-point scale, representing the best recently released wines available in U.S. wine shops, liquor stores and supermarkets. The ratings and recommendations are *Wine Spectator's* alone, stemming from independent wine tastings conducted by *Wine Spectator* magazine over the past sixteen months.

For those of you who don't know us, *Wine Spectator* is the world's largest-circulation consumer wine magazine. We pack each of our 18 issues per year with wine-buying advice based on our exclusive "blind" tastings of wine. Plus, we feature informative articles that stimulate our readers' interests in wine, dining, travel, cooking and collectibles.

This book presents in one convenient pocket-sized package the essential information to understand, buy and enjoy a wide variety of reasonably priced wines from around the world. It includes all the major types of wine that you might look for, from California Chardonnay to French Beaujolais. It can also introduce you to exciting new wines on the scene, like Merlot from Washington state and Sauvignon Blanc from South Africa.

Our thanks to staffers Ann Berkhausen, Kathy McGilvery, Donna Morris, Tara Collins and Amy Lyons for putting the book together.

If, like us, you love a bargain almost as much as a great-tasting bottle of wine, this book is for you.

Marvin R. Shanken

Editor and Publisher

Table of Contents

FOREWORD V

INTRODUCTION 1

STORING AND SERVING WINE 4

MATCHING WINE WITH FOOD 9

GREAT WINE VALUES 15

    Australia 15

    Chile 33

    France 51

    Germany 78

    Italy 85

    Portugal 102

    South Africa 109

    Spain 118

    U.S.A. 131

    Other Countries 227

INDEX 231

Introduction

BY JIM GORDON

Y ou don't have to spend a lot of money to buy a
really good bottle of wine. Forget the alarming prices
on many restaurant wine lists and the headlines about
rare Burgundy and Bordeaux selling for tens of thou-
sands of dollars at auction. The world of wine still
contains hundreds of treasures at $10 a bottle and less.

In fact, if you take our advice and buy at least a
few of the more than 1,000 wines recommended in
this up-to-date pocket guide, you'll discover—as we
did—that there has never been a better time to find
great values in wine.

For the purposes of this book, we define a good
value as any wine that our editors awarded at least 80
out of 100 points in a *Wine Spectator* tasting, and that
has a suggested retail price of $10 or less. In other
words, every wine reviewed here carries a solid rec-
ommendation. As you begin to use this guide to
shop, you will find that wines rated 85 or higher,
and those priced as low as $4 or $5, may be the
very best values you can find.

The tasting notes and ratings that form the core of
this book all come from "blind" wine tastings conducted exclusively by our own editors. By "blind," we
mean that the tasters do not know the prices or the wine

producers' names when they are tasting and assigning rating points to the wines. This practice is designed to make their reviews as objective as possible.

The reviews published here originate from tastings conducted largely within the 16 months prior to when this book went to press. They are the most current and most specific recommendations you will find in any book of this type. They are designed to help you go shopping.

Following the lead of most wine shops, we grouped the wines by country of origin, then by specific region or grape variety, depending on the custom in that country. For each specific region and type, we list the highest scoring wines on top, to make it easy to know which wines to look for, or ask for, first.

If you take this guide to the wine shop, as we hope you do, use the index in back to quickly find our review for a wine you spot on the shelf. If it's not listed in our guide, it means one of two things: either we reviewed it and it didn't rate high enough to be included, or we didn't review it.

Wine Spectator strives to review all of the widely available wines from important regions that are sold in America. Our total of wines tasted in 1995 will surpass 7,000. Still, it hasn't been possible to review every wine sold in America at $10 or less. The ones you find here, however, are great-value reds, whites, rosés, sparkling wines and dessert wines from California, Washington, Oregon, France, Italy, Spain, Portugal, Germany, Chile, South Africa and other regions.

This guide is as fresh and complete as we could make it. Because new vintages are constantly coming to market, however, we added an extra feature that will give it longer shelf life. For each country, we have created a special list of wines that we know from our tasting experience to be consistent from year to year. These are called "Most Reliable Values." If, for example, you cannot find the vintage we recommend, you can feel safe in buying a more recent vintage from the same company. (Be cautious buying older vintages, however, because most of the wines in this book are meant to be drunk while young and fresh.)

When you turn the page you will find two essays designed to help new wine consumers understand the topic. The first explains how to store and serve wine, and the second has tips for choosing an appropriate wine for a meal.

Following these are the chapters on different wine-producing countries, with specific reviews. Each begins with a brief explanation of that country's important value-oriented wine types, an illustration of how to make sense of its wine labels, and a map showing the major viticultural areas. Each chapter introduction is written by the *Wine Spectator* editor who specializes in wines of that country.

The wine tasting notes and scores, taken together, tell you how much our editors liked the wines, and what styles or flavors you should expect to find. Here is an explanation of what the ratings mean:

WINE SPECTATOR'S 100-POINT SCALE

95-100: Classic quality, a great wine.

90-94: Outstanding quality, a wine of superior character and style.

80-89: Good to very good quality, a wine with special qualities.

70-79: Average quality, a drinkable wine that may have minor flaws.

60-69: Below average quality, not recommended.

50-59: Poor quality, undrinkable, not recommended.

Jim Gordon is managing editor of Wine Spectator *magazine.*

Storing and Serving Wine

By Bruce Sanderson

A few basic guidelines in storage and service will go a long way to enhance your enjoyment of wine. The idea is to recognize which of your needs are most important when selecting a wine, its proper serving temperature, and glassware to accommodate the occasion, whether casual or formal.

STORAGE

Once you have purchased wine, whether it's a few bottles or several cases, the issue of storage must be addressed. Since most wine is consumed within 24-48 hours of purchase, for many wine lovers a small rack away from a direct heat source provides an ideal solution. If you plan to collect fine wines that benefit from additional bottle maturation, proper storage is essential. Before choosing a space be sure it will be large enough to accommodate future purchases. In some cases, vacant space beneath a stairway is sufficient, in others it may be necessary to allow for hundreds of wines stored both as individually racked bottles and full cases.

One of wine's greatest enemies is extreme heat. Temperatures greater than 70 degrees Fahrenheit will age a wine more quickly, and can also "cook" a wine until the fruit character becomes blunted, resulting in flat aromas and flavors. Equally important is the rate at which temperature changes. Rapid temperature fluctuations may cause pressure changes within a bottle, forcing the cork upwards and allowing leaks while permitting air to enter the bottle. Air is another of wine's enemies. Any prolonged exposure will lead to oxidation, which produces a brownish color and sherry-like flavors.

Therefore it is important to have a cool space with constant temperature for long-term storage. If your storage area is naturally cool (for example, a below-ground cellar), that's fine; if not, it may be necessary to invest in a cooling unit. Light may also harm wine over time. Bottles should be kept from direct sunlight, preferably in darkness, and should be stored on their sides, either in cases or racked.

Humidity is a more controversial subject but it's nothing to worry about unless you're keeping wines for the long-term. Some experts advocate a constant humidity of 70% to prevent corks from drying out, while others maintain that if a bottle is on its side, the cork is constantly in contact with moisture inside the bottle and external humidity is ineffectual.

SERVING WINES

Most wines may simply be opened and served. Sparkling wines, dessert wines and light-bodied whites need to be chilled to preserve their freshness and fruitiness (34-50 degrees Fahrenheit), while fuller-bodied whites such as Chardonnay and white Rhônes may be served slightly warmer. Light reds (most Beaujolais, Pinot Noir, Cabernet Franc from the Loire valley) benefit from being served slightly cooler than full-bodied reds like Australian Cabernet and Shiraz, California Cabernet and Meritage blends,

Bordeaux and Rhône, which are best at cellar temperature (55-65 degrees Fahrenheit). Of course these are general guidelines and individual tastes may vary.

Most wines are finished with a cork, covered by a capsule of either metal or plastic. To open, cut the capsule around the neck just below the lip of the bottle and remove the top of the capsule. Wipe the top of the bottle with a damp towel or cloth if necessary. Use a corkscrew to remove the cork. There are several different models of corkscrew available; again, the choice is a matter of individual taste.

Champagne and sparkling wines have a different closure, and must be handled carefully since the contents are under pressure and could cause injury. Remove the foil, and with a thumb over the metal crown to prevent the cork from ejecting, loosen the wire fastener. Without removing the wire, grasp the cork firmly and with the other hand turn the bottle, slowly releasing the cork. This process is easier when the wine is well chilled.

In certain instances, it will be necessary to decant a wine. Fine reds with bottle age produce a natural sediment as color pigments and tannins bond together and fall out of solution. Decanting is simply the process of separating the clear wine from the sediment. Before decanting, the bottle should be upright for a minimum 24 hours for the best results. Remove the capsule and cork, and with a light under the neck of the bottle (a candle or flashlight works well), pour the wine into a clean vessel in a single, steady motion until you can see the sediment reach the neck of the bottle. The wine is now ready to serve.

WINE GLASSES

Wine appreciation involves all the senses, and the choice of glassware will influence the sight, aroma, and taste of a wine. Georg Riedel, director of the

Riedel glass company in Austria, has done extensive experimentation using blind tasting trials with professional tasters. He divides glass design into three elements: Clarity and thinness are important for visual perception. The size and shape of the bowl determine the intensity and complexity of the bouquet, and the shape of the rim determines where the wine initially lands on the tongue, affecting the perception of its taste.

White Wine

Clear glass and a thin-rimmed bowl reduce the barriers between the wine lover and the wine. The clearer the glass, the richer the wine's color appears. The thinner the rim, the less the glass distracts from the wine as it enters the mouth. The stem should be long enough so that the hand doesn't touch the bowl, obscuring the glass with fingerprints or warming the wine above proper serving temperature. If the stem is too long, however, the glass will tip too easily. The stem should be about as long as the bowl is tall.

A large bowl and a narrow opening work together to magnify the

Red Wine   **Port**

ILLUSTRATIONS BY HARRY AUNG

Champagne

wine's bouquet. They give plenty of space for the aromas to expand, but only a narrow escape. If the bowl's widest point is too high or too low, a normal serving of wine won't have the maximum surface area for aeration. If the opening is too small, drinking will be difficult.

Many glasses are too small; few are too large. Our evaluations suggest that a good red-wine glass will have a capacity of at least 12 ounces. Generally, glasses for red table wines are wider than those for white, but beyond that it's really up to your personal preference.

Champagne flutes should hold 6 1/2 ounces or more. Sherry and Port glasses traditionally are small, because Port and sherry are fortified wines, and usually drunk in small quantities.

With the exception of sparkling wines, it's best not to fill a wine glass more than half full. This will leave enough air space to release the aromas. Most importantly, find a balance of wine-friendliness, aesthetic appeal and price, and settle on the glass that seems best for you.

Bruce Sanderson is Wine Spectator's *New York tasting coordinator.*

Matching Wine With Food

By Harvey Steiman

The first thing to remember about matching food and wine is to forget the rules. Forget about shoulds and shouldn'ts. Forget about complicated systems for selecting the right wine with the food on the table. This is not rocket science. It's common sense. Follow your instincts.

The most important rule is to choose a wine that you want to drink by itself. Despite all the hoopla about matching wine and food, you will probably drink most of the wine without the benefit of food—either before the food is served or after you've finished your meal. Therefore, you will not go too far wrong if you make sure the food is good and the wine is, too. Even if the match is not perfect, you will still have an enjoyable wine to drink.

Some of today's food-and-wine pontificators suggest that mediocre wines can be improved by serving them with the right food. The flaw in that reasoning, however, is the scenario described above. If the match does not quite work as well as you hope, you're stuck with a mediocre wine. So don't try to get too fancy. First pick a good wine.

As for which (good) wine to choose, that's where common sense comes in. The old rule about white wine with fish and red wine with meat made perfect sense in the days when white wines were light and fruity and red wines were tannic and weighty. But today, when most California Chardonnays are heavier and fuller-bodied than most California Pinot Noirs, and even some Cabernets, color coding does not always work.

Red wines as a category are distinct from whites in two main ways: tannins—many red wines have them, few white wines do—and flavors. White and red wines share many common flavors; both can be spicy, buttery, leathery, earthy or floral. But the apple, pear and citrus flavors in many white wines seldom show up in reds, and the currant, cherry and stone fruit flavors of red grapes usually do not appear in whites.

In the wine-and-food matching game, these flavor differences come under the heading of subtleties. You can make better wine choices by focusing on a wine's size and weight. Like human beings, wines come in all dimensions. To match them with food, it's useful to know where they fit in a spectrum, with the lightest wines at one end and fuller-bodied wines toward the other end.

A Spectrum of Wines

To help put the world of wines into perspective, consult the following lists, which arrange many of the most commonly encountered wines into a hierarchy based on size, from lightest to weightiest. If you balance the wine with the food by choosing one that will seem about the same weight as the food, you raise the odds dramatically that the match will succeed.

Yes, purists, some Champagnes are more delicate than some Rieslings and some Sauvignon Blancs are bigger than some Chardonnays, but we're trying to paint with broad strokes here. When you're searching for a lightish wine to go with dinner, pick one from the top end of the list. When you want a bigger wine, look toward the end.

SELECTED DRY AND OFF-DRY WHITE WINES, LIGHTEST TO WEIGHTIEST:

Soave and Orvieto
Riesling
Muscadet
Champagne and other dry sparkling wines
Chenin Blanc
French Chablis and other unoaked Chardonnays
Sauvignon Blanc
White Bordeaux
Mâcon
Gewürztraminer
Barrel-fermented or barrel-aged Chardonnay

SELECTED RED WINES, LIGHTEST TO WEIGHTIEST:

Beaujolais
Valpolicella
Dolcetto
Rioja
Burgundy and Pinot Noir
Barbera
Chianti Classico
Merlot
Bordeaux
Zinfandel
Cabernet Sauvignon (U.S., Australian)
Rhône and Syrah

More Common Sense

Hearty food needs a hearty wine, because it will make a lighter wine taste insipid. With lighter food, you have more leeway. Lighter wines will balance nicely, of course, but heartier wines will still show you all they have. Purists may complain that full-bodied wines "overwhelm" less hearty foods, but the truth is that anything but the blandest food still tastes fine after a sip of a heavyweight wine.

These are the secrets behind some of the classic wine-and-food matches. Muscadet washes down a plate of oysters because it's just weighty enough to match the delicacy of a raw bivalve. Cabernet complements lamb chops or roast lamb because they're equally vigorous. Pinot Noir or Burgundy makes a better match with roast beef because the richness of texture is the same in both.

To make your own classic matches, follow the same path as the first person who tried Muscadet with oysters. Try a dry Champagne or a dry Riesling, which are on either side of Muscadet on our weight list, for a similar effect. Don't get stuck on Cabernet with lamb. Try Zinfandel or Côtes du Rhône. Instead of Burgundy or Pinot Noir with roast beef, try a little St.-Emilion or Barbera. That's the way to put a little variety into your wine life without straying too far from the original purpose.

At this point, let us interject a few words about sweetness. Some wine drinkers recoil at the thought of drinking an off-dry wine with dinner, insisting that any hint of sweetness in a wine destroys its ability to complement food. In practice, nothing can be further from the truth. How many Americans drink sweetened iced tea with dinner? Lemonade? Or sugary soft drinks? Why should wine be different? The secret is balance. So long as a wine balances its sugar with enough natural acidity, a match can work. This opens plenty of avenues for fans of German Rieslings, Vouvrays and White Zinfandel.

One of the classic wine-and-food matches is Sauternes, a sweet dessert wine, with *foie gras*— which blows the sugarphobes' theory completely. The match works because the wine builds richness upon richness. The moral of the story is not to let some arbitrary rules spoil your fun. If you like a wine, drink it with food you like, and you're bound to be satisfied.

Harvey Steiman is editor-at-large of Wine Spectator.

Australia

By Harvey Steiman

Two factors have contributed to the eye-opening percentage of good values from Australia. One, the Australian dollar is in even worse shape than the U.S. dollar, and two, the wine industry there has worked hard to satisfy a market of Aussies who like to drink wine and prefer to spend as little as possible on it.

The past decade has seen an explosion of interest in Australia for wines that Americans like, too: Chardonnay and Cabernet Sauvignon. These two types, plus Australia's red wine specialty, Shiraz, make up the bulk of Down Under exports to the United States. Riesling is big in Australia itself, where it has long been the quaffing white wine of choice, but few producers bother to export the stuff in this direction.

Australia, like America, labels its best wines with varietal names. The rules are similar, in that varietal wines are made entirely or mostly from the single grape variety named on the front label. Often, more than one variety is named, in which case Shiraz-Cabernet has more Shiraz in it and Cabernet-Shiraz has more Cabernet.

As is true anywhere else, the narrower and more prestigious the geographical appellation, the higher the price of the wine. As a result, most value-oriented wines carry broad appellations, such as Southeastern

Australia—which encompasses a region nearly 600 miles wide—or simply Australia.

Australian vineyards tend to produce grapes with prominent fruit flavors that bring a certain charm even to lesser wines. Aussie winemakers are also brilliant at blending wines from various regions and giving them judicious cellar treatments to achieve a consistent style. Chardonnays such as Lindemans Bin 65 and Yalumba Oxford Landing are perennial Best Buys in *Wine Spectator* for precisely these reasons.

Other than Chardonnay, Sémillon is the white variety Aussies prize most for the herbal, tobacco and lanolin flavors that sneak in around the fruit. At lower prices, however, we go for Sémillon blended with either Sauvignon Blanc or Chardonnay. The few Rieslings that make it over the Pacific are worth trying, too.

Among the reds, the best values are often Cabernet-Shiraz blends, which tend to carry lower prices than either varietal sold separately. Australian Shirazes in the under-$10 range tend to spill over with delicious fruit. The Cabernets edge toward supple drinkability as well. The blends, though less distinctive, are usually sturdy wines which are drinkable when young.

Finally, don't miss the dessert wines. Australia makes some of the best in the world, including Tawny Ports that live up very well to the Portuguese bottlings they are modeled after, at a fraction of the price. The fortified Muscats may not be fashionable, but they are delicious.

No summary of Australia's best values would be complete without a nod in the direction of Tyrrell's Long Flat Red and Long Flat White, both consistent Best Buys from a longtime Hunter Valley winery.

Harvey Steiman is editor at large of Wine Spectator.

Most Reliable Values

These wines have proven to be of consistently good quality, year in and year out. Even if a particular vintage is not reviewed here, you may purchase these wines with confidence.

RED WINES

Lindemans Cabernet Sauvignon Bin 45

Rosemount Cabernet Sauvignon

Lindemans Shiraz Bin 50

Rosemount Shiraz

Seppelt Shiraz Reserve Bin

Penfolds Cabernet-Shiraz Koonunga Hill

Rosemount Shiraz-Cabernet

Yalumba Cabernet Sauvignon Shiraz Oxford Landing

Tyrrell's Long Flat Red

WHITE WINES

Lindemans Chardonnay Bin 65

Penfolds Chardonnay South Australia

Yalumba Chardonnay Oxford Landing

Lindemans Sémillon Bin 77

Rosemount Sémillon-Chardonnay

Tyrrell's Long Flat White

How to Read an Australian Wine Label

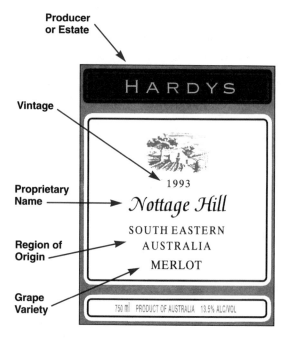

Producer or Estate

Vintage

Proprietary Name

Region of Origin

Grape Variety

HARDYS

1993

Nottage Hill

SOUTH EASTERN
AUSTRALIA

MERLOT

750 ml   PRODUCT OF AUSTRALIA   13.5% ALC/VOL

1. Clare
2. Barossa Valley
3. Coonawarra
4. Goulburn Valley
5. Yarra Valley
6. Hunter Valley

Red

Cabernet Blend

87 ROSEMOUNT Shiraz Cabernet 1994 **$8.00**
Light but hardly fragile, smooth and generous with its
blueberry, vanilla, pepper and spice flavors that extend
into the lively finish. Tasty now; should be best in 1996.

87 SEPPELT Cabernet Shiraz South Australia
Classic 1992 **$6.00** A stylish wine; ripe, smooth
and generous, just a little short of opulent, with spicy
plum and berry flavors on a polished, supple frame. A
lighter style with plenty of flavor.

85 BROWN BROTHERS King Valley Everton
Family Selection 1992 **$9.00** Ripe and generous in
flavor, firm and almost aristocratic in structure, this
has the dark cherry and meaty flavors and the balance
to develop well past 2000.

85 HARDY'S Cabernet Shiraz South Eastern
Australia Nottage Hill 1993 **$7.00** Bright and
sharply focused, chewy in texture, with plum and
berry flavors that remain vibrant through the finish.

85 PENFOLDS Cabernet Shiraz South Australia
Koonunga Hill 1991 **$9.00** Lean and a little chunky,
but the ripe currant and plum flavors carry through on
the finish. Maybe best from 1997.

84 TYRRELL'S Cabernet Merlot South Eastern
Australia Old Winery 1992 **$8.00** A lighter style of
Cabernet, almost transparent in texture, with light currant and blackberry fruit playing against an herbal,
slightly tarry edge. Best from 1996.

84 YALUMBA Cabernet Sauvignon Shiraz South Eastern Australia Oxford Landing 1992 **$7.00** Lean in structure but supple in texture and showing a spicy, slightly leathery edge to the plum and prune fruit. Approachable now; best from 1996.

82 COLDRIDGE Cabernet Shiraz South Eastern Australia 1994 **$7.00** Youthful, fruity and appealing; light and soft in texture and showing pretty raspberry notes on the finish.

82 MITCHELTON South Eastern Australia 1993 **$10.00** Lean and distinctly herbal, with a minty-eucalyptus edge to the basic black cherry flavors. Smooth and drinkable now.

82 QUEEN ADELAIDE Shiraz Cabernet South Eastern Australia 1992 **$6.00** Ripe in flavor and crisp in texture, this is a tightly wound wine that should be at its best from 1997.

81 BROWN BROTHERS Victoria Everton Family Selection 1990 **$7.00** Lean and supple, strongly herbal in flavor, with a strong smoky edge to the modest Cabernet flavors.

Cabernet Sauvignon

87 HARDY'S Cabernet Sauvignon Coonawarra 1992 **$10.00** Firm and focused, lean in structure, with a bay leaf and tobacco overlay to the earthy plum and black cherry fruit. Packed with flavor, it needs until 1997-1998 to settle down.

86 BLEASDALE Cabernet Sauvignon Longhorne Creek 1990 **$8.50** Herbal, slightly gamy flavors add an extra dimension to the soft prune and black cherry fruit. Ready now; better in 1996-1997.

86 CHATEAU REYNELLA Cabernet Sauvignon McLaren Vale Basket Pressed 1992 **$10.00** Bright and focused, and jam packed with herbal, tobacco-scented black cherry flavors; an earthy wine with style and distinction. Best from 1997-1998.

86 LINDEMANS Cabernet Sauvignon South Eastern Australia Bin 45 1992 **$7.00** Firm and chewy, packed with minty, spicy black cherry and currant flavors that keep fanning out of the finish. Best from 1997-1998.

85 JABIRU Cabernet Sauvignon 1993 **$8.00** An oddball range of flavors—spicy, toasty and a little like candied orange peel on the finish, but it has style and remains nicely balanced.

85 ROSEMOUNT Cabernet Sauvignon South Australia 1993 **$10.00** Soft and simple, and generous with its black cherry and raspberry fruit. The finish is supple and appealing.

84 NORMANS Cabernet Sauvignon South Australia Family Reserve 1993 **$10.00** Smooth and flavorful, a nice mouthful of berry and currant fruit, approachable now.

83 ASHWOOD Cabernet Sauvignon Riverland 1992 **$9.00** Light and supple, with a tinge of beet flavor sneaking in with the modest plum and berry notes.

83 TYRRELL'S Cabernet Sauvignon South Eastern Australia Old Winery 1992 **$8.00** Firm in texture, a sturdy wine with clear berry and currant fruit lingering on the smooth finish. Best from 1996.

83 WYNDHAM Cabernet Sauvignon South Eastern Australia Bin 444 1991 **$7.00** Lean and velvety, with a modest level of black cherry and smoke flavors persisting into the finish.

81 HANWOOD Cabernet Sauvignon 1993 **$8.00** Soft and a little chewy, with modest blackberry and currant flavors; finishes with an earthy streak. Best from 1996.

81 HARDY'S Cabernet Sauvignon South Eastern Australia No Preservatives Added 1994 **$8.00** Focused and flavorful, balanced toward berry and currant fruit, generous and appealing to drink now.

Shiraz

87 BLEASDALE Shiraz Langhorne Creek 1992 **$7.50** Broad and supple, wrapping its gamy plum and blackberry flavors in a chewy package that promises fullest pleasure in 1997-1998.

87 SEPPELT Shiraz South Australia Reserve Bin 1992 **$7.00** A little chewy in texture, with plenty of plum and blackberry fruit coming through; fresh and inviting through the finish. Best from 1996.

85 EVANS & TATE Shiraz Gnangara 1993 **$10.00** Light and fruity, a simple wine with appealing cherry and spice flavors. Gets a little richer on the finish. Maybe best from 1996.

85 LEASINGHAM Shiraz Clare Valley Domaine 1992 **$9.00** Bright, open-textured and disarmingly fruity; juicy with blackberry and black cherry flavors. Only a little tannic on the finish, so maybe best from 1996.

85 MITCHELTON Shiraz South Eastern Australia 1993 **$10.00** A light, fruity style that echoes with pleasant berry and currant flavors.

83 ASHWOOD Shiraz Riverland 1992 **$9.00** Smooth, elegant and almost refined; unusual for a Shiraz. Showing slightly gamy prune and spice flavors.

83 ROSEMOUNT Shiraz South Australia 1993 **$10.00** Not as good as recent vintages, but it's smooth, almost silky, and has modest tannins to balance the sweet plum and spice flavors. Best from 1996.

83 TYRRELL'S Shiraz Hunter Valley Old Winery 1990 **$8.00** Lean and spicy, a chewy wine with modest fruit and tobacco overtones. Best from 1996.

82 LINDEMANS Shiraz South Eastern Australia Bin 50 1992 **$7.00** Earthy flavors against a coarse texture add up to a red struggling to find its balance. Maybe best from 1997.

82 MCLARENS Shiraz South Eastern Australia 1992 **$9.00** Soft and generous, and showing a bright, spicy edge to the plum and blackberry flavors; finishes with a touch of tea leaf. Drinkable now.

81 KOOKABURRA Shiraz South Eastern Australia 1992 **$6.00** On the lighter side, with pleasant plum, vanilla and earthy flavors that echo on the crisp finish.

81 PETER LEHMANN Shiraz Barossa Valley 1992 **$10.00** Relatively light and smooth, modestly fruity, with a prune edge to the spicy flavors.

Other Red

88 TYRRELL'S Pinot Noir South Eastern Australia Old Winery 1993 **$8.00** Delicate and distinctive, delicious with pure plum and berry flavors, and supported by fine tannins and textbook balance. A beautifully made Pinot that should be at its best from 1996.

87 LINDEMANS Merlot South Australia Bin 40 1993 **$8.00** Light and nicely focused, with spicy black cherry and currant flavors that ride smoothly to a polished finish. Appealing now; best from 1996.

86 HARDY'S Merlot South Eastern Australia Nottage Hill 1993 **$7.00** Light and airy, showing nicely focused currant and blackberry fruit that expands and becomes supple on the finish. Appealing.

85 MCGUIGAN BROTHERS Merlot South Eastern Australia Bin 3000 1993 **$8.00** Smooth and sweet, with a honeyed edge to the cherry flavors. Very unusual, rather like a cough drop. Tasty through the finish. Best from 1996.

83 BROWN BROTHERS Victoria Tarrango 1993 **$8.00** Bright and fruity, a light, simple Beaujolais-like red with appealing grapey flavors. Serve cool.

83 TYRRELL'S South Eastern Australia Long Flat Red 1992 **$6.00** Smooth, easy-drinking red with a spicy edge to the raspberry and plum fruit that keeps it going right through the finish.

WHITE

Chardonnay

90 SEAVIEW Chardonnay McLaren Vale 1994 **$7.00** Ripe and resonant, a vibrant wine that pours out its beautiful pear, spice and honey flavors and lets them linger on the polished finish. Impressive now.

88 WYNDHAM Chardonnay South Eastern Australia Oak Cask 1993 **$9.00** Smooth and buttery, rich with pear, caramel and vanilla flavors that balance beautifully on the finish.

87 NORMANS Chardonnay South Australia Family Reserve 1994 **$10.00** Round and generous, a fruity wine with nice spice and mineral nuances to the pear and vanilla flavors at the core.

87 PENFOLDS Chardonnay South Australia 1993 **$9.00** Bright and tightly structured, a lighter style of Chardonnay that shows off its pear and spice flavors as they linger on the finish.

86 YALUMBA Chardonnay South Eastern Australia Oxford Landing 1994 **$7.00** Fresh, floral and smooth, a broad-textured wine that never gets heavy. Tasty to drink while it's fresh.

85 LINDEMANS Chardonnay South Eastern Australia Bin 65 1994 **$7.00** Light and fruity, with a greenish, citrusy tinge to the apple flavor, echoing on the finish.

85 TYRRELL'S Chardonnay South Eastern Australia Old Winery 1993 **$8.00** Ripe and generous, supple enough to show off the peach and spice flavors to best advantage.

84 HANWOOD Chardonnay 1993 **$8.00** Simple, fruity and appealing, and playing out its pear and delicately toasty flavors.

84 HARDY'S Chardonnay South Eastern Australia Nottage Hill 1994 **$7.00** Bright and fruity, a youthful, straightforward wine with appealing apple and slightly resiny flavors.

84 JABIRU Chardonnay South Eastern Australia 1994 **$8.00** Light and piney, a zippy white that comes off more like a snappy Riesling than a Chardonnay. Pleasant.

84 LEASINGHAM Chardonnay Clare Valley 1993 **$9.00** Ripe and focused, with a resiny edge to the spicy pear and apple fruit; balanced a little toward oak.

83 WYNDHAM Chardonnay South Eastern Australia Bin 222 1993 **$7.00** Clean and sharply focused, with lively apple and apricot flavors that linger on the finish.

82 HARDY'S Chardonnay South Eastern Australia 1994 **$8.00** Light and simple, pleasantly fruity with pear and apple flavors that remain bright through the finish.

82 MITCHELTON Chardonnay Victoria 1994 **$10.00** Bright and fruity, a fresh-tasting wine with simple pear fruit and leafy overtones.

82 ROSEMOUNT Chardonnay Hunter Valley 1994 **$10.00** Youthful and exuberant, a little coarse but lively with pear and pineapple fruit.

81 NORMANS Chardonnay South Australia Chandlers Hill 1994 **$8.00** Light and fruity, with a sappy edge to the basic nectarine flavors.

81 QUEEN ADELAIDE Chardonnay South Eastern Australia 1993 **$6.00** Fresh and fruity, with flavors similar to fruit cocktail; light and refreshing.

80 KOOKABURRA Chardonnay South Eastern Australia 1993 **$6.00** Sharp-edged and a little coarse, but the bright pineapple and pear fruit comes through on the finish.

Sémillon/Sémillon Blend

85 LINDEMANS Sémillon Chardonnay South Eastern Australia Bin 77 1994 **$7.00** Distinctive for its nectarine and pear flavors that remain exuberant right through the finish.

85 PETER LEHMANN Sémillon Barossa Valley 1994 **$10.00** Bright and spicy, a refreshing wine with citrusy pineapple flavors that echo on the light finish.

85 ROSEMOUNT Sémillon Chardonnay 1994 **$8.00** Bright, fruity and appealing. Centers around pear and fig flavors, and has a spicy finish.

83 MCLARENS South Eastern Australia Sémillon Chardonnay 1992 **$9.50** Soft, appealing, simple and spicy, with modest fig and pear flavors.

83 PENFOLDS Sémillon Chardonnay South Australia Koonunga Hill 1993 **$9.00** Broad in texture, with fig and toast flavors that ride nicely on the finish.

82 COLDRIDGE Sémillon Chardonnay South Eastern Australia 1994 **$7.00** Fresh and inviting, a simple, fruity wine with nice pear flavor.

82 MCLARENS Sémillon Chardonnay South Eastern Australia Classic Dry White 1993 **$7.00** Subdued in aromas, but the flavors have the distinctive floral, piney, green apple notes of clean, dry Riesling.

81 MARIENBERG Sémillon Sauvignon Blanc McLaren Vale Lavinia Classic Dry White 1994 **$10.00** Lean and tight, with focused pineapple and tobacco flavors, maybe best in 1996.

80 ASHWOOD Sémillon Sauvignon Blanc Riverland 1994 **$8.00** Soft and floral, and a little sweet; showing some nice pineapple notes on the finish.

Other White

87 CHATEAU TAHBILK Marsanne Goulburn Valley 1993 **$10.00** Soft, ripe and generous, a lively wine with fruit bowl flavors that keep glowing on the finish.

85 PENFOLDS Chardonnay-Sauvignon Blanc Clare Valley Organically Grown Grapes 1993 **$10.00** Smooth, spicy, light-textured and round, with melon, apple and vanilla flavors and a lingering finish.

85 ROSEMOUNT South Eastern Australia Traminer Riesling 1994 **$8.00** Soft and appealingly fruity, with flavors centered around peach and delicate spices; fresh and inviting.

84 BLEASDALE Langhorne Creek White Burgundy 1994 **$7.50** Broad in texture with a floral, leafy strand of flavor that opens up on the citrusy finish. Lively and ready now.

84 MARIENBERG Riesling McLaren Vale Cottage Classic 1994 **$10.00** Unusual tropical fruit and floral flavors combine in this reticent style of

Riesling. Tasty now, but might be worth waiting until 1997.

84 TYRRELL'S South Eastern Australia Long Flat White 1994 **$6.00** Simple, fruity and tremendously appealing; generous with its pear, tropical fruit and spicy flavors.

83 BROWN BROTHERS Sauvignon Blanc King Valley Family Selection 1993 **$10.00** A zinger. Strong herbal flavors pervade this crisp, lemony white. Definitely Sauvignon.

82 SEAVIEW Sauvignon Blanc McLaren Vale 1993 **$8.50** Crisp and distinctively herbal, a silky wine with a touch of onion skin to the melony fruit flavors. Drinkable now.

DESSERT

87 BROWN BROTHERS Muscat Victoria Lexia Family Selection 1993 **$9.00** Soft, sweet and appealing, with honey, litchi and pineapple flavors that spread out nicely on the finish.

87 WOODLEY Port South Australia Queen Adelaide Tawny NV **$7.00** Lean in structure with rich spice and cigar box flavors that cut through the sweetness. Has a welcome sense of elegance and impressive length.

86 BROWN BROTHERS Port Victoria Family Selection Wood Matured Reserve NV **$8.00** Smooth and spicy like a tawny, this is a rich wine with a remarkable range of spice, toast and raisiny flavors that linger on the balanced finish.

86 HARDY'S Tall Ships Tawny Port NV **$10.00** Smooth and rich, offering coffee, raisin, spice and slightly tarry flavors that meld nicely on the finish.

82 DRAYTON'S Port Fine Old Pioneer NV **$10.00** Coffee, tea and spice notes mingle with a touch of plum and vanilla in this solid, forthright tawny. Nicely balanced.

81 TYRRELL'S Port 8 Year Old Fine Aged Tawny NV **$9.00** Smooth and sweet, a lighter style of tawny with modest tea and spice flavors.

Chile

By Thomas Matthews

Chile makes wines that Americans like to drink. These wines are fresh and fruity, have straightforward varietal character, and sell for reasonable prices. That's why this small, dynamic wine producer has become the third-largest exporter to the United States, led only by Italy and France.

Simplicity is the key to Chile's success. The wines are made from grapes Americans already know and like: Cabernet Sauvignon and Merlot for the reds, Sauvignon Blanc and Chardonnay for the whites. Vintages hardly matter, because Chile's vineyards enjoy temperate, semi-arid weather conditions that ripen the grapes consistently from year to year. The appellation system is relatively primitive and the big wineries tend to blend fruit from widely-spread grow-ing regions, so regional character is still blurred (though beginning to emerge). Most of the Chilean wines we see in America are produced by a handful of large companies, so labels are few and brands are consistent. It's simply hard to go wrong.

Chile's wine industry was founded in the 1850s by wealthy aristocrats who modeled their estates after the châteaux of Bordeaux. Most of the wineries were established in the Maipo Valley just south of Santiago, Chile's capital. This is still the heart of Chile's wine country, which extends 250 miles through the coun-try's Central Valley, a narrow, fertile plain at the foot of the Andes. Chile's best wines are still made from

Bordeaux's traditional grape varities: Cabernet Sauvignon, Merlot and Sauvignon Blanc.

The style of Chilean wines tends to resemble the elegance of Europe rather than the power of the New World. The reds are the best bets so far. Refreshing, and a great accompaniment to food, they are polished, rarely heavy or jammy, and have bright fruit, firm acidity and light tannins. Most are ready to drink two or three years after harvest; few reward extended cellaring. The top Cabernets still come from the Maipo Valley, but look also for Cabs and Merlots from Colchagua, a sub-region of the Rapel Valley south of Maipo.

The whites have played second fiddle so far. Chardonnay has only been widely planted for about ten years, and though good examples are available, it lacks the overall consistency and character of the other varietal wines, mostly offering straightforward fruit with some oak influence. Sauvignon Blanc is more exciting, especially wines coming from the newest vineyard region, Casablanca; crisp and exuberant, they mix fruit and herb flavors in refreshing balance.

Chilean wines vary in price from under $5 per bottle to nearly $15, and overall you get what you pay for. Because the soil is fertile and irrigation permitted and often overused, the vines can be made to yield enormous harvests; the result can be simple wines with little concentration or varietal character at the low end of the price range. But the top wineries are seeking out better matches of site and grape variety, reducing yields and improving their vinification methods, with the result that wines in the $8 to $12 range are better now than ever. (Chile's more expensive prestige wines, unfortunately, are sometimes over-ambitious, suffering from overoaking and overextraction.)

Today, Chile's top wineries offer clean, accessible wines in food-friendly styles at reasonable prices, which are likely to remain attractive bargains to

Most Reliable Values

These wines have proven to be of consistently good quality, year in and year out. Even if a particular vintage is not reviewed here, you may purchase these wines with confidence.

RED WINES

Carmen Rapel Reserve Merlot

Casa Lapostolle Colchagua Selection Merlot

Concha y Toro Rapel Marqués de Casa Concha Peumo Vineyard Merlot

Los Vascos Colchagua Cabernet Sauvignon

Santa Rita Rapel 120 Cabernet Sauvignon

Undurraga Maipo Valley Reserve Cabernet Sauvignon

WHITE WINES

Canepa Rancagua Chardonnay

Carmen Rapel Sauvignon Blanc

Miguel Torres Curicó Sauvignon Blanc

Concha y Toro Maipo Marqués de Casa Concha Santa Isabel Vineyard Chardonnay

---

American wine drinkers. But over the next few years, the top players and emerging boutique wineries will push wine quality higher. Don't be surprised to find outstanding wines, still at fair prices, emerging from Chile before too long.

Thomas Matthews is New York bureau chief of Wine Spectator.

How to Read a Chilean Wine Label

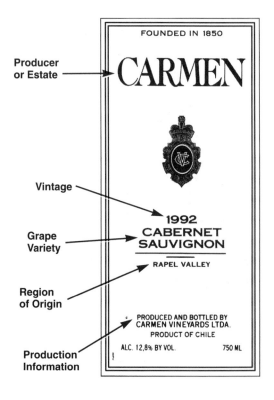

Producer or Estate → CARMEN

FOUNDED IN 1850

Vintage → 1992

Grape Variety → CABERNET SAUVIGNON

Region of Origin → RAPEL VALLEY

Production Information → PRODUCED AND BOTTLED BY CARMEN VINEYARDS LTDA.
PRODUCT OF CHILE
ALC. 12,8% BY VOL.   750 ML

1. Aconcagua   4. Rapel

2. Casablanca   5. Colchagua

3. Maipo   6. Maule

RED

Cabernet Sauvignon

88 CANEPA Cabernet Sauvignon Maipo Valley Private Reserve 1992 **$8.00** There's plenty of ripe fruit here, with jammy black cherry and currant flavors, and plenty of tannin, too; the wine needs some time to come together, but it's an ambitious effort that should be better in 1996.

88 UNDURRAGA Cabernet Sauvignon Maipo Valley Reserve 1991 **$9.00** Rich toast and coffee flavors of new oak give this wine punch, and ripe, concentrated plum and currant flavors give it depth. It has good structure for Chile, and a lingering fruit finish. Approachable now, it will improve through 1997.

87 CARMEN Cabernet Sauvignon Rapel 1992 **$6.00** This well-made, sophisticated wine has polished texture, firm structure and enough cherry and raspberry flavors to fill it out. Minty and light toasty notes add interest and keep you coming back for more. Drink now through 1996.

87 VINA PORTA Cabernet Sauvignon Valle del Cachapoal 1992 **$9.00** Nice complexity here, a mix of sweet oak, appealing herbal accents and plenty of bright berry and cherry fruit. The tannins are firm but in balance with the fruit and crisp acidity. It makes good drinking now but should hold through 1996.

86 CRANE LAKE Cabernet Sauvignon Colchagua Valley 1992 **$5.00** Lush ripe fruit gives this wine immediate appeal. Layers of plum, black cherry and raspberry flavors are underpinned by chocolate notes and bright acidity. There's enough tannin to give it grip. Drink now.

85 ALAMEDA Cabernet Sauvignon Maipo Valley Vintner's Selection 1992 **$5.00** Ripe, jammy berry fruit, accented by peppery and earthy notes give this rich wine liveliness; firm tannins give it structure. A straightforward wine that is pleasant to drink.

85 CONO SUR Cabernet Sauvignon Selection Reserve 1992 **$10.00** A dose of oak adds sweet vanilla and spicy notes to this round, fruity wine. The plum and black cherry flavors are clean and linger on the finish. Generous and lively, this makes pleasant drinking now through 1996.

85 DOMAINE RABAT Cabernet Sauvignon Colchagua Valley Apalta Vineyard Reserva 1990 **$7.50** Attractive tobacco and cedar aromas give way to soft, fresh fruit flavors of cherry and berry and a touch of oak still toasty and sweet on the finish. It's well-integrated and drinks nicely now.

85 DONA SOL Cabernet Sauvignon Colchagua Valley 1992 **$6.00** Alluring aromas of black cherry, licorice and smoke give way to bright fruit on the palate. Balanced and clean, it offers varietal character and a bit of personality.

85 LOS VASCOS Cabernet Sauvignon Colchagua 1993 **$7.00** Good presence here. The cassis and plum flavors are concentrated, and firm tannins give the wine structure. It has clean, ripe varietal character, good balance and though drinkable now, should hold through 1996.

85 MIGUEL TORRES Cabernet Sauvignon Curicó 1993 **$8.00** A nice balance of fruit and oak, coupled with good concentration, gives this wine appealing depth. The flavors range from spicy black cherry to toast and licorice.

85 SANTA RITA Cabernet Sauvignon Rapel 120 1992 **$7.00** A focused wine with ripe berry, cherry flavors accented with light cinnamon and chocolate flavors. The tannins are light but present, and the balance is good. This wine is fresh and clean.

84 CANEPA Cabernet Sauvignon-Malbec Sagrada Familia 1993 **$5.00** Fresh and fruity, this soft red offers bright cherry and blackberry flavors with hints of spice and herbs. There's just enough tannin to keep it refreshing.

84 SANTA CAROLINA Cabernet Sauvignon Maipo Valley Reserva Santa Rosa Vineyard 1990 **$8.00** Ripe and blowsy, this still has enough underlying tannin to give it shape; the flavors are roasted red fruits and earth. There's a hint of herbal Cabernet character, too. Drink now.

84 UNDURRAGA Cabernet Sauvignon Maipo Valley 1992 **$6.50** This ripe, fleshy wine is thick with cassis, plum and chocolate flavors, full-bodied for Chile, with just enough tannin for grip. Can stand up to a steak. Drink now.

83 MONTES Cabernet Sauvignon Curicó Villa Montes 1992 **$6.00** Bright perfumey raspberry and cherry aromas are attractive and carry through on the palate, which is rather soft and light but still balanced and fresh. Pleasant to drink now.

82 CARTA VIEJA Cabernet Sauvignon Maule 1993 **$4.00** Bright and vivid, this shows lively tart cherry and raspberry flavors with crisp acidity and soft tannins. It's fresh and clean on the palate, but finishes a bit short.

82 CONCHA Y TORO Cabernet Sauvignon Maipo Valley Casillero del Diablo 1992 **$8.00** Pleasant minty and black cherry aromas and flavors give this wine appeal, but the fruit thins out on the palate, dominated by oak tannins. It has Cab character, but winds up a bit simple.

82 CONO SUR Cabernet Sauvignon 1993 **$6.00** A straightforward wine with good varietal character, this shows ripe plum and cherry flavors with a slight herbaceous note and soft tannins. It's balanced and easy to drink now.

82 DE MARTINO Cabernet Sauvignon Maipo Valley "Prima" Santa Ines Vineyard 1991 **$8.00** A soft, well-knit wine for drinking now. Pleasant cherry fruit marries well with a mature tobacco note; the tannins are well-integrated and fade gently into a lingering finish.

81 CANEPA Cabernet Sauvignon Maipo Valley "Finisimo" Estate Reserve 1989 **$9.00** A pleasant, simple wine at full maturity. The flavors run from dried cherry through tobacco and cedar, and linger on the soft, slightly drying finish.

81 SANTA RITA Cabernet Sauvignon Maipo Valley Reserva 1992 **$9.00** A light, crisp wine for drinking now. The flavors mingle light cherry and berry with a marked herbal, green bean note; the tannins are light but dry.

81 VILLARD Cabernet Sauvignon Rancagua 1992 **$8.00** A sturdy red, with firm tannins and straightforward cherry and light earthy flavors. It'll stand up to food, but doesn't have much to say on its own.

80 CARMEN Cabernet Sauvignon Maipo Valley Reserve 1991 **$9.00** A ripe-smelling but lean-tasting Cabernet that has more tannin than fruit. Its mineral and herb flavors turn tight and astringent on the finish.

Merlot

89 CONCHA Y TORO Merlot Rapel Marqués de Casa Concha Peumo Vineyard 1993 **$10.00** A beauty. Striking aromas of chocolate, coffee and ripe black plums give way to richly concentrated flavors of plums, toast, licorice and chocolate. It's ripe and balanced and lingers on the finish. A well-made wine; drink now.

88 CARMEN Merlot Rapel Reserve 1993 **$9.00** Vibrant blackberry and plum aromas follow through on the velvety palate in this ripe wine. It's lush and fruity and shows toasty oak character; the flavors carry through on the finish. Appealing now, it should improve through 1996.

87 CASA LAPOSTOLLE Merlot Colchagua Selection 1994 **$9.00** Ripe and concentrated. Clean, fresh flavors of plum and licorice are supported by firm tannins in this balanced, well-made wine. Drink now. Made by Pomerol star Michel Rolland.

86 SANTA CAROLINA Merlot Maipo Valley Santa Rosa Vineyard 1993 **$6.00** Pretty plum, smoke and toast flavors run through this lush, appealing wine. The flavors are bright and forward, the tannins soft, and it finishes with plenty of sweet fruit. Easy to like.

86 SANTA CAROLINA Merlot San Fernando Valley Gran Reserva Cinco Estrellas 1993 **$10.00** Round yet well-defined, this shows clean Merlot character in its black cherry, light herbal and smoke flavors. It's balanced, with enough tannin for grip. Drinkable now, it should open up through 1996.

86 WALNUT CREST Merlot Rapel 1993 **$5.00** A rich, ripe, brawny red for Chile, this wine shows deep color, aromas of plum and smoke, and ripe plum, light herbal and toast flavors in good balance. Try now.

85 CARMEN Merlot Maipo Valley Reserve 1993 **$9.00** A densely flavored and lavishly oaked Merlot that's deep in color, almost chewy in texture, with firm tannins and a long finish. Drink now.

85 CONCHA Y TORO Merlot Rapel Casillero del Diablo 1994 **$8.00** This shows good intensity for Chilean Merlot, from the bold cherry, toast and spice aromas to the firm flavors of fruit, oak and smoke. Drinkable now, it could benefit with a bit more time in the bottle.

Other Red

85 SANTA CAROLINA Merlot/Cabernet
Sauvignon San Fernando Valley 1993 **$6.00** Ripe
fruit flavors of currants, raspberries and cherries give
this wine appeal. It's fresh and lush, and if it lacks the
structure for aging, it gives plenty of pleasure now.

81 CONO SUR Pinot Noir Selection Reserve
1994 **$10.00** Smoke and toast notes get the upper
hand over the soft plum fruit in this round, fleshy
wine. It's clean and the fruit is ripe, it lacks well-
defined Pinot character.

80 CONO SUR Pinot Noir 1994 **$6.50** Here's a
soft, supple wine for immediate drinking. The flavors
run through cherry, tomato and herbal notes, then finish a bit short. Shows a bit of Pinot character, and it's
quaffable.

White

Chardonnay

88 VILLARD Chardonnay Aconcagua
Casablanca Vineyard 1993 **$8.00** Fresh and lively,
from the alluring peach and toast aromas through the
ripe fruit and crisp acidity on the palate. The oak is
deftly used, and adds interest to the solid, concentrated fruit. A well-made wine that should improve
through 1996.

87 CARMEN Chardonnay Maipo Valley Reserve
1994 **$9.00** Complete, balanced and harmonious.
Not a flashy wine, it shows deft use of oak, ripe, crisp

fruit, full body and a long finish. More sophisticated than most South American Chardonnays; fine now but will show more in 1996.

86 CARTA VIEJA Chardonnay Maule Proprietor's Reserve 1993 **$8.00** Packs a healthy punch of oak and rich fruit. The flavors range from smoke and nuts to melon and pear, with firm acidity for structure. Shows balance and intensity.

85 CONCHA Y TORO Chardonnay Maipo Marqués de Casa Concha Santa Isabel Vineyard 1994 **$10.00** Balanced and clean, this fresh, fruity wine mingles pear, melon and vanilla flavors with good acidity and a firm texture. Brings you back for another sip.

84 ALAMEDA Chardonnay Maipo Valley Santa Maria Vineyard 1994 **$6.00** This ripe, oaky wine shows good intensity, with crisp acidity and fresh pineapple and butter flavors. The oak is a bit heavy, but the wine has verve and style.

84 CANEPA Chardonnay Rancagua 1994 **$6.00** This is clean, subtle and charming. The peach, floral and light citrus flavors are fresh and crisp, not weighed down by oak influence. It's pretty and easy to drink.

84 CANEPA Chardonnay Rancagua Private Reserve 1993 **$8.00** Bright and flavorful, if a bit over-oaked, this bold wine marries tingly acidity, crisp fruit and plenty of vanilla and butter flavors. If the Chardonnay character gets lost, the wine is still intense and attractive.

84 CARMEN Chardonnay Rapel 1994 **$6.00** A clean, fresh-tasting Chardonnay with pleasant fruit flavors and a touch of buttery complexity. Smooth, soft and almost sweet on the palate.

84 DONA SOL Chardonnay Colchagua Valley 1993 **$6.00** Aggressive use of oak gives this wine appealing toast, hazelnut and vanilla flavors, along with underlying ripe apple and pear flavors that seem a bit overwhelmed at the moment. There's enough acidity for grip. For fans of oak.

84 MONTES Chardonnay Curicó Oak Barrel Fermented 1994 **$8.00** Vanilla notes add interest to this round, yet crisp wine, and mingle nicely with the pear, apple and citrus flavors. It holds together well, and has good Chardonnay character.

83 CASA LAPOSTOLLE Chardonnay Colchagua Selection 1994 **$9.00** Soft and lush, this ripe wine shows pear, honey, butter and floral notes that carry through to a lingering finish. It could use a bit more crispness, but the style is bold and rich.

83 UNDURRAGA Chardonnay Maipo Valley 1994 **$6.50** Vivid pineapple and citrus aromas give way to a lively wine with tart acidity. It has a different profile than most South American Chards we've tasted; fresh and zingy.

82 SANTA MONICA Chardonnay Rancagua 1993 **$5.50** A delicate, silky wine with light lemon, pear and vanilla flavors and a nice balance of creaminess and crispness on the palate. It's clean and shows some elegance.

82 SANTA RITA Chardonnay Maipo Valley Reserva 1994 **$9.00** A tight wine in a subdued style, this shows crisp acidity, a hint of smoky oak and straightforward apple fruit. It seems simple at first, but grows on you; a good food wine.

81 DONA SOL Chardonnay Colchagua Valley 1994 **$6.00** Crisp and fruity, this lean wine offers green apple and citrus flavors; the lack of oak will please those who like their fruit fresh and pure.

80 SANTA RITA Chardonnay Maule Valley 120 1994 **$7.00** Appealing floral and appley aromas fade on the rather diluted palate; it's straightforward and clean.

Sauvignon Blanc

87 CARMEN Sauvignon Blanc Rapel 1994 **$6.00** A bold wine with plenty of Sauvignon Blanc character. It shows lemon, light herbal, melon and fig flavors in a taut package with good acidity for backbone. A touch of oak lingers on the finish. Solid and well-made.

87 CASABLANCA Sauvignon Blanc Casablanca Valley Santa Isabel Estate 1993 **$8.00** This rich wine shows a hint of Sauternes character—honeyed and spicy—but then the acidity kicks in and it finishes crisp and clean. A bold wine with plenty of Sauvignon Blanc character.

86 CONCHA Y TORO Sauvignon Blanc Maipo Valley Casillero del Diablo 1994 **$8.00** Appealing aromas of melon and vanilla give way to a round, soft wine. It's still crisp, though, and the fruit lingers on the finish. It draws you back for another sip.

86 VINOS DE CHILE Sauvignon Blanc Lontue Gato Blanco 1994 **$5.00** Vibrant and bright with gooseberry and fig flavors and very crisp acidity, this is reminiscent of New Zealand in style. The flavors persist and the finish is clean. A well-made wine. Tasted twice with consistent results.

85 CANEPA Sauvignon Blanc Curicó 1994 **$5.00** A big wine with lush body, crisp acidity and ripe flavors of pineapple, vanilla and melon. The first impression is a bit clumsy, but the wine has a lot going for it; needs food to show its best.

85 CASA LAPOSTOLLE Sauvignon Blanc Colchagua 1994 **$7.00** Rich texture and ripe melon fruit, along with plenty of vanilla oak character, give this wine good intensity. It's full-bodied, and though the acidity is a bit low, it's still luscious.

85 SANTA RITA Sauvignon Blanc Maule Valley Reserva 1994 **$8.00** Smooth and fleshy, this wine delivers clean grassy and herbal Sauvignon Blanc character with a bit of spice in the finish. It's richer than many Chilean Sauvignons, yet still clean and fresh.

85 VILLARD Sauvignon Blanc Aconcagua Casablanca Vineyard 1994 **$7.00** An exotic fruit salad with a very distinctive style. Vibrant citrus, pineapple, hay and herbal notes mingle in this tart, vivid wine. May be too rambunctious for timid palates; really makes a statement.

84 MIGUEL TORRES Sauvignon Blanc Curicó 1994 **$7.00** Light and very crisp, with well-defined grassy, herbal flavors that are balanced, true and not aggressive. It's not complex, but it is appealingly fresh and lively.

Other White

84 CASABLANCA Gewürtztraminer Casablanca Valley Santa Isabel Estate 1993 **$8.00** This bright, lively wine offers vivid grapefruit and lichi flavors with tangy acidity and a smoky finish, with more the structure than the flavors of Gewürtztraminer. It's a vibrant, well-made wine that would show well with shellfish dishes.

84 VINA SEGU OLLE Moscatel Maule Valley De Alejandria Doña Consuelo 1993 **$6.00** Smooth yet crisp, this clean wine shows herbal, smoky and light honey flavors in a tight, well-integrated package. The fig and apple flavors are light but fresh. It's subtle, but grows on you. Don't expect obvious Muscat character.

82 SANTA MONICA Semillon Rancagua 1993 **$4.00** A crisp, straightforward wine with forward pear and citrus flavors, accented with a pleasant herbal note. It's round and easy to drink.

France

BY JAMES SUCKLING

When most people think of France, they think of the great and expensive wines from such areas as Bordeaux, Burgundy and the Rhône Valley. However, the French also make a wealth of interesting and reasonably priced wines, from both renowned and little known regions.

All the areas included in the country's rather complex system of wine designations, the *appellation controlée*, produce wines offering good value for the money—even in regions where the top wines cost several hundred dollars per bottle. The key regions to look for include Alsace, Beaujolais, Bordeaux, Burgundy, and the Loire and Rhône Valleys. Most of these regions make wines from different grape varieties, so it's helpful to know what grape variety or region you prefer. For instance, a vintner in Beaujolais makes light and refreshing red wines, which are best consumed young, from Gamay grapes. In Bordeaux, the red wines are made predominantly from Cabernet Sauvignon and Merlot, and are generally better for aging.

A recent trend toward making varietal wines with the name of just one grape variety on the label has made things easier for many people, although most of these wines do not come from areas within the *appellation controlée* system. The majority are produced in the Midi, a huge wine producing area in the southeast of France which encompasses a number of regions including Languedoc-Roussilion and Provence. Wines labeled as Cabernet Sauvignon, Syrah, Chardonnay and Sauvignon Blanc from here all usually carry the designation "Vin de Pays," which loosely translates to "Country Wine."

Regardless of which region or grape variety you choose, it's often best to buy wines by the producer's name—one with a reputation for consistent quality and value. Many of the wines listed in this year's guide are made by producers who, nearly every vintage, make wines which impress us with their high quality and reasonably low prices.

Perhaps the most impressive producer of values is Georges Duboeuf, often called the "King of Beaujolais." In this year's guide, you will find no less than 17 wines from this firm that our editors found to be good quality for the money. From white Burgundy to Syrah from the deep South of France, Duboeuf knows how to select the best wines to be bottled under his label. His Beaujolais from the district of Brouilly, the Château de Pierreux 1994, tied for the best value wine from France; it's a giveaway at $10 a bottle. If you can't find this wine, try some of his other '94 Beaujolais in this guide, including his Beaujolais-Village, Morgon, Beaujolais Château de Varennes, Brouilly, and Brouilly Nervers. All are priced between $7 and $10 a bottle.

Fortant de France was another producer we found this year with several good value wines, and this fast-growing wine company is leading the new wave of varietal wines from the South of France. Its 1993 Cabernet Sauvignon, 1993 Chardonnay and 1993 Sauvignon Blanc all received 83 points and sell for between $7 and $8 a bottle.

THE FRENCH MAKE A WEALTH OF INTERESTING AND REASONABLY PRICED WINES, FROM BOTH RENOWNED AND LITTLE KNOWN REGIONS.

La Vieille Ferme is yet another producer with a string of good wines this year. If you like the big, rich reds of the Rhône Valley, you can't lose with the wines of La Vieille Ferme, whose owners also control one of France's best red estates, Château de Beaucastel in Châteauneuf-du-Pape. La Vieille Ferme's Côtes du Rhône Réserve sets the standard for the bread-and-butter reds of the region, and at $10 a bottle, it's often better quality than other reds costing two or three times the price. We gave the '92 Réserve Côtes du Rhône a score of 85 points, and the '93 a score of 81 points.

The dominance of Pierre Sparr in the region of Alsace is similar to La Vieille Ferme's in the Rhône; its Rieslings and Gewürztraminers are some of the best produced in the area—and the most reasonably priced. Sparr's '92 Riesling Carte d'Or received the highest score for any white wine in this year's guide, 88 points, and at $9 a bottle, the price looks like a misprint.

All in all, France continues to offer a bounty of good wines for the money, despite its rather elitist reputation. The biggest difficulty is deciding what to buy.

James Suckling is European bureau chief of Wine Spectator.

Most Reliable Values

These wines have proven to be of consistently good quality, year in and year out. Even if a particular vintage is not reviewed here, you may purchase these wines with confidence.

BEAUJOLAIS

Georges Duboeuf Beaujolais-Villages Flower Label

Georges Duboeuf Brouilly Flower Label

Georges Duboeuf Morgon Flower Label

Louis Jadot Beaujolais-Villages

Mommessin Beaujolais-Villages

BORDEAUX RED

Jean-Pierre Moueix Merlot

Mouton-Cadet

RHÔNE

E. Guigal Côtes du Rhône

Paul Jaboulet Aîné Côtes du Rhônes Parallèle "45"

La Vieille Ferme Côtes du Lubéron

La Vieille Ferme Côtes du Rhône Reserve

La Vielle Ferme Côtes du Ventoux

OTHER RED WINES

Château de Jau Vin de Pays des Côtes Catalanes Le
 Jaja de Jau

Château Lagrezette Cahors

Fortant de France Vin de Pays d'Oc Cabernet
 Sauvignon

Fortant de France Vin de Pays d'Oc Merlot

ALSACE

Pierre Sparr Riesling Carte d'Or

Leon Beyer Pinot Blanc

Alsace Willm Pinot Blanc

Hugel Gentil Hugel

Pierre Sparr Gewürztraminer Carte d'Or

OTHER WHITE WINES

Château Bonnet Entre-Deux-Mers Vinifié en Fûte
 Neuf

Domaine Deletang Touraine Sauvignon de Touraine

Georges Duboeuf St.-Véran Mâcon

Fortant de France Vin de Pays d'Oc Chardonnay

Fortant de France Vin de Pays d'Oc Sauvignon Blanc

Marquis de Goulaine Muscadet de Sèvre et Maine
 Sur Lie

How to Read a French Wine Label: I

Producer or Estate

Region of Origin

GEORGES DUBŒUF

BEAUJOLAIS-VILLAGES

APPELLATION BEAUJOLAIS-VILLAGES CONTROLÉE
RED BEAUJOLAIS WINE

MIS EN BOUTEILLES PAR
LES VINS GEORGES DUBŒUF
71570 ROMANÈCHE-THORINS
FRANCE

PRODUCED AND BOTTLED IN FRANCE

ALC. 12.5 % BY VOL.   PRODUCE OF FRANCE   750 ML
IMPORTED BY : W.J. DEUTSCH & SONS LTD., ARMONK, NY.

Importer

Production Information

How to Read a
French Wine Label: II

**Brand or
Proprietary
Name**

**Grape
Variety**

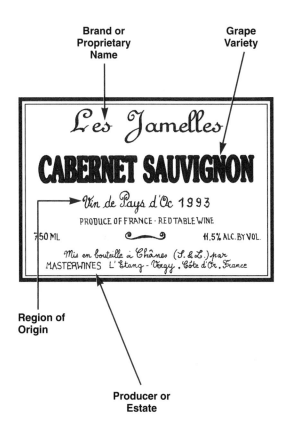

**Region of
Origin**

**Producer or
Estate**

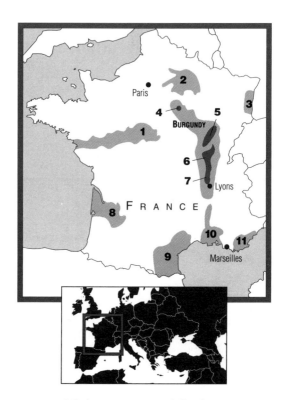

1. Loire
2. Champagne
3. Alsace
4. Chablis
5. Côte d'Or
6. Mâcon
7. Beaujolais

8. Bordeaux
9. Languedoc-
   Roussillion
   (d'Oc)
10. Rhône
11. Provence

RED WINES BY REGION

Beaujolais

88 GEORGES DUBOEUF Brouilly Château de Pierreux 1994 **$10.00** Subtle chocolate and coffee flavors add complexity to this ripe, firm Brouilly. The plum and black cherry notes are ripe, and the wine is balanced and long. This is rich enough to accompany a meal, and should improve through 1996.

87 GEORGES DUBOEUF Beaujolais-Villages Flower Label 1994 **$7.00** Tropical flavors and aromas are matched by some nice strawberry flavors. It has good structure, richness and moderate tannins. There's also some good spice on the lingering finish.

87 GEORGES DUBOEUF Morgon Flower Label 1994 **$9.00** An attractive combination of round fruit and firm tannins, this chewy wine offers fresh ripe plum, gamy and spicy flavors. A fine expression of the appellation. Drink now.

86 GEORGES DUBOEUF Beaujolais-Villages Château de Varennes 1994 **$8.00** Fruity and exuberant with a nice touch of richness and spice. Appealling plum and cherry flavors makes this a delicious quaff. Drink slightly chilled.

86 GEORGES DUBOEUF Brouilly Flower Label 1994 **$9.50** There's real flair here, with floral and bright berry notes giving immediate appeal and crisp acidity keeping it taut and fresh. It's no blockbuster, but does have lots of personality.

85 GEORGES DUBOEUF Brouilly Château de Nervers 1994 **$10.00** Polished, firm, even a bit hard, this wine offers black cherry, light chocolate and herbal flavors on a tannic frame. It has concentration, and may open and show more in 1996.

85 JEAN-MARC AUJOUX Fleurie RT 1994 **$10.00** There's good concentration here, with fleshy fruit and muscular tannins, but the flavors are still closed, hinting at plum, spice and chocolate. Drinkable now, but better in 1996.

84 GEORGES DUBOEUF Beaujolais-Villages Domaine du Granit Bleu 1994 **$8.00** Moderately rich and tannic, with appealing spice and plum flavors, this wine also has a tropical fruit component that begins in the aroma and carries through to the finish.

84 JEAN-MARC AUJOUX Brouilly RT 1994 **$8.00** Pleasant spice and cinnamon notes add interest to this soft, fruity wine. The cherry and berry flavors are ripe but simple, while soft tannins give it structure.

84 LOUIS JADOT Beaujolais-Villages Jadot 1994 **$10.00** Tastes like a light Pinot Noir with some nice spice and chocolate notes. The fruit flavors are dominated by plum and cherry, which iinger on the finish.

83 GEORGES DUBOEUF Beaujolais-Villages Château des Vierres 1994 **$8.00** Moderately rich and flavorful, with good strawberry flavors and a slightly green quality. The tropical, banana flavors linger on the finish.

83 MOMMESSIN Beaujolais-Villages Château du Carra 1994 **$8.00** Fruity and youthful, with a dollop of tannin and spice. Strawberry and banana flavors put their stamp on this medium-bodied wine.

83 MOMMESSIN Beaujolais-Villages 1994 **$8.00** A good, well-rounded wine, though a bit tannic on the finish. It offers moderate fruit flavors of strawberry and red plum.

82 GEORGES DUBOEUF Beaujolais-Villages Château de la Grande Grange 1994 **$8.00** Good strawberry and cherry flavors dominate this medium-bodied wine. It has moderate tannins and a nice dried-fruit finish.

82 MOMMESSIN Beaujolais Brouilly 1994 **$10.00** Clean and fruity, this offers bright simple flavors of cherry, banana and hard candy. It's friendly, but not complex.

81 GEORGES DUBOEUF Flower Label 1994 **$7.00** Robust for a Beaujolais, this shows round plum and grapey flavors and a mild jolt of tannin. Spice and bubblegum flavors linger on the finish.

Bordeaux Red

87 CHATEAU HAUT-MAZIERES 1990 **$10.00** Ripe fruit and a judicious use of oak give this wine chewy concentration and age-worthiness. It's firm, and a bit austere now, but balanced and fresh. A mini-Pauillac. A good value. Better in 1996.

86 CHATEAU LE BOUSCAT Grand Réserve 1990 **$9.00** Here's a harmonious, balanced wine with a solid core of black cherry and plum fruit, attractive accents of tobacco and herbs and a firm frame of tannins. It only lacks complexity. Drink now.

80 CHATEAU PITRAY Côtes de Castillon 1992 **$8.00** Spicy cherry and plum fruit flavors are framed by firm tannins in this straightforward, medium-bodied wine. It's simple yet balanced, and rich enough for food.

Burgundy Red

82 JEAN CLAUDE BOISSET Pinot Noir de Bourgogne 1992 **$9.00** A nicely balanced, modest style of Burgundy that's fruity and spicy in aroma, firm in texture and offers enough cherry and strawberry flavor to make it satisfying. If it only didn't turn stemmy and murky on the finish.

82 OLIVIER LEFLAIVE Pinot Noir 1992 **$9.00** Modest plum and strawberry aromas, matched with smoky, spicy flavors and a dry, tannic finish add up to a typical, solid Burgundy. Drink now while the fruit lasts.

Rhône

85 CHATEAU MONT-REDON Côtes du Rhône 1992 **$9.00** A rich and round, fruity, full-bodied red that's meaty in its flavor and texture. Tannic, but ready to drink now.

85 E. GUIGAL Côtes du Rhône 1991 **$10.00** A lively Rhône, with plenty of plum, cherry and spice flavors. It has good acidity to match the fruit, as well as a pleasant gameyness. Firmly textured and flavorful. Drink now through 1996.

84 LA BOUVERIE Costières de Nimes 1992 **$5.00** Ripe and interesting in flavor and aroma, blending herb, smoke, pepper and tart cherry. Full-bodied, and not too tannic.

84 LA VIEILLE FERME Côtes du Ventoux 1992 **$7.00** Agreeably jammy in flavor, full-bodied, peppery and fresh. A good, solid mouthful of wine for current drinking.

83 LUCIEN DESCHAUX Côtes du Rhône Le Vieux Presbytere 1991 **$8.00** Spicy and rich with pleasant plum and cherry flavors. There are some nice cinnamon notes that linger on the finish, but the wine is a little tired.

83 PAUL JABOULET AÎNÉ Côtes du Rhône Parallèle "45" 1993 **$9.00** A full-bodied, deep-flavored, sturdy Rhône with ample blackberry, pepper and smoke flavors. It's tannic and dry; best to drink soon.

82 DOMAINE DE LA MORDORÉ Côtes du Rhône 1992 **$8.00** Fruity in aroma, but very dry and lean in flavor with tart cherry and smoke accents and firm tannins. Rather rustic, spare, almost austere. A good wine but we would like more ripeness and depth.

82 GEORGES DUBOEUF Côtes du Rhône Domaine des Moulins 1993 **$6.00** A young, dark and tannic Rhône with peppery, herbal and dried fruit aromas, but flavors that thin out on the finish. It's hearty and impressive, but we could wish for more richness and depth. Drink now through 1996.

Other Red

84 CATHERINE DE ST.-JUERY Côteaux du Languedoc 1993 **$8.50** A concentrated, full-bodied, firmly tannic red with a deep color, peppery, berrylike flavors and a sense of intensity. Drink now through 1996.

83 CHATEAU DE JAU Vin de Pays des Côtes Catalanes Le Jaja de Jau 1993 **$7.00** This light, fruity red makes pleasant summertime quaffing, with fresh cherry and strawberry flavors, soft tannins and a peppery kick. Try it slightly chilled.

83 CHATEAU LAGREZETTE Cahors 1990 **$10.00** Deep color and intriguing anise and smoky aromas promise more than the wine delivers right now; on the palate it's smooth and firm but lacking in fruit. Still, there's some concentration.

83 GEORGES DUBOEUF Vin de Pays d'Oc Domaine de Bordeneuve 1993 **$5.50** You can almost taste the southern French sun here, with its dark color, flavors of ripe plums and grilled meat and firm tannins. Enjoy this simple, vivid wine in its youth.

82 CHATEAU ROUTAS Côteaux Varois 1993 **$7.00** A fresh, grapey wine that seems barely out of the cradle, it's still balanced and firm enough to marry well with simple food.

82 DOMAINE DE LA COSTE Côteaux du Languedoc Cuvée Sélectionnée Saint Christol 1993 **$7.00** A sturdy, hearty red that reminds us of a Côtes du Rhône with its peppery, grapey flavor profile and moderate tannins.

81 CHATEAU PECH DE JAMMES Cahors 1989
$8.50 This lively wine offers bright acidity and firm
tannins, but the ripe cherry and berry fruit flavors are
a bit subdued. It's clean and refreshing, but needs food
to soften and round it into attractiveness.

80 MAS STE.-BERTHE Côteaux d'Aix en
Provence Cuvée Tradition 1992 **$10.00** Promising
roasted aromas are followed by greener, leaner fruit
flavors. Interesting but limited.

WHITE WINES BY REGION

Alsace

88 PIERRE SPARR Riesling Carte d'Or 1992
$9.00 Smooth texture and beautifully integrated fla-
vors of apple, peach and grapefruit combine for a fine
taste on the palate and a long finish. This is intriguing
to drink now for its fruit and liveliness, but it should
improve if cellared until about 1996.

87 DOMAINES SCHLUMBERGER Pinot Blanc
1993 **$10.00** Exotic accents of honey and pineapple
make this an especially ripe and fruity tasting Pinot
Blanc. Almost like a Chardonnay, with buttery notes
lingering on the finish.

87 LEON BEYER Pinot Blanc 1993 **$10.00**
There's good depth of flavor in this round, soft wine.
Orange, melon and vanilla notes marry nicely and follow through on the long finish; the wine is well-balanced and fresh.

86 HUGEL Gentil Hugel 1993 **$10.00** A spicy, floral-tasting white wine that's exuberant and fresh, quite dry and refreshing. Solid, flavorful and interesting.

86 J.B. ADAM Pinot Blanc Réserve 1992 **$9.75** Light, delicate flavors and a smooth, solid texture make this floral-scented wine a real charmer. It has thin layers of peach, apple, cream and spice notes, and a lingering, soft finish.

86 MEYER-FONNE Pinot Blanc 1993 **$10.00** True to type Pinot Blanc, dry and full-bodied, tasting like melons, almonds and minerals, with a fine tangy acidity and a lingering finish. Should be very food-friendly.

85 PIERRE SPARR Gewürztraminer Carte d'Or 1992 **$10.00** Lively, fruity and fresh, with zesty lemon and orange flavors and great balance. Firm acidity keeps it clean and helps the flavors linger on the finish.

84 DOMAINES SCHLUMBERGER Schlumberger Reserve 1990 **$10.00** A taste of the big time, at a reasonable price. A rich, lush-textured, broadly flavorful wine with ample aromas of rose petal, honey and papaya and flavors that are ripe and exotic. Gives you all it's got upfront then turns leaner on the finish.

84 PIERRE SPARR Pinot Gris Carte d'Or 1992 **$10.00** Expressive yet subtle, this generous wine offers pear, honey and butter flavors, soft and clean. It's balanced and easy to drink.

83 ALSACE WILLM Pinot Blanc 1993 **$8.00** A smooth, flavorful wine with notes of peach and hazelnut; has enough underlying acidity to keep it lively, yet gives a round, full feeling without tartness. Easy to drink; best as an apéritif.

83 PIERRE SPARR Chasselas Vielles Vignes 1992 **$8.00** Attractive floral aromas lead to peach and grapefruit flavors in this dry, delicate wine. With refreshing acidity and soft flavors, it has enough charm to while away a summer afternoon.

82 J. BECKER Pinot Blanc 1992 **$10.00** A feather pillow of a wine, soft and generous. Apple and lime flavors are delicate and light; the wine is appealing without much structure.

82 SELTZ Pinot Blanc 1992 **$9.00** Made in a delicate style, this offers grapefruit and hazelnut flavors in a clean, almost austere frame. It's crisp yet still soft.

Bordeaux White

89 CHATEAU HAUT-MAZIERES 1991 **$10.00** A very good wine from an off vintage. Clean, balanced, complex and gaining an intriguing maturity. It blends toasty, figgy, coconut and pineapple flavors in a harmonious mix that lingers a long time on the finish. Keeps you coming back for more.

86 CHATEAU BONNET Entre-Deux-Mers Vinifié en Fùts Neuf 1992 **$10.00** Well made and balanced, featuring a subtle, grassy note and butter, orange and honey flavors.

84 MOUTON-CADET 1992 **$10.00** A brightly fruity wine with pear, melon and slightly herbal flavors and good richness and body. Attractive and generous in flavor, yet well-balanced with acidity.

83 CHATEAU LE BOUSCAT Grand Réserve 1992 **$9.00** An oaky style of white Bordeaux, with seductive aromas of toast and vanilla, but not much fruit flavor to back them up. Clean and balanced, yet lacking richness and focus.

83 LUCIEN DESCHAUX Blanc 1991 **$8.00** A basically tight and austere wine that has developed some attractively nutty, toasty flavors that make it interesting. It's mature and ready to drink now.

82 LUCIEN DESCHAUX Graves 1991 **$9.00** A robust white Graves with buttery, earthy flavors and a smooth texture. Full-bodied and assertive, but we would like to taste more fruit.

81 AUGEY 1992 **$6.00** A soft, easy-to-drink white wine with fresh fruit and herb flavors. Clean, if a bit lacking in concentration. Good value.

Burgundy White

86 GEORGES DUBOEUF Mâcon-Lugny Chardonnay Fête des Fleurs 1994 **$8.00** Concentration and clean, varietal fruit give this wine depth and appeal. The fruit flavors run from apple to melon to pear, with just enough oak for structure and acidity for balance. A well-made wine.

86 GEORGES DUBOEUF Mâcon St.-Véran 1994 **$9.00** Tropical fruit and buttery flavors stand out in this exuberant wine, which still has a crisp core of citrusy acidity. It doesn't go very deep, but offers harmony and even elegance in a fruit-driven style.

86 JEAN CLAUDE BOISSET Challonaise Rully 1992 **$9.50** A pleasing, well-rounded Chardonnay with toasty aromas, solid flavors of pear and nutmeg and a lingering finish. Lively and well-balanced, too.

85 BARTON & GUESTIER Mâcon Saint-Louis Chardonnay 1993 **$8.00** An aroma dominated by cider gives way to a wine that is clean and straightforward. It's rich and solid with appealing apple and pear flavors, and a hint of licorice.

84 DOMAINE MAURICE PROTHEAU Challonaise Rully 1992 **$8.00** A thick, buttery-tasting Chardonnay with a broad, smooth texture, lots of vanilla and fig flavor and a lingering finish. Balanced on the soft, fat side.

81 GEORGES DUBOEUF Mâcon-Villages Domaine les Chenevières 1994 **$8.50** Straightforward apple flavor and a fat palate feel are strengths, but there's little complexity or depth. It's clean and offers easy drinking now.

Loire

85 CHATEAU DU COING DE ST.-FIACRE
Muscadet de Sèvre et Maine Sur Lie 1993 **$8.00**
Ripe, full flavors move from apple to melon and pear
in this generous wine. It's round on the palate and
long in the finish, and though plenty crisp for food
isn't dominated by acidity.

85 DOMAINE DE LA BATARDIERE Muscadet
de Sèvre et Maine 1992 **$7.00** A round wine with
almond and pear flavors and good depth on the palate.
The acidity is well-integrated and the wine is still
fresh. It's smooth, clean and has enough weight to
match up well with chicken on the grill.

84 HERITIERS GUILBAUD Muscadet de Sèvre
et Maine Clos de Beauregard Sur Lie 1992 **$8.00**
Appealing aromas of apples, butter and herbs give
way to round, fresh fruit on the palate, marred just a
bit by a slightly sour finish, which might not matter so
much with food.

84 CHATEAU DE LA RAGOTIERE Muscadet de
Sèvre et Maine Sur Lie 1992 **$9.50** The aromas
have evolved into pleasant butter and vanilla notes,
and the wine is smooth and round. It lacks the sharp
edge of acidity, but is still fresh and fruity.

84 DOMAINE DE LA QUILLA Muscadet de
Sèvre et Maine Sur Lie 1993 **$9.50** This crisp,
clean, lightly fruity wine is basically neutral in character. It has some pleasant citrus and pear character,
and is tart and refreshing.

84 HENRI POIRON Muscadet de Sèvre et Maine Château des Grandes Noëlles Sur Lie 1993 **$9.00** Floral notes add interest to the light lemon and green apple flavors in this light-bodied, crisp wine. It has a pleasing delicacy.

84 LES FRERES COUILLAUD Vin de Pays du Jardin de la France Domaine Couillaud 1992 **$10.00** A smooth, full-bodied wine with vanilla and buttery notes that blend well with apple and peach flavors. It's soft and well-integrated, not complex or long, but appealing for drinking now.

84 MARQUIS DE GOULAINE Muscadet de Sèvre et Maine Sur Lie 1993 **$7.00** Hints of nuts and spice give this round, firm wine an appealing complexity; it's crisp but not overly tart, with more substance than many Muscadets. Nicely balanced.

83 ANDRE-MICHEL BREGEON Muscadet de Sèvre et Maine Sur Lie 1992 **$10.00** A year in the bottle has softened this wine nicely, turning the citrus notes into rounder apple flavors, and a slight spritz keeps it refreshing. It's smooth and polished, as Muscadets go.

83 CHATEAU DE LA CHESNAIE Muscadet de Sèvre et Maine Sur Lie 1993 **$8.00** Light floral and herbal aromas are attractive, and the wine has a bracing austerity on the palate, with lively grapefruit flavors. It's clean and very tart; refreshing with food.

83 DOMAINE DELETANG Touraine Sauvignon de Touraine 1993 **$10.00** Fresh herbal and lemon aromas and flavors give this wine character and typicity. It's very dry and crisp and the herbal note carries through on the finish. A good picnic wine.

83 M. BONNIGAL Touraine Domaine la Prévötè Sauvignon de Touraine 1993 **$7.00** There's not much varietal character in this tart, appley wine, but it's light, clean and refreshing. A simple, snappy wine.

82 DOMAINE BARRE Muscadet de Sèvre et Maine 1993 **$9.00** This crisp, lemony wine goes down quick and clean. It's light-bodied and basically neutral, with tart green apple and citrus notes.

81 B. CHEREAU Muscadet de Sèvre et Maine Cuvée des Ducs 1993 **$6.00** Light and crisp, this delicate wine offers apple and light melon flavors, with a hint of bread dough on the finish. It's clean and short.

80 DONATIEN BAHUAUD Muscadet de Sèvre et Maine Cuvée des Aigles 1992 **$6.00** Crisp, simple and light—nothing to fault, nor to get excited about. The light green apple and lemon flavors are clean and fresh.

Other White

83 CHATEAU ROUTAS Côteaux Varois Pyramus 1993 **$8.00** A spicy white wine with modest green apple and fig flavors. Straightforward and refreshing with a fairly alcoholic finish.

81 LA VIEILLE FERME Côtes du Rhône Reserve 1993 **$10.00** Fresh and clean, a refreshing and basic white wine with good acidity, but not a lot of flavor.

81 LA VIEILLE FERME Côtes du Lubéron 1993 **$7.00** A simple, enjoyable white wine with basic apple flavors and good acidity. Refreshing in a straightforward style.

80 GEORGES DUBOEUF Vin de Pays d'Oc Chasan 1994 **$6.00** Floral aromas and soft peach flavors are pleasant in this soft, simple wine. It shows some delicacy and would make a good apéritif.

RED WINES BY GRAPE VARIETY

Cabernet Sauvignon

83 FORTANT DE FRANCE Vin de Pays d'Oc Cabernet Sauvignon 1993 **$7.50** A robust, enjoyable Cabernet that is firm-textured, full-flavored and fairly tannic.

82 LES JAMELLES Vin de Pays d'Oc Cabernet Sauvignon 1993 **$7.00** Appealing fruit flavors and firm tannins make this a good, straightforward Cabernet to drink tonight.

82 LIONEL GALLULA Vin de Pays d'Oc Cabernet Sauvignon 1992 **$8.00** This ripe, concentrated wine shows plum, tar and menthol flavors, but the tannins are a bit hard and there's a green note in the finish.

81 CHANTEFLEUR Vin de Pays d'Oc Cabernet Sauvignon 1993 **$5.00** A simple, appetizing red with fresh plum and cherry flavors and moderate tannnins.

80 ALEXIS LICHINE Vin de Pays d'Oc Cabernet Sauvignon 1993 **$6.00** An herbal smelling, plummy flavored, tough-textured red wine that is simple and sturdy.

Merlot

84 GEORGES DUBOEUF Vin de Pays d'Oc Merlot Domaine de Bordeneuve 1994 **$7.00** A dark and tannic red wine with attractive aromas and flavors of smoke, cherry and herbs. Has enough complexity of flavor to make it interesting, but it's firm with tannins.

83 DELAS Vin de Pays d'Oc Merlot 1993 **$9.00** A smooth drinking, nicely flavored red wine with blackberry and cherry accents and light tannins. It is rich in fruit, appealing in texture, and ready to drink.

83 GEORGES DUBOEUF Vin de Pays d'Oc Merlot 1994 **$7.00** Deep in color, smoky and herbal in aroma, with modest plum and licorice flavors and moderate tannins. Promises more flavor than it delivers, but is still enjoyable.

83 MOREAU Vin de Pays de Cassan Merlot 1992 **$6.00** Solid fruit flavors are rounded out by spicy accents in this fully mature red. Drink now for its smooth texture and cherry-plum flavors.

82 CHANTEFLEUR Vin de Pays d'Oc Merlot 1993 **$5.00** A robust, fairly tannic and fruity red with jammy flavors and a nice bite to the texture.

82 FORTANT DE FRANCE Vin de Pays d'Oc Merlot 1992 **$7.00** This fresh, clean wine shows plum and cherry flavors with a pleasant herbal accent; it's medium-bodied, with moderate, well-integrated tannins. Not that expressive, but well-balanced and accessible now.

82 JEAN-PIERRE MOUEIX Merlot 1990 **$10.00** Sweet, toasty new oak is the dominant flavor in this round but tannic wine. There's cherry fruit, but it's not concentrated enough for balance. A tasty but slightly unbalanced effort.

81 BARTON & GUESTIER Vin de Pays d'Oc Merlot 1993 **$6.00** A straightforward, medium-bodied Merlot with light tannins and pleasant plum and herb flavors.

Syrah

82 DOMAINE DES FONTANELLES Vin de Pays d'Oc Shiraz-Syrah 1993 **$7.00** A strong earthy streak runs through this dark, tannic, meaty red. It's big and tough, but if you like Syrah on the wild side, this is good.

82 GEORGES DUBOEUF Vin de Pays d'Oc Syrah 1994 **$6.00** Like a Côtes du Rhône but fresher. Deep in color, smoky and peppery in aroma, yet mild in flavor. Light on tannins and easy to drink.

80 CHANTEFLEUR Vin de Pays d'Oc Syrah 1993 **$5.00** A full-bodied, dry, tannic red with blackberry and black peppper flavors that persist on the finish. Good and solid, if a bit rough.

80 LES JAMELLES Vin de Pays d'Oc Syrah 1992 **$7.00** A mature and mellow red that is full-bodied, light in tannins, with modest plum and herb flavors.

WHITE WINES BY GRAPE VARIETY

Chardonnay

86 GEORGES DUBOEUF Vin de Pays d'Oc Chardonnay 1994 **$7.00** A touch of oak adds interest to this wine, and toasty flavors that complement the appley fruit. It's clean and well-balanced. A classy wine for the appellation.

84 LA PORCII Vin de Pays d'Oc Chardonnay 1992 **$10.00** A big, rich wine with toast, butter and fig flavors, it's deep, soft and ready to drink. Oak lovers will appreciate it, but it could use more fruit for balance.

83 BARTON & GUESTIER Vin de Pays d'Oc Chardonnay 1993 **$6.00** Fairly rich and buttery, with good apple and honeydew melon flavors. This wine is clean and well-made but doesn't have much of a finish.

83 FORTANT DE FRANCE Vin de Pays d'Oc Chardonnay 1993 **$8.00** Packs a punch with some good apple and peach flavors. Crisp and lively with a good acidity and a clean finish.

80 MOREAU Vin de Pays d'Oc Chardonnay 1993 **$6.50** A basic white wine that is pleasant enough, but lacks excitement. The green apple flavors are straightforward, with a little grapefruit tang.

Sauvignon Blanc

83 FORTANT DE FRANCE Vin de Pays d'Oc Sauvignon Blanc 1993 **$7.50** This fresh white has bright fruity flavors and a rich texture, without much complexity. It makes pleasant quaffing now.

82 DOMAINE DES FONTANELLES Vin de Pays d'Oc Sauvignon Blanc 1993 **$7.00** This fresh, lively wine shows typical and appealing grapefruit and herbal flavors in a lighter style. It's clean and bright, but lacks a bit of concentration.

81 GEORGES DUBOEUF Vin de Pays d'Oc Sauvignon 1994 **$6.00** Basically neutral in flavor, this rugged white has enough body and acidity to hold its own with food. It's simple and straightforward, a good refresher.

SPARKLING

80 CADEAUX Brut Royal Crown NV **$9.00** An easy-to-drink bubbly with mature flavors, a soft texture and a bit of sweetness. Simple but good.

Germany

BY BRUCE SANDERSON

Germany produces a compelling variety of wines in 13 wine-growing regions (including two in the former East German Republic). Selecting a German wine appears to be a daunting task, due to the large number of types and styles, and confusion resulting from label nomenclature. With the help of a few basic guidelines, however, selecting a German wine is not difficult, given the generally high quality standards of most producers.

Undoubtedly, the best German wines are made from Riesling. While few of these fall into the "under $10" category, there are still good-value Rieslings to be found. While some originate from a single vineyard site, such as Piesporter Goldtröpfchen, most are usually blends of different sites, bottled under a *Grosslagen* or collective name, for example Zeller Schwarze Katz or Bernkasteler Kurfürstlay. Others may be blends of two or more grape varieties. German wine law requires a varietally labelled wine to contain at least 85% of the specified grape variety. Varieties commonly blended with Riesling are Sylvaner, Müller-Thurgau and Elbling.

Müller-Thurgau is the most widely planted white variety, and is capable of producing good value wines if the yields are low enough to coax some character out of the grapes. There is some red wine production, mainly from Pinot Noir (called Spätburgunder in Germany), but the values are more likely to be from varieties such as Blauer Portugieser, Trollinger and Lemberger. The red wine reviewed below is a blend of the latter two varieties cultivated in Württemberg. With German wines, the region often provides an indication of style. Mosel wines tend to be the most delicate, Rheinhessen rounder and fruity, while Nahe wines fall somewhwere between the two. Rheingau produces firm, spicy wines. The richest, fullest versions come from Pfalz. Because of their vibrant acidity, fruitiness and hint of sweetness, German white wines are terrific with food, particulary seafood, chicken, pork, smoked meats and fish, and spicy Asian dishes. Served slightly chilled, the red can accompany light meats, charcuterie and mild cheeses.

Bruce Sanderson is Wine Spectator's *New York tasting coordinator.*

WITH THE HELP OF A FEW BASIC GUIDELINES, SELECTING A GERMAN WINE IS NOT DIFFICULT.

How to Read a German Wine Label

Producer or Estate

Region of Origin

Village

Vintage

Vineyard

SCHMITT SÖHNE

750 ml e

MOSEL-SAAR-RUWER
1993
PIESPORTER
GOLDTRÖPFCHEN
RIESLING - SPÄTLESE
Qualitätswein mit Prädikat - A. P. Nr. 3 907 027 067 94
Shipped by: Weinkellerei H. Schmitt Söhne GmbH, Longuich/Mosel
Bottled by: Herhen Kellerei GmbH, D-54340 Longuich/Mosel-Germany

Grape Variety

Government approval no.

Quality Level

Ripeness level at harvest

1. Mosel-Saar-Ruwer   4. Rheinhessen
2. Nahe   5. Pfalz
3. Rheingau

Riesling

84 SCHMITT SOHNE Spätlese Mosel-Saar-Ruwer Piesporter Goldtröpfchen 1993 **$9.50** Pleasant and rich, with ripe peach and apple flavors and a good finish. The fruity aromas give way to a well-made Riesling. A flavorful and satisfying wine.

84 SICHEL SOHNE QbA Rheingau Bereich Johannisberg 1992 **$8.00** Classic petrol aromas give way to a crisp, austere wine, with just a touch of sweetness. Good mineral and spice flavors.

83 VON HOVEL Kabinett Saar-Ruwer Balduin Von Hövel 1993 **$9.00** Plenty of body, with apple pie aromas and flavors. Medium bodied and fruity with an appley after taste.

82 LEONARD KREUSCH Spätlese Mosel-Saar-Ruwer Bernkasteler Kurfürstlay 1992 **$9.50** A solid wine with minerally aromas and peach and apple flavors. Clean and well-made with a good, crisp finish. Good for a summer picnic.

82 MOSELLAND Spätlese Mosel-Saar-Ruwer Graacher Himmelreich 1992 **$10.00** A good middle-of-the-road wine with strong peachy aromas and flavors. Typical for the vintage with appealing, soft, fruit flavors. The finish is appley and minerally.

81 DEINHARD Kabinett Mosel-Saar-Ruwer Piesporter Goldtropfchen 1991 **$10.00** Very crisp and lean, with green-apple flavors accented by smoke and mineral. It's flavorful within a narrow spectrum. Clean and austere overall.

81 SCHMITT SOHNE Kabinett Mosel-Saar-Ruwer Piesporter Goldtröpfchen 1993 **$7.50**
Firm, with moderate peach and apple flavors. A citrus note runs throughout this cleanly-made wine, which gives it a nice crispness.

80 LEONARD KREUSCH QbA Mosel-Saar-Ruwer Piesporter Goldtröpfchen 1992 **$9.00** A soft, neutral wine with flavors typical of this vintage. Smooth textured, apparently low in acidity but with a clean finish. Has fairly light peach and apple flavors.

Other White

86 WEINGUT KLEIN Müller-Thurgau Kabinett Trocken Rheinhessen Niersteiner Spiegelberg 1992 **$10.00** A serious, dry Müller-Thurgau. It's a rich wine with nice, concentrated fruit flavors and a lingering finish. Appealing aromas of bread dough and apples. A good value at $10.00 for this one-liter bottle.

82 SCHMITT SOHNE Mosel-Saar-Ruwer Zeller Schwarze Katz 1993 **$5.50** Peach and apple flavors dominate this solid and cleanly-made wine. Its acidity adds some nice zip and makes for a good, slightly-sweet quaff.

81 SCHMITT SOHNE Mosel-Saar-Ruwer Bernkasteler Kurfürstlay Auslese 1993 **$9.50** A soft, simple wine with moderate apple and tangerine flavors. The flavors are clean, however, with a hint of rich sweetness on the finish.

80 SCHMITT SOHNE Mosel-Saar-Ruwer
Piesporter Michelsberg 1993 **$5.50** This is a fairly
neutral wine, with moderate tangerine and apple flavors. Light and refreshing, but nothing exciting.

Red

80 GRAF VON NEIPPERG Rotwein QbA 1993
$10.00 This deep-colored, spicy wine has attractive
peppery and herbal flavors with a tannic intensity that
seems to be due more to extraction than ripeness.

Italy

By Per-Henrik Mansson

More than any other European country, Italy has come of age in recent years as a producer of high quality—and sometimes very expensive—wines. Yet riding on the coattails of the more famous wines are a slew of great values. Italy already has a favorable climate and fine vineyard land. Now, improvements to wine cellars and vineyards have enabled the Italians to compete in the world marketplace.

From Piedmont in the north to Sicily in the south, Italy is a cornucopia of wine regions that grow dozens of indigenous grape varieties. To be sure, Cabernet Sauvignon, Chardonnay and Merlot are making some inroads, but these are a drop in the bucket compared to wines made with local varieties.

Italian wine labels often fail to mention the grapes used to make the wine. For example, the backbone of Chianti Classico is Sangiovese, a grape that produces a red wine with a refreshing, crisp texture. But several other grape varieties are included as well, and the percentages can change from year to year.

The geographic origins of Italian wines are prominently highlighted on the labels. Thus, names such as Barolo, Chianti Classico and Brunello di Montalcino indicate the regulated districts, or appellations, that the wines come from.

The Piedmont region, with its upscale Barolo and Barbaresco, and Tuscany, with its Brunello di

Montalcino, produce the bulk of the expensive red Italian wines exported to the United States. Yet these regions also produce their fair share of good values.

From Tuscany, try Antinori's perennial bargain, the widely available Santa Cristina. And if you find a Chianti Classico at $10 or below from the outstanding 1990 vintage—like Saccardi Chianti Classico—don't hesitate to buy it for its fresh character and excellent concentration.

When the price is right, we also have a weakness for Dolcetto and Barbera, two Piedmont grape varieties that produce deliciously grapey, very aromatic and not-too-tannic wines. A dozen producers make fine Dolcettos and Barberas at attractive prices in top years; among them are Pio Cesare and Michele Chiarlo.

Valpolicella, a wine region just outside Verona in northeastern Italy, makes a juicy, soft red primarily from the Corvina grape. Even better is the Valpolicella Classico. The best of these, like a good vintage from producer Masi, will retail for under $10 and score very well in *Wine Spectator* tastings.

For an easy, light red, don't overlook Bardolino, grown in the Verona area on the eastern side of Lake Garda. It uses the same grape varieties as Valpolicella but tends to make a distinctly lighter wine.

Although the real action in Italy is in red wines, the white wines of northeastern Italy are making progress, as evidenced by the Anselmi Soave Classico Sanvincenzo and 1993 Vignalta Siriol from the Veneto. In Umbria, Lungarotti remains a top producer of good values in any year, and its 1993 Pinot Grigio is worth looking for.

Like no other cuisine in the world, Italian cooking lends itself to light, youthful and often inexpensive wine. What better match for pasta, risotto or pizza than a glass of fresh, vibrant, slightly chilled Chianti

Classico, Dolcetto, Barbera, Valpolicella or Rosso di Montalcino? Or try a thirst-quenching white like Soave, Pinot Grigio or Verdicchio with grilled fish sprinkled lightly with olive oil and lemon juice.

Per-Henrik Mansson is a senior editor of Wine Spectator.

Most Reliable Values

These wines have proven to be of consistently good quality, year in and year out. Even if a particular vintage is not reviewed here, you may purchase these wines with confidence.

RED WINES

Pio Cesare Barbera d'Alba

Michele Chiarlo Barbera d'Asti

Baccardi Chianti Classico

Cecchi Chianti Classico

Renzo Masi Chianti Rufina

Antinori Santa Cristina

Masi Valpolicella Classico Superiore

WHITE WINES

Castellare di Castellina Bianco

Lungarotti Torre di Giano Bianco di Torgiano

Tiefenbrunner Alto Adige Chardonnay

Lungarotti Pinot Grigio

Tiefenbrunner Alto Adige Pinot Grigio

Masi Soave Classico Superiore

Santa Sofia Soave Classico Superiore

How to Read an Italian Wine Label

Brand or Proprietary Name

Grape Variety

Region of Origin

RED TABLE WINE · PRODUCT OF ITALY

SANTA CRISTINA.

SANGIOVESE TOSCANO

1993

ANTINORI

750 ML

ALC. 12% BY VOL.

Producer or Estate

Vintage

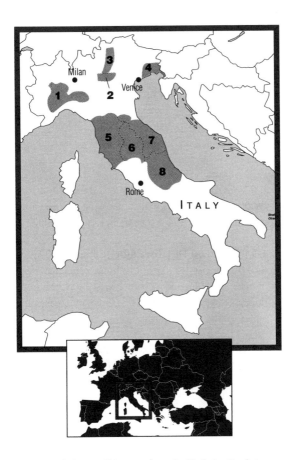

1. Piedmont (Piemonte):
   Barbera, Dolcetto

2. Verona: Bardolino,
   Soave, Valpolicella

3. Trentino/Alto Adige

4. Friuli-Venezia

5. Tuscany: Chianti,
   Rosso di Montalcino

6. Umbria: Orvieto

7. The Marches:
   Verdicchio

8. Abruzzi:
   Montepulciano
   d'Abruzzo

RED

Barbera

86 PIO CESARE Barbera d'Alba 1991 **$10.00**
Perfumy with rose petal and violet overtones to the
black cherry and raspberry fruit, showing enough
concentration to balance the modest tannins. A little
peppery on the finish.

85 MICHELE CHIARLO Barbera d'Asti 1993
$9.00 Fresh and fruity, a generous wine with youthful
berry and cherry fruit that tastes ripe and appealing.

83 FONTANAFREDDA Barbera d'Alba 1990
$10.00 Almost over the hill with interesting mature
aromas of truffles and mushrooms. The flavors are
dominated by dried cherries that turn a bit astringent
and dried out on the finish.

82 TENUTE COLUE Barbera d'Alba 1992
$10.00 A very rustic style with dried cherry and
stewed plum flavors. A little dull and a bit astringent.

Bardolino

83 MASI Bardolino Classico Superiore 1992
$8.00 Soft and round, this wine has generous black
cherry, coffee and smoky flavors and just enough tannin for grip. A bit more structured than most
Bardolinos; drinking well now.

81 BOLLA Bardolino Classico 1993 **$7.00** A dark
rosé in color, this soft, light-bodied wine offers strawberry and tart cherry flavors in an easy-drinking style.
Try it slightly chilled.

80 MOSCA Bardolino 1993 **$5.00** An easy-to-drink, soft red wine. Light and fruity with appealing sweet cherry and raspberry flavors. It has cedary aromas and light tannins.

Chianti

87 SACCARDI Chianti Classico 1990 **$10.00**
Here's a juicy, generous wine with fresh, ripe flavors of plum, tart cherry, chocolate and spice. It's round on the palate, with a firm tannic core; good with food now, it will benefit with a year or two more in the bottle.

86 CECCHI Chianti Classico 1992 **$8.00**
Attractive smoke and spice notes weave through this round, fruity wine and linger on the finish. It has balance and some concentration.

84 CAPEZZANA Chianti Montalbano 1993 **$8.00**
A good, firmly-structured wine with lots of strawberry and cherry fruit. Finishes a little earthy, but still appealing.

84 RENZO MASI Chianti Rufina 1993 **$6.00**
Tight, vivid and still showing the grapiness of youth, this offers fresh cherry and smoky flavors, light, firm tannins and good balance.

82 SPALLETTI Chianti 1993 **$7.50** Firm and flavorful with good cherry and almond flavors. A straightforward and fairly light wine, with a stemmy quality in the aroma.

81 CASTELLO DI VOLPAIA Chianti Borgianni 1992 **$8.00** A full-bodied wine with cherry and plum flavors and some richness. Simple and cleanly made, but nothing to get excited about.

80 BARONE RICASOLI Chianti 1994 **$6.50** Straightforward, fruity Chianti with light tannins and a crisp finish. Pleasant glass of wine. Drink now.

80 BARONE RICASOLI Chianti Classico 1993 **$8.50** Light, simple and fully mature wine. Plenty of plummy, red fruit character. Just a touch of dilution, but it makes for easy drinking upon release. Serve slightly chilled.

80 CASTELLO D'ALBOLA Chianti Classico 1991 **$9.00** Lean and a bit hard, this wine offers modest cherry and strawberry fruit along with coffee and chocolate accents. It's balanced and drinkable.

Dolcetto

86 RENATO RATTI Dolcetto d'Alba 1993 **$10.00** Ripe and round, this wine marries lush blackberry fruit flavors with a light earthy note. There's a good balance of fruit and tannin, and impressive concentration.

83 CA' DE MONTE Dolcetto d'Alba 1993 **$8.00** Cherry and nutmeg flavors are brightened by lively acidity in this brisk, light-bodied wine. This is light and fresh, ready to drink.

83 PIO CESARE Dolcetto d'Alba 1992 **$10.00** Plum and floral aromas are attractive, and there's some depth to the plum and cherry flavors, but the finish is a bit hollow and dry. Still, it provides some muscular pleasure.

Merlot

85 CA'VIT Trentino Merlot Riserva 1991 **$8.00**
Well-balanced and complex; made in a Bordeaux
style. A deeply flavored red that blends ripe plum,
tomato and tobacco flavors with good acidity and
modest tannins. Enjoy now.

83 BOLLA Piave Merlot 1993 **$7.00** Pleasant
cherry and smoke aromas and flavors mingle in this
fresh, light-bodied wine. The tannins are light and it's
drinking well now.

82 CIELO Merlot 1992 **$5.00** Chocolate and herbal
flavors give this soft, round wine presence; black
cherry fruit keeps it fresh. Good drinking now.

82 ZONIN Merlot-Cabernet del Friuli 1992 **$6.00**
A straightforward, nicely fruity red wine that's fresh
and ready to drink.

80 COLLAVINI Grave del Friuli Campo Olivio
Merlot 1991 **$7.00** Dry and austere in texture, but
with enough fruit flavor to flesh it out. Has raspberry,
tomato and herb accents. Light in tannins.

Montepulciano d'Abruzzo

86 MASCIARELLI 1992 **$6.00** Has loads of black-
berry and blueberry fruit flavors, accented by nice
earthy and meaty notes. It tastes chewy, dense and
fairly well concentrated. A great bargain.

84 VILLA CERVIA 1992 **$4.00** Peppery, fruity and concentrated with blackberry and currant flavors. Seems slightly sweet, with a good shot of tannin and fruit on the finish.

83 CANALETTO 1993 **$6.00** Soft and easy-going, with fresh strawberry flavors. Fresh, light, and medium-bodied. A supple and dry red wine.

82 COCORA ORTONA Farnese 1992 **$5.00** Well-balanced and dominated by interesting blackberry and prune flavors. A fairly tannic wine that becomes astringent on the finish.

82 DARIO D'ANGELO 1993 **$4.00** A fruity, medium-bodied red wine with fresh berry flavors and a hint of licorice. Easy-to-drink, with a simple finish.

81 BARONE CORNACCHIA 1992 **$8.00** A rustic, ripe red wine with leathery and peppery flavors. Flirts with vinegary and overly earthy components. Still, a fairly gutsy red.

Valpolicella

83 LA SORTE Valpolicella Classico Superiore 1991 **$6.50** An inviting fruity aroma gives way to tart, cranberry-like flavors. A tight, lean style of red wine, with nuances of cedar and some depth.

82 MOSCA 1993 **$5.00** This well-balanced wine has a raisiny quality that is matched by moderate tannins. Medium-bodied and fruity with upfront flavors of cherry and berry.

80 MASI Valpolicella Classico Superiore 1992
$8.00 Strong aromas of menthol and licorice give
way to cherry and smoky flavors in this distinctive but
slightly disjointed wine. It's firm and silky, with nice
fruit on the finish.

Other Red

85 INFERNOTTO Barolo 1990 **$9.00** A good
example of Barolo from a great vintage. Clean, spicy
aromas, and rich, meaty flavors make this an appealing wine to drink now through 1997. Moderately tannic, long on the finish.

85 VILLA PIGNA Vellutato 1990 **$7.00** This com-
bines thick texture with sharp focus; the flavors range
from coffee and licorice to raisins and spice. It has
enough tannin for grip, and a lingering finish.

84 ANTINORI Santa Cristina 1993 **$7.00** Always
an excellent value. Light-bodied and fresh, with fra-
grant raspberry and black cherry character and a clean
finish. 90% Sangiovese.

84 CAPEZZANA Barco Reale 1993 **$10.00** An
herbal note runs through this wine and the fruit flavors are dominated by cranberry and green cherry.
Fairly tight and still tannic.

84 CASTELLO ROMITORIO Brio 1992 **$10.00**
Solid fruit flavors and a firm texture make this a
hearty, likeable red. Moderately tannic, nicely balanced with acidity and well-made.

84 TERRALE Rosso 1993 **$5.00** Sweet fruit and soft tannins make this an appealing quaff. Cherry, raisin and spice flavors are fresh and graceful. Try it slightly chilled; drink now.

83 FOSSI Vanti 1992 **$8.00** A little light, but still flavorful with cherry and leathery flavors. Simple and pleasant with modest spice notes on the finish.

83 FRESCOBALDI Sangiovese di Toscana 1993 **$9.00** Delicious medium- to light-bodied red. Very aromatic, it unfolds seductive cassis, cherry and plum layers. Fine tannins on the finish.

82 CECCHI Sangiovese di Toscana 1993 **$6.00** A firmly-structured wine with cranberry and currant flavors. Fairly rich and concentrated with a tart finish.

82 COLLAVINI Grave del Friuli Roncaccio Cabernet 1991 **$8.00** A mature, meaty-tasting Cabernet that's nice in aroma, turning lean and a bit astringent on the palate. Good, but drink it soon.

82 FONTANA CANDIDA Villa Fontana 1993 **$6.00** Light and soft, this offers strawberry and raspberry flavors without much depth or tannin. Crisp acidity holds it together, though; try it slightly chilled.

80 CASTELLO BANFI Rosso di Montalcino 1992 **$9.00** Much better than when we first tasted this wine. Very fresh and easy with soft tannins and a lovely berry fruit. Drink slightly chilled.

80 MONTE ANTICO 1990 **$9.00** A bit heavy and plodding, with plum and stewed fruit flavors and aromas. Still tannic on the finish. An unfocused wine.

WHITE

Chardonnay

84 PIO CESARE Chardonnay del Piemonte 1993 **$10.00** A solid Chardonnay that is fruity and generous, with ample pear and spice flavors that linger on the crisp finish.

82 TIEFENBRUNNER Alto Adige Chardonnay 1993 **$8.00** Light and bright, a tight little wine with pretty green apple fruit, even if it finishes a little short.

81 BOLLA Chardonnay 1993 **$7.00** Light and crisp, this wine has pleasant mineral, flinty flavors on a lean frame, with enough apple fruit for balance. It's refreshing and simple.

80 PIGHIN Grave del Friuli Chardonnay 1993 **$10.00** Lean and green, marked by a pleasant note of sweet peas and flowers, finishing chalky and crisp.

Pinot Grigio

87 LUNGAROTTI Pinot Grigio 1993 **$10.00** A good change of pace. An interesting but very dry and lean white with herb and grapefruit flavors, a touch of mineral to add complexity and a nicely austere finish.

84 TIEFENBRUNNER Alto Adige Pinot Grigio 1993 **$9.00** A well-made Pinot Grigio that delivers much pleasure, with focused pear, grapefruit and floral flavors, and lots of harmony. Light, delicious and quite smooth.

83 CIELO Pinot Grigio 1993 **$5.00** Clean, crisp and elegant; will be good as an apéritif. This wine has lively apple and floral flavors, a smooth texture and a clean finish.

82 ALOIS LAGEDER Alto Adige Pinot Grigio 1993 **$10.00** A lovely wine, showing lots of life and fresh character; has lime galore that jumps out from the glass with notes of orange peel, apple skin and banana. Light and crisp.

81 GAIERHOF Atesino Pinot Grigio Mosaico 1992 **$6.00** Light and supple, a smooth-textured wine with an earthy edge to the lemony pear flavors.

81 GAIERHOF Trentino Pinot Grigio Mosaico Torre di Luna 1993 **$10.00** Simple but direct, a fruity wine with straightforward pear, apple and citrus flavors. Sings a clear song, but without complexity.

80 CANALETTO Pinot Grigio delle Tre Venezie 1994 **$6.00** A smooth, light-bodied white wine with a soft texture, light melon flavors and a short finish.

Soave

86 ANSELMI Soave Classico Sanvincenzo 1993 **$9.00** Really puts some interest in a too-often bland type of wine. Nicely balanced and intriguing in flavor, this has expansive aromas—pear, pineapple, toasted almond—yet stays rather light and lively on the palate.

85 BOLLA Soave Classico 1993 **$7.00** A clean, very crisp wine with pleasant notes of oranges and herbs on the finish. It's light-bodied and firm-textured and doesn't miss the influence of oak at all.

84 SANTA SOFIA Classico Superiore 1993
$9.00 Balanced and straightforward, this wine shows
pear and light almond flavors; it's round on the palate
and finishes clean. Fresh and easy to drink.

83 MASI Soave Classico Superiore 1993 **$8.00**
This wine is bigger than most Soaves, with almond flavor and a creamy texture; firm yet unobtrusive acidity
keeps it lively. More fruit would increase its appeal.

Verdicchio

85 UMANI RONCHI Verdicchio dei Castelli di
Jesi Classico CaSal di Serra 1993 **$9.00** A
sophisticated toasty oak aroma and flavor makes this
wine interesting. Not typical, but seductive. Good
acidity and modest flavors of apple and pear.

84 GAROFOLI Verdicchio dei Castelli di Jesi
Classico Macrina 1993 **$8.00** Citrus aromas and
flavors with a hint of grassiness. Crisp, clean and
slightly nutty with a vivid acidity. Try with seafood.

83 FAZI-BATTAGLIA Verdicchio dei Castelli di
Jesi 1993 **$10.00** Refreshing, with grapefruit and
lemon flavors. Floral aromas framed by a nice tropi-
cality. A bit soft and simple, but attractive.

81 UMANI RONCHI Verdicchio dei Castelli di
Jesi Classico Villa Bianchi 1993 **$8.00** An unusu-
ally buttery tasting Verdicchio. Tastes mature for its
age, and gets a little thin on the finish.

Other White

85 CASTELLARE DI CASTELLINA Bianco 1992 **$8.00** Has round, complete fruit flavors of pear and apple accented by nutmeg in a smooth, medium-bodied style. Mature and ready to enjoy.

85 VIGNALTA Sirio 1993 **$10.00** Smooth, almost opulent, a spicy, floral wine with layers of citrus, pear and floral flavors that keep echoing on the finish. A dry Moscato.

84 BARBI Orvieto Classico Secco 1992 **$8.00** A blend of apple, fig and spice flavors and a smooth, well-balanced texture gives this more interest than most Italian whites. A lingering finish, too.

84 LUNGAROTTI Torre di Giano Bianco di Torgiano 1993 **$9.00** Lively and crisp in texture, and light and lean in flavor, with enough peach and almond accents to give it interest. Appetizing and well-balanced.

83 PALLAVICINI Frascati Superiore 1993 **$9.00** An appealing white with clean, floral, melonlike aromas; smooth in texture with a pleasant, slightly astringent finish.

83 VILLA FRATTINA Lison-Pramaggiore Vigneto Quartarezza 1993 **$10.00** Light and fresh, with bracing acidity; this wine has pear and almond flavors that linger on the palate. It would be a graceful accompaniment to lighter foods.

82 ANTINORI Orvieto Classico Campogrande 1993 **$8.00** This wine is fresh-smelling, crisply balanced and grapefruity in flavor. A pleasantly tart, lean wine with earthy accents.

82 ANTINORI Villa Antinori 1993 **$8.00** A bracingly crisp white wine with subtle herb and mineral flavors. Refreshing, dry, even a bit astringent on the finish. Needs food.

82 CA' DE MONTE Gavi 1993 **$8.00** A smooth and modestly fruity white, with banana and fig flavors and a hint of vanilla on the finish. Straightforward.

82 PLOZNER Grave del Friuli Pinot Bianco 1993 **$10.00** Light and simple, showing some bright pear flavor, a nice drink on a modest scale.

80 CAVALCHINA Bianco di Custoza 1993 **$10.00** Fresh and bright, a light, narrow beam of a wine that accents its apple flavors with hints of mineral and vanilla.

SPUMANTE

86 TOSTI Asti Spumante NV **$9.00** A sweet, spicy, minty, smooth-textured bubbly with a refreshing balance and distinctive flavors. A very good example of the style.

80 CA' DE MONTE Moscato d'Asti NV **$8.00** Sweet, honeyed and herbaceous, with extremely youthful flavors, like just-pressed grape juice. Appealing for its fresh fruitiness, but sweet and simple.

Portugal

BY KIM MARCUS

Portugal is fast securing a place for itself on the short list of the world's great wine values. We're not talking Port, though. Instead, it is Portugal's red table wines that offer some of the best bargains. Good wines priced at $6 and under are common.

Most Portuguese wines are made out of native grape varieties; at their best, these wines are fruity and ripe. Traditionally, many Portuguese table wines were subjected to extended aging. This practice survives today in wines with the "garrafeira" designation, which denotes extended aging in wood vats and in the bottle. Many wineries have abandoned this style because of the deadening effect it can have on fruit flavors, though many good to very good garrafeiras are made.

Some of the best and most widely available Portuguese table wines today come from the Douro and Dão appellations. The Douro may be best known for its Port vineyards, but it is home to high-quality table wines as well.

In the Dão, situated in hilly country south of the Douro, the wines have benefited greatly from Portugal's 1986 entry into the Common Market. Before that time, government control of several large cooperatives in the region meant that quality was sacrificed for quantity. Growers were paid for bringing in the biggest harvest possible, and that made for flat-tasting wines. Now, many of the region's wineries are replanting vineyards with an eye to lower yields and higher quality, and are concentrating on a traditional grape variety of the region, Touriga Nacional.

The Alentejo region of southern Portugal also offers good to very good wines. The best taste something like a rich Beaujolais, with a jammy aroma and a lingering, fruity finish.

Most wines now on the market are from the 1990, 1991 and 1992 vintages, though older garrafeira selections are available. Most white wines from Portugal in this price range don't appeal to us.

Kim Marcus is assistant managing editor of Wine Spectator.

Most Reliable Values

These wines have proven to be of consistently good quality, year in and year out. Even if a particular vintage is not reviewed here, you may purchase these wines with confidence.

RED WINES

Caves Aliança Dão Reserva

Caves Dom Teodosio Dão Teodosio Garrafeira

Caves Velhas Dão

Aveleda Douro Charamba

Caves Aliança Douro Foral Garrafeira

Quinta do Cotto Douro

Sogrape Alentejo Vinha do Monte

Terra de Lobos Ribatejo

How to Read a Portuguese Wine Label

Brand or Proprietary Name

Region of Origin

Vintage

Production Information

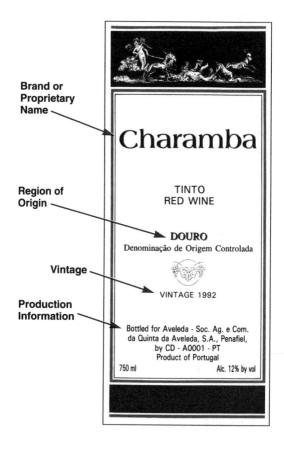

Charamba

TINTO
RED WINE

DOURO
Denominação de Origem Controlada

VINTAGE 1992

Bottled for Aveleda - Soc. Ag. e Com.
da Quinta da Aveleda, S.A., Penafiel,
by CD - A0001 - PT
Product of Portugal

750 ml   Alc. 12% by vol

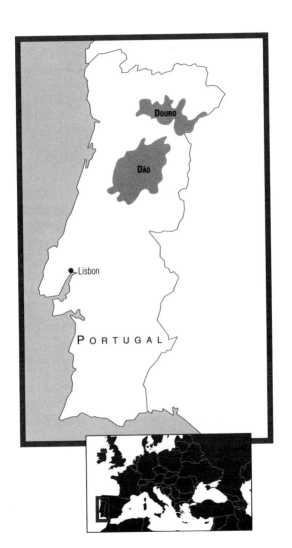

Red

89 SOGRAPE Douro Reserva 1990 **$10.00**
Deep color and lively fruit testify to this wine's youth
and concentration. It's big, with ripe plum and cassis
flavors and plenty of tannin for backbone. Fruit and
spice flavors outlast the tannins on the long finish.

88 QUINTA DO COTTO Douro 1992 **$10.00** A
delicious, hearty red wine with grapey, peppery aromas and flavors. It's smooth textured, full-bodied and
not too tannic. Drink now through 1996.

87 CAVES ALIANÇA Douro Foral Garrafeira
1990 **$6.00** Aromatic, with cedar and cranberry
notes, it's firm and flavorful on the palate, with sweet
currant, herbal and eucalyptus character. Very tannic
now, it needs until 1996 to open.

86 AVELEDA Douro Charamba 1992 **$5.50**
A great buy. Deep color and lots of ripe fruit in the
aromas and flavors mark this as a concentrated, very
enjoyable red. A refreshing dose of tannins and acidity helps carry the fruit into the lingering finish. Drink
now through 1996.

86 CAVES ALIANÇA Douro Foral 1991 **$5.00** A
firm wine with ripe fruit, licorice, and black pepper
flavors and light barnyard aromas. It's polished and
harmonious, and still young; drink now or hold
through 1996.

86 CAVES DOM TEODOSIO Dão Teodósio Garrafiera 1985 **$8.50** Rich and full-bodied, with good mint and spice flavors, all wrapped around a sold core of plum and cherry. It has a nice, mouth filling texture and long finish. Fairly mature, but still fresh and vibrant.

86 CAVES VELHAS Dão 1990 **$8.00** A well-made, fruity wine with muscular tannins; has the stuffing to age, and needs some time to harmonize the cherry, licorice and black pepper flavors. It's a bit austere now, but should come around.

86 SOGRAPE Alentejo Vinha do Monte 1991 **$9.00** The mineral and cedar aromas remind us of Bordeaux's Graves, and the palate isn't a letdown. The wine is rich, with ripe plum and sweet currant flavors and plenty of tannin for backbone. Drink or hold through 1996.

86 TERRA DE LOBOS Ribatejo 1992 **$5.00** A tremendous value. Tastes like a rich Beaujolais, from the fresh, jammy aromas to the moderate tannins and lingering, fruity finish. Drink now while it's fresh.

85 CAVES ALIANÇA Dão Garrafiera 1989 **$6.00** An attractive wine with clean, ripe flavors. Notes of plum, licorice and tar mingle in this soft, full-bodied wine. Drink now with hearty food.

85 CAVES ALIANÇA Dão Reserva 1992 **$5.00** Spicy and flavorful, with a nice rich taste of plum and black cherry. It is full-bodied, jammy and full of gusto. Finishes with good chocolate and coffee notes.

85 CAVES DOM TEODOSIO Dão Cardeal 1989
$5.00 A well-balanced, mature wine with nice plum and cherry flavors and aromas. Full-bodied and a bit tannic, but still enjoyable. Finishes with some good spice flavors.

85 CAVES VELHAS Dão Reserva 1985 **$10.00**
A round, soft wine that has benefited from time in the bottle. The cherry and cedar flavors are balanced, the tannins firm but a bit dry. This makes a good match with roast meats and should hold through 1997.

84 CAVES VELHAS Palmela Romeira 1990
$7.00 Ripe fruit and soft tannins make this an attractive wine for drinking now. It tastes of black cherry and licorice, and shows an attractive light herbal note in the finish.

80 SOGRAPE Douro Mateus "Signature" 1990
$7.00 This is not your father's Mateus. It's firm, still young, with herb and tar notes. A bit lean; drink through 1996.

South Africa

BY JAMES SUCKLING

Following a change in government in 1994 and an aggressive policy of expanding exports, South Africa has emerged as a solid source of quality wines at reasonable prices. Images of vineyards growing in arid grasslands dotted with zebras and giraffes may come to mind when someone speaks of South Africa; in fact, most of its quality vineyards are located in or near the seaside city of Cape Town, and benefit from the cooling influence of its maritime climate.

For the most part, South African wine nomenclature resembles that of the United States. Wines are usually made from a predominant grape; Chardonnay, Sauvignon Blanc and Cabernet Sauvignon are extremely popular and produce the best wines. Nonetheless, the variety with the largest plantings is Chenin Blanc, called "Steen" locally, which can produce everything from crisp, clean dry white wines to oaky brandy. Another favorite grape is Pinotage, which is a cross between the refined Pinot Noir and the coarse Cinsault. It can make light and refreshing rosés as well as powerful, long-lived reds.

The selection of South African wines available in America remains rather limited, although many producers in such quality regions as Constantia, Paarl, and Stellenbosch have their eyes on the U.S. market. One producer already making a name for itself is the Backsberg winery in Paarl. In this year's *Great Wine Values* pocket guide, this family-run winery has four very good wines; its 1993 Chardonnay and 1993

Merlot both received 87 points. Both sell for $10 a bottle and both would give solid competition to similar wines from California or France costing $15 or more a bottle. Groot Constantia—part of the original property where the South African wine industry was founded in the 1680s—is another winery with several very good wines for less than $10, especially its whites such as Sauvignon Blanc and Riesling.

James Suckling is European bureau chief of Wine Spectator.

Most Reliable Values

These wines have proven to be of consistently good quality, year in and year out. Even if a particular vintage is not reviewed here, you may purchase these wines with confidence.

Red Wines

Backsberg Paarl Cabernet Sauvignon

Backsberg Paarl Merlot

Backsberg Paarl Pinotage

White Wines

Backsberg Paarl Chardonnay

Stellenryck Coastal Region Chardonnay

Boschendal Paarl Sauvignon Blanc

Villiera Estate Paarl Sauvignon Blanc

Dessert Wine

KWV Coastal Region Noble Late Harvest

How to Read a South African Wine Label

Brand or Proprietary Name

Grape Variety

FLEUR DU CAP

CHARDONNAY

Wine of Origin Coastal Region

WHITE WINE **1 9 9 4** VINTAGE

Produced, matured and bottled by The Bergkelder Ltd., Stellenbosch

PRODUCE OF THE REPUBLIC OF SOUTH AFRICA

ALC. 13% BY VOL. NET CONTENTS 750ML

Producer or Estate

Region of Origin

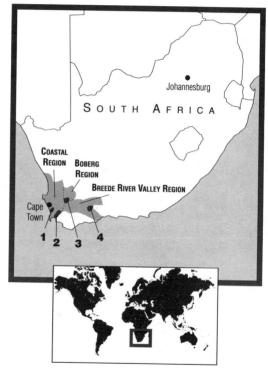

1. Constantia   **3.** Paarl

2. Stellenbosch   **4.** Robertson

WHITE

Chardonnay

87 BACKSBERG Chardonnay Paarl 1993
$10.00 Everything nice and spice in this one.
Medium-bodied with a viscous texture and plenty of
apple, spice and honey flavors. Fresh acidity.

87 STELLENRYCK Chardonnay Coastal Region
1992 **$9.00** Deft winemaking with incredible youth.
Full-bodied with firm acidity and masses of pear,
apple, hay and earth character. Still, give it time.

86 DE WETSHOF Chardonnay Robertson
Lesca 1994 **$8.00** A ringer for a very good Chablis.
This Chardonnay shows loads of apple, mineral and
honey aromas and flavors. Medium-bodied with super
fresh, green apple acidity on the finish.

86 SPRINGBOK Chardonnay Coastal Region
1994 **$6.50** Rich with flavor and lively with acidity,
a spicy, buttery, generous wine that offers a lot of satisfaction. Has fine balance and a lingering finish.

85 FLEUR DU CAP Chardonnay Coastal Region
1994 **$8.00** Not really giving much at the moment
but shows some pretty lemon, vanilla and spice notes.
Medium-bodied, medium acidity and an oaky finish.

80 ROOIBERG Chardonnay Robertson 1994
$8.00 Delicate lemon and floral aromas give way to
clean, simple flavors of apple and pear in this smooth,
chewy wine. It's clean and easy to drink.

Sauvignon Blanc

87 BOSCHENDAL Sauvignon Blanc Paarl 1994 **$9.00** Subtle and intriguing wine with mineral, pine needle and peaches on the nose and palate. Medium-bodied and almost off-dry with a fresh and fruity finish. A blend of 40 percent Sauvignon and 60 percent Chenin Blanc. Drink or hold.

86 VILLIERA ESTATE Sauvignon Blanc Paarl 1994 **$10.00** Plenty of Sauvignon character in this one. Rich and refreshing with grapefruit, mineral aromas and flavors, and a hint of grass. Medium-bodied and oily, yet very fresh on the finish.

85 BOSCHENDAL Sauvignon Blanc Paarl Grand Cuvée 1993 **$10.00** Rich and full-bodied, and with enough acidity to keep it fresh, this wine offers ripe melon and apple flavors, along with a touch of vanilla from oak-aging.

85 ROOIBERG Sauvignon Blanc Robertson 1994 **$8.00** A wine with an interesting lemon custard, chalky, mineral character. Medium-bodied with fresh acidity and good flavors.

84 GROOT CONSTANTIA Sauvignon Blanc Constantia 1994 **$10.00** Pretty and easy with a floral, tropical fruit character. Medium-bodied with an oily texture and fruity finish. A bit simple.

80 SPRINGBOK Sauvignon Blanc Coastal Region 1993 **$6.00** Melon and pear flavors mingle in this full-bodied yet very crisp wine. It has good structure, but lacks depth and finishes a bit short.

Other White

84 GROOT CONSTANTIA Constantia Weisser Riesling 1994 **$9.00** This tastes bright, slightly sweet and very fruity, with peach flavors and a fairly smooth, rich texture. Hints of ripe fruit linger on the finish.

81 NEDERBURG Paarl Prelude Sauvignon Blanc/Chardonnay 1993 **$10.00** A full-bodied, modestly flavorful white that tastes crisp and grape-fruitlike. It's clean, fresh, bracing, and subtle in flavor.

80 GROOT CONSTANTIA Constantia Blanc 1994 **$7.00** A simple, straightforward white wine with appley, herbal flavors and good balance. Dry and nicely crisp.

RED

87 BACKSBERG Merlot Paarl 1993 **$10.00** Very concentrated Merlot with tobacco, cherry, berry, and black olive aromas and flavors. Full-bodied with velvety tannins and a long rich finish. Drink or hold.

86 BACKSBERG Pinotage Paarl 1992 **$8.00** Plenty of character with meaty, berry and smoky aromas and flavors. Medium-bodied with firm tannins and soft finish. Drink now or hold.

85 BACKSBERG Cabernet Sauvignon Paarl 1992 **$10.00** This solid wine shows good balance, with firm structure and ripe fruit. It's clean and well-made and should improve through 1996.

85 CATHEDRAL CELLAR Cabernet Sauvignon Coastal Region 1992 **$10.00** Already at its peak with lovely chocolate, tobacco and blackberry flavors. Medium-bodied with silky tannins and a cedary finish.

84 FLEUR DU CAP Merlot Coastal Region 1992 **$8.00** Pretty herbal, tobacco styled Cabernet with medium body, medium tannins and a succulent, silky finish.

84 FLEUR DU CAP Pinotage Coastal Region 1989 **$8.50** A wine with big ambitions but falls slightly short of the mark. Full-bodied with lovely cherry, raspberry aromas and flavors, full tannins and a medium finish. Drinkable now but better after 1996.

84 ROOIBERG Pinotage Robertson 1992 **$8.00** Delicious red with tobacco and plum aromas and flavors. Medium-bodied and firm yet velvety texture and a slightly dry finish.

Dessert

86 KWV Full Cream Sherry NV **$7.00** A nicely balanced sweet wine with mature flavors and a lingering finish. It smells like molasses, tastes like black walnut pie, yet remains subtle and enjoyable.

85 KWV Breede River Valley Jerepigo Hanepoot 1975 **$10.00** A thick-textured, mature, fortified wine that's amber in color, nutty in aroma, and tastes like coffee and herbs. It's strong, not elegant, but has gained some nuances with age.

84 KWV Renasans Pale Medium Dry Sherry NV **$7.00** Tastes like a well-aged sherry, with briny, nutty aromas, seemingly dry, bracing flavors and a long-lasting finish.

84 KWV Coastal Region Noble Late Harvest 1988 **$10.00** A sweet, late-harvest style wine with mature, intriguing nutty aromas and peachy flavors. It's smooth, still fresh and lively.

Spain

By Thomas Matthews

Spain has long been proud of its national traditions, and its wineries have staunchly resisted the international style of oaky Chardonnays and tannic Cabernets. This Mediterranean country's top values continue to be made with native grape varieties in traditional styles. They reward exploration by adventurous wine drinkers.

The most successful wines in every price category are red, primarily those made from the Tempranillo grape, which dominates the regions of Rioja, Ribera del Duero, Navarra and Toro. Rioja, traditionally the most prestigious Spanish red wine region, now faces plenty of competition, especially in the $6 to $10 price range. Cabernet Sauvignon has begun to make an appearance, often blended with Tempranillo, while obscure local grape varieties contribute to the distinctive character of wines from Penedés, Priorato and Somontano.

Most wineries offer reds in four quality levels, which correspond to the amount of aging (in wooden barrels or in bottle) the wines receive before release; in order of increasing age (and price), they are "sin crianza," "crianza," "reserva" and "gran reserva." For the best values and the freshest fruit, look for "crianza" and "reserva" level red wines. The 1990 and '91 vintages are the best currently on the market.

Sparkling wines, made by the classic Champagne methode but using indigenous grapes, also provide good value. Called *cava*, these come primarily from the Penedés region near Barcelona. Don't worry too much about special designations or vintages; the non-vintage cuvées offer the best value and a hearty, straightforward taste perfect for parties or punches.

Whites are hit or miss in Spain. White Riojas and Ruedas, made from Viura, are fresh and clean, while "reservas," aged in American oak, are voluptuous and herb-scented. Spanish Chardonnays and other white varietals have few advantages over those from other countries, but a few indigenous grapes make distinctive wines from northern regions such as Penedés and Galicia.

Thomas Matthews is New York bureau chief of Wine Spectator.

Most Reliable Values

These wines have proven to be of consistently good quality, year in and year out. Even if a particular vintage is not reviewed here, you may purchase these wines with confidence.

RED WINES

Bodegas Montecillo Rioja Viña Cumbrero Crianza
Bodegas Martinez Bujanda Rioja Conde de
  Valdemar Crianza
Marques de Caceres Rioja
Hijos de Antonio Barcelo Ribera del Duero Viña
  Mayor Crianza
Farina Toro Gran Colegiata Crianza

WHITE WINE

Marques de Riscal Rueda Sauvignon Blanc

SPARKLING WINES

Paul Cheneau Blanc de Blancs
Codorniu
Freixenet
Segura Viudas

How to Read a Spanish Wine Label

Region of Origin

Importer

Producer & Estate Information

Brand or Proprietary Name

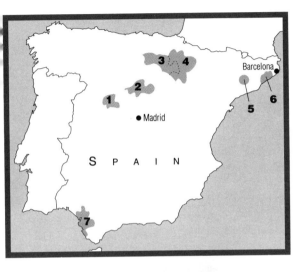

1. Rueda
2. Ribera del Duero
3. Rioja
4. Navarra
5. Priorato
6. Penedès
7. Jerez

Rioja Red

87 BODEGAS MONTECILLO Rioja Viña Cumbrero Crianza 1990 **$7.00** This wine is like a cup of good coffee — rich and full-flavored. Fresh and lively with nice cherry and bittersweet chocolate flavors that follow through on the finish with spice and vanilla.

86 AGE Rioja Siglo Reserva 1986 **$10.00** Silky and elegant, this wine shows traditional Rioja vanilla, spice and coffee flavors, but retains a core of spicy cherry fruit. It's well-balanced and firm. Drinkable now but should hold through 1996.

86 BODEGAS CORRAL Rioja Don Jacobo Crianza 1989 **$7.00** Round but firm, this polished wine marries plum and chocolate notes in a seamless package. It could use more concentration, but the flavors are true and it should improve with age.

86 LORINON Rioja 1990 **$9.00** The ripe cherry and plum flavors stretch out on an ample frame, with good concentration and firm tannins; a slight earthy note detracts from the spice and vanilla accents. A good example of traditional Rioja.

86 MARQUES DE GRINON Rioja 1991 **$10.00** Full-bodied and rich with mature flavors of plum, prune and spice. Balanced and smooth, with a pleasant gamey component throughout and a dollop of brown sugar on the finish.

86 SONSIERRA Rioja Viña Mindiarte Reserva 1988 **$9.00** Cinnamon and tobacco aromas carry through on the silky palate; it's balanced and shows complex coffee, spice and cherry flavors. Subtle and appealing, it offers the pleasures of maturity without the weakness of old age.

85 BODEGAS MARTINEZ BUJANDA Rioja Conde de Valdemar Crianza 1991 **$8.50** A fairly complex wine, with appealing cedar and berry flavors and aromas, fringed by spice and sugar. Lively and appealing, it tastes like a Pinot Noir.

85 BODEGAS SIERRA CANTABRIA Rioja Crianza 1989 **$7.00** Chewy and concentrated, with delicious chocolate and plum flavors and a nice, tarry aroma. Loads of vanilla and spice to boot. Ready to drink now.

84 AGE Rioja Siglo Crianza 1990 **$8.00** A light, elegant style of Rioja that's dominated by sweet-seeming vanilla and cherry flavors. Smooth on the palate, lingering on the finish.

84 BODEGAS BERBERANA Rioja Tempranillo "Dragon Label" 1992 **$9.00** Finely proportioned, with some nice spice and fruit components to its flavor profile. An upfront and brash wine that turns a bit astringent on the finsh.

84 BODEGAS LAN Rioja Lancorta Crianza 1989 **$9.00** An intriguing blend of cedar, coffee and cherry flavors combine in this firm-textured, rather tannic wine. Drink now through 1996.

84 CUNE Rioja Viña Real 1990 **$9.00** Good spice and berry flavors run through this well-made wine. Balanced, though not particularly intense, with cinnammon and cloves on the finish.

84 MARQUES DE CACERES Rioja 1991 **$10.00** A good, solid middle-of-the-road wine that delivers appealing plum and cherry flavors. Spicy and sugary notes come through on the finish.

81 BODEGAS FAUSTINO MARTINEZ Rioja Faustino VII 1991 **$6.00** Earthy, barnyardy aromas and vanilla and cherry flavors add up to a traditional style of Rioja. It's silky in texture, long on the finish, but it won't appeal to everyone.

81 BODEGAS SENDA GALIANA Rioja Cosecha Reserva 1987 **$10.00** Delicate, even a bit diluted, this is fully mature, with vanilla, berry and nutmeg flavors. The tannins are rather firm for the light fruit.

81 BODEGAS SENDA GALIANA Rioja Conde Alegre 1993 **$5.00** A weedy aroma gives way to a fairly soft wine dominated by cherry, berry and smokey flavors. It finishes with a nice silky texture.

80 SONSIERRA Rioja 1993 **$5.00** Tannic, though not out of balance, with good berry and cherry flavors. Turns a bit astringent on the finish.

Other Red

88 BODEGAS MANUEL SANCHO Penedès Mont-Marçal Tinto Reserva 1989 **$9.00** A well-built wine with concentration and balance. The attractive flavors run from plum and cocoa to licorice and spice. It's still fresh, with enough muscle to stand up to rich food. Drink now or hold through 1996.

88 VINA MAGANA Navarra Eventum Crianza Finca Paso de la Reina 1990 **$9.00** A gutsy, "chewy" red with nicely smoky aromas, gobs of fruit flavor, nice oak accents and a lingering finish. Packed with fine tannins, it's drinkable now through 1997.

86 HIJOS DE ANTONIO BARCELO Ribera del Duero Viña Mayor Crianza 1991 **$8.00** A strong jolt of sweet vanilla oak is the dominant flavor here, but there's enough pretty cherry fruit to back it up. The wine has good texture and grip; drink now through 1997.

86 ONIX Priorato Collita 1992 **$7.00** Rich and dense, this brawny red shows ripe plum and tomato flavors, muscular tannins and enough acidity to keep it all in balance. A straightforward wine that makes an impact. Try now.

85 SCALA DEI Priorato Negre Crianza 1991 **$9.00** A round, harmonious wine with expressive flavors of blueberry, cranberry and plum; shows firm tannins and good balance. Not a blockbuster, but tasty and approachable now.

83 SOLANA Valdepeñas Cencibel 1993 **$8.00**
Lively and bracing, fruity and fresh. Cranberry and
raspberry flavors and moderate tannins give it some
punch.

83 VICENTE GANDIA Utiel-Requena Merlot
1993 **$6.00** A solidly-built wine, with firm tannins,
ripe cherry fruit and an attractive mineral note.

82 FARINA Zamora Gran Peromato Vino de
Mesa 1989 **$9.00** Nicely developed aromas of spice
and mint lend interest to this oak-influenced, mature
and lean-flavored red.

82 SCALA DEI Priorato 1993 **$7.50** Vivid fruit
aromas of blueberries and plums give way to a tannic
wine with bright fruit and black pepper flavors.
Lighter than many Prioratos, it could use more depth
and length.

81 AGRICOLA DE BORJA Campo de Borja
Borsao 1993 **$4.00** A very fruity, rather light red
with peppery aromas and raspberry-strawberry flavors. Drink now while it's fresh.

81 FARINA Toro Gran Colegiata Crianza 1990
$10.00 A ripe, supple red with spicy vanilla aromas,
plenty of prune, plum and chocolate flavor and a simple finish. Not very tannic; drink now.

81 FARINA Zamora Peromato Vino de la Tierra
1991 **$5.00** Smooth and mellow, with subtle plum
and cranberry flavors and moderate tannins.

80 AGE La Mancha Vega Serena 1993 **$5.00** A pleasant, easy-drinking red wine with a soft texture and simple, clean, berry flavors.

White

87 MARQUES DE RISCAL Rueda Sauvignon Blanc 1992 **$9.00** Worth discovering. A distinctive, full-bodied and smooth-textured wine that smells smoky and flinty, and tastes ripe, with generous apple and pear flavors. Gains more interest on the lingering, lively finish.

85 AGE Rioja Siglo 1993 **$6.00** A tasty white that blends mature, figgy aromas with intriguing fruity and floral flavors that linger on the finish. Silky in texture, too.

85 MARQUES DE RISCAL Rueda 1993 **$7.00** Tastes like a full-bodied Sauvignon Blanc, with pineapple and ripe grapefruit flavors overlain with herbal accents. A buttery, smoky aroma and lingering finish add interest.

85 VINAS DEL VERO Somontano Saint Marc Estate Chardonnay 1993 **$7.00** A smooth and subtle, full-bodied white with spicy, pearlike flavors and good balance. Nutmeg and vanilla accents develop on the finish.

84 MARQUES DE CACERES Rioja 1993 **$7.00** Grapefruit and herbal flavors are refreshing in this clean, crisp wine, and it has enough body to stand up to food. It's balanced and has some richness.

80 ANTONIO BARBADILLO Jerez Castillo de San Diego Vino de la Tierra de Cadiz 1993 **$6.00** Earthy, fennellike aromas and dry, austere flavors make this a very lean white wine. Good if you like lightness and simplicity.

80 FARINA Toro Colegiata 1994 **$7.00** Clean, well-balanced, it's almost neutral in flavor, but light pear and hazelnut flavors linger on the finish. It's simple but well-made.

80 MARQUES DE MURRIETA Rioja Crianza 1991 **$10.00** Mature aromas of vanilla and fig lend some interest to this woody, spicy and tart white wine. Not for everybody, because there's little fruit, but it's different.

SPARKLING

86 FREIXENET Brut Nature Cava 1988 **$10.00** Age has made this dry sparkling wine into something flavorful and interesting. Floral aromas, melon and vanilla flavors and a supple texture add up to a lot of enjoyment at a great price.

84 FREIXENET Brut Rosé Cava NV **$10.00** An attractive rosé that is dry and appealing. Light salmon in color, subtly fruity in flavor and clean on the finish.

83 CODORNIU Blanc de Blancs Penedés 1989 **$9.00** A good quality, dry, mature bottle of bubbly that smells toasty, tastes buttery and pearlike and has a clean finish. Fine to drink now.

83 VALLFORMOSA Penedés Gran Baron NV
$10.00 A good value. It tastes fruity and crisp, with banana and citrus flavors and a lively balance. Bright, light and simple.

83 XENIUS Brut Penedés Cava Reserva NV
$9.00 Vibrant fruit flavors, a crisp, lively texture and a clean finish make this a cut above the average cava. Fine quality at this price.

82 PAUL CHENEAU Brut Cava Blanc de Blancs NV **$7.00** A good, inexpensive off-dry cava with straightforward fruit and spice flavors and a soft texture. Simple and clean tasting.

82 SUMARROCA Brut Cava NV **$9.00**
Straightforward, generally fruity sparkling wine with honey and pine flavors. Nearly dry, smooth in texture. Clean and simple in style.

81 SUMARROCA Brut Nature Cava NV **$9.00**
Refreshing but nearly neutral in flavor. This is a well-balanced, crisp and clean sparkling wine with simple fruit flavors.

80 FREIXENET Brut Cava Cordon Negro NV
$10.00 An enjoyable, soft and simple sparkling wine with easy going fruit and spice flavors.

80 SEGURA VIUDAS Brut Cava Reserva NV
$7.00 Fresh and lively, with decent fruit flavors and a crisp feel in the mouth.

U.S.A.

By Harvey Steiman

As wines such as Chardonnay, Cabernet Sauvignon, Merlot and Pinot Noir have become more popular, their prices have risen correspondingly, and searching for good values among them has become trickier. The lion's share of U.S.-made wine values comes in two basic areas: good wines made from less popular grape varieties, and well-made, mass-produced wines from big wineries.

Traditionally, the best buys were generic, blended wines—those that used to be labeled Chablis or Burgundy, and are now usually simply called table wine. More recently, some of the largest wineries in California and Washington have also found success selling Chardonnays, Cabernets, and other prestigious varietals—that is, wines made entirely or mostly from the single grape variety named on the front label—at less than $10.

When carefully made, these wines represent excellent value. How do they do it? They use grapes from less-prominent regions, age the wine in barrels already used for expensive wines, or blend judiciously to make good wine at a fair price.

Smart buyers also know that top-ranked Rieslings, Gewürztraminers, and to a lesser extent, Sauvignon Blancs, cannot command the prices Chardonnay can. These can be crowd-pleasing white wines, full of fruit flavor and personality, yet they have not thus far achieved the recognition they deserve.

Lesser-known wine regions often present some of the best values. Areas of California such as San Luis

Obispo and the Sierra Foothills lack the cachet of Napa and Sonoma, so their wines carry more appealing price tags. And vineyard land in Washington and Idaho is cheaper than land in California, which makes it possible for those states to price good wines attractively.

Unfortunately, the same does not hold true for wine regions in the eastern United States. Capricious weather makes it tough for good wineries in Virginia, New York and Texas to match the quality-to-price ratio California and Washington can achieve. Eastern wineries can turn out distinctive wines, but prices tend to be higher than similar-quality wines from the west.

You might also think that new-to-the U.S., relatively untested grape varieties would offer good values, but such is not the case. Recent enthusiasm in California for Rhône varieties (Syrah, Mourvèdre, Viognier) and Italian varieties (Sangiovese, Nebbiolo) has translated into interesting wines, but at high prices. Few cost less than $10, except for the occasional Grenache or Barbera.

Other less-celebrated wines can also qualify as good values, including Pinot Gris and Riesling from Oregon, Zinfandel and Chardonnay from Mendocino, Chenin Blanc and Lemberger from Washington, and Riesling from New York and Virginia. The secret to finding value in an American wine is to ignore pedigree and explore lesser-known regions and wines.

Harvey Steiman is editor at large of Wine Spectator.

Most Reliable Values

These wines have proven to be of consistently good quality, year in and year out. Even if a particular vintage is not reviewed here, you may purchase these wines with confidence.
(Note: Wines not designated otherwise are from California)

CABERNET SAUVIGNON/CABERNET BLENDS

Arrowood Cabernet Sauvignon Domaine du Grand Archer

Bandiera Cabernet Sauvignon

Columbia Crest Cabernet Sauvignon (Washington)

Dunnewood Cabernet Sauvignon Barrel Select

Hess Select Cabernet Sauvignon

Husch Cabernet Sauvignon La Ribera Red

Laurel Glen Cabernet Sauvignon Terra Rosa

J. Lohr Cabernet Sauvignon Cypress

Robert Mondavi Woodbridge Cabernet Sauvignon

Napa Ridge Cabernet Sauvignon

Parducci Cabernet Sauvignon

Paul Thomas Cabernet Merlot (Washington)

MERLOT

Arrowood Merlot Domaine du Grand Archer

Columbia Crest Merlot (Washington)

Dunnewood Merlot Barrel Select

Estancia Merlot

Louis M. Martini Merlot

Napa Ridge Merlot

Paul Thomas Merlot (Washington)

continued on next page

Most Reliable Values *continued*

PINOT NOIR
Argyle Pinot Noir (Oregon)
Louis M. Martini Pinot Noir
Napa Ridge Pinot Noir
Pepperwood Grove Pinot Noir
Shooting Star Pinot Noir
Sokol Blosser Pinot Noir
Tualatin Pinot Noir (Oregon)
Villa Mt. Eden Pinot Noir Cellar Select

ZINFANDEL
Beringer Zinfandel
Bogle Zinfandel
Hop Kiln Marty Griffin's Big Red Zinfandel

OTHER RED WINES
Bogle Petite Sirah
Parducci Petite Sirah
Bonny Doon Clos de Gilroy
Llano Estacado Signature Red (Texas)
Preston Gamay Beaujolais
Trefethen Eshcol Red

CHARDONNAY
Bridgeview Chardonnay Oregon Barrel Select
  (Oregon)
Columbia Crest Chardonnay (Washington)
Estancia Chardonnay Monterey County
Geyser Peak Chardonnay
Hess Select Chardonnay
Hogue Chardonnay (Washington)
Knudsen Erath Chardonnay (Oregon)
Louis M. Martini Chardonnay

Napa Ridge Chardonnay Coastal Vines
Paul Thomas Chardonnay (Washington)
Sokol Blosser Chardonnay (Oregon)
Vichon Chardonnay Coastal Selection
Villa Mt. Eden Chardonnay Cellar Select
Stephen Zellerbach Chardonnay

CHENIN BLANC

Chappellet Chenin Blanc
Chateau Ste. Michelle Chenin Blanc (Washington)
Hogue Chenin Blanc Dry (Washington)
Husch Chenin Blanc La Ribera

GEWÜRZTRAMINER

Claiborne & Churchill Gewürztraminer Alsatian
    Style Dry
Columbia Gewürztraminer (Washington)
De Loach Gewürztraminer Early Harvest
Geyser Peak Gewürztraminer
Husch Gewürztraminer

RIESLING

Argyle White Riesling (Oregon)
Chateau Ste. Michelle Johannisberg Riesling
    (Washington)
Claiborne & Churchill Riesling Alsatian Style Dry
Columbia Johannisberg Riesling (Washington)
Elk Cove White Riesling (Oregon)
Hidden Cellars Johannisberg Riesling
Dr. Konstantin Frank Johannisberg Riesling (New York)
Lamoreaux Landing Johannisberg Riesling (New York)

continued on next page

Most Reliable Values *continued*

Riesling *continued*
Rapidan River Riesling (Virginia)
Renaissance Johannisberg Riesling Dry
Tualatin White Riesling (Oregon)
Ventana Johannisberg Riesling

Sauvignon Blanc/Fumé Blanc
Chateau Souverain Sauvignon Blanc
Hogue Fumé Blanc (Washington)
J. Lohr Fumé Blanc Cypress
Llano Estacado Sauvignon Blanc (Texas)
Markham Sauvignon Blanc
Robert Mondavi Fumé Blanc
Navarro Sauvignon Blanc Cuvee 128
Preston Cuvée de Fumé
Voss Sauvignon Blanc
Waterbrook Sauvignon Blanc (Washington)

Other White Wines
Columbia Sémillon (Washington)
Columbia Crest Sémillon (Washington)
Hogue Sémillon (Washington)
Montinore Pinot Gris (Oregon)
Oak Knoll Pinot Gris (Oregon)
Ca' del Solo Big House White
Navarro Edelzwicker
Tualatin Müller-Thurgau (Oregon)

Other Categories
Bonny Doon Vin Gris de Cigare (Blush)
Quady Electra Orange Muscat (Dessert Wine)
Quady Elysium Black Muscat (Dessert Wine)

How to Read an American Wine Label

Vintage

Brand or Proprietary Name

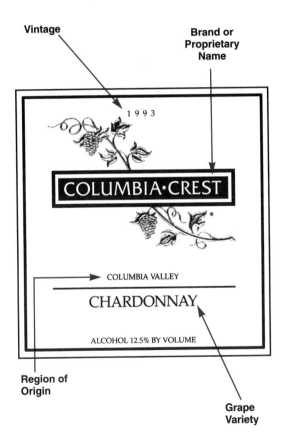

Region of Origin

Grape Variety

1. Willamette Valley
2. Yakima Valley
3. Columbia Valley
4. Mendocino & Lake Counties
5. Sonoma
6. Napa
7. Central Coast
8. Central Valley
9. South Central Coast

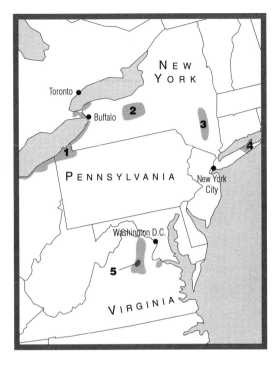

1. Lake Erie   **4.** Long Island

2. Finger Lakes   **5.** Monticello

3. Hudson Valley

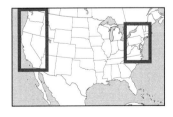

Red

Cabernet Blend

California

85 DICKERSON Napa Valley Ruby Cabernet 1992 **$10.00** Ripe and chunky, with spicy black cherry, currant and plum flavors that finish with a firm tannic grip.

84 MOUNT KONOCTI Cabernet Franc Lake County Kelsey 1992 **$7.50** Light, with an herb and cedary oak edge to the berry flavors.

84 SHOOTING STAR Cabernet Franc Clear Lake 1992 **$9.00** This wine has a weedy, herbal edge to the light berry and currant notes, but it holds its focus and gains complexity on the finish.

81 HOPE FARMS Paso Robles Claret 1991 **$10.00** Light with spicy herb and cedar notes. Finishes with a hint of cherry and currant and mild tannins.

80 MASO Napa Valley 1991 **$8.00** Hard and tannic, with a tight band of herb and oak-laced Cabernet fruit. Turns smoky, dry and leathery on the finish; a tough wine to like. A curious blend of Sangiovese (35%), Pinot Noir (5%), Cabernet (30%) and Cabernet Franc (30%).

80 TREFETHEN Napa Valley Eshcol NV **$8.75** Light and herbal with simple cherry and currant notes.

WASHINGTON

87 HEDGES Washington Cabernet Merlot 1993 **$9.50** Ripe and generous, showing nicely articulated berry and black cherry flavors that extend into a delicious finish shaded with herb flavors at the end.

87 PAUL THOMAS Columbia Valley Cabernet Merlot 1993 **$9.00** A delicious blend offer elegant ripe plum, berry and spicy vanilla flavors that remain focused and bright on the finish. Best from 1996.

86 BARNARD GRIFFIN Columbia Valley Cabernet Merlot 1992 **$10.00** A little chewy, but the berry and currant flavors come through nicely. Give it until 1996 or 1997 to polish the tannins.

85 SNOQUALMIE Columbia Valley Cabernet Merlot 1992 **$8.00** Serves up an attractive medium-weight range of wild berry and cherry fruit.

84 HYATT Yakima Valley Cabernet Merlot 1992 **$9.00** Lighter than most, a chewy wine that picks up enough berryish flavor to remain in balance. Drink now.

83 TEFFT Yakima Valley Red Table Wine NV **$10.00** A minty character keeps running through the chunky black cherry flavors in this mouthfilling wine. Drinkable now.

83 WASHINGTON HILLS Columbia Valley Cabernet Merlot 1992 **$8.00** Currant and berry flavors emerge smoothly through a chewy layer of fine tannins, making the wine approachable now.

83 WHITE HERON Washington Chantepierre 1990 **$10.00** A chunky wine with modest cedar-tinged berry flavors, edging toward tobacco and herbs on the finish.

OTHER U.S.A.

83 LLANO ESTACADO Texas Red Signature Edition 1992 **$8.00** Light and somewhat spicy, fresh tasting, with berry flavors and a hint of mint. Drinkable now.

Cabernet Sauvignon

CALIFORNIA

88 LAUREL GLEN Cabernet Sauvignon North Coast Terra Rosa 1992 **$10.00** Ripe with smooth, supple cherry, berry, spice and attractive buttery oak flavors; offers good depth and intensity, finishing with firm tannins.

88 SHENANDOAH Cabernet Sauvignon Amador County 1992 **$10.00** Another solid effort from this producer, with its bright, juicy black cherry, plum and currant flavors and a nice touch of spice and toasty oak on the finish.

87 ARROWOOD Cabernet Sauvignon Sonoma County Domaine du Grand Archer 1992 **$9.50** Firm and intense, with a good dose of smoky, toasty oak up front; the currant and cherry flavor hangs on to the finish. Has the tannins to age, but is drinkable now.

87 HESS SELECT Cabernet Sauvignon California 1992 **$9.50** Ripe and fruity, with a pretty array of black cherry, plum, cedar and spice, finishing with mild tannins, good length and a hint of mint. Ready now through 1997.

87 VICHON Cabernet Sauvignon California Coastal Selection 1992 **$9.00** Complex and elegant, with tiers of black cherry, spice and cedar flavors. Drinkable now.

86 BARON HERZOG Cabernet Sauvignon California 1992 **$9.00** Smooth, ripe and generous, with vanilla aromas and cranberry-currant flavors. Has a supple finish and it's drinkable now.

86 RUTHERFORD RANCH Cabernet Sauvignon Napa Valley 1991 **$10.00** Tart and intense, with spicy black cherry and currant notes that pick up an anise and cedar edge on the finish. Holds together nicely. Best after 1997.

85 BANDIERA Cabernet Sauvignon Napa Valley 1991 **$6.50** Herb and light oak shadings mark this excellent Bandiera Cabernet. It delivers plenty of currant and cherry flavors at a price that's hard to beat. Best now through 1998.

85 DOMAINE ST. GEORGE Cabernet Sauvignon California Vintage Reserve 1992 **$6.00** Supple and generous, with ripe, bright, fleshy cherry and plum flavors. Very appealing and easy to drink now.

85 SEBASTIANI Cabernet Sauvignon Sonoma County 1991 **$10.00** Distinctive for its spicy, minty notes, this elegant red serves up pretty currant and berry flavor, finishing with spice and firm tannins. Best after 1997.

85 ST. FRANCIS Cabernet Sauvignon Sonoma County 1992 **$10.00** Serves up a nice array of bright, ripe Cabernet fruit, but it's still a little rough around the edges when the tannins kick in. Ready now through 1998.

85 WEINSTOCK Cabernet Sauvignon Sonoma County 1992 **$9.00** Smoky, herbal flavors finish with a cedary bite, a tough wine that needs until 1997 or so to smooth out the tannic wrinkles.

84 CEDAR BROOK Cabernet Sauvignon Napa Valley 1992 **$8.00** Firmly oaked and tannic, compact, youthful and tightly wound, offering hints of cherry and currant before the tannins clamp down. Best after 1997.

84 CONCANNON Cabernet Sauvignon Central Coast Selected Vineyard 1992 **$10.00** Supple and spicy, with an herb and cedar edge to the Cabernet flavors. Still, plenty of fruit comes through on the finish.

84 DOMAINE ST. GEORGE Cabernet Sauvignon Sonoma County Premier Cuvée Reserve 1989 **$9.00** A solid, chunky red displaying earth, herb and currant flavor and finishing with firm tannins.

84 DUNNEWOOD Cabernet Sauvignon North Coast Barrel Select 1991 **$7.50** Firm, austere and tannic with rough edges, but there's enough plum and currant-laced Merlot fruit here to admire.

84 HOPE FARMS Cabernet Sauvignon Paso Robles 1990 **$9.00** An oaky Cabernet marked by toasty, buttery notes, but enough anise and cherry flavor emerges on the finish to merit attention.

84 MONTEREY PENINSULA Cabernet Sauvignon Monterey County 1986 **$10.00** A good value in mature Cabernet, with supple herb and currant notes that pick up a chocolate edge on the finish. Best now through 1998.

84 MOUNT KONOCTI Cabernet Sauvignon Lake County Kelsey 1992 **$10.00** Young and still a bit grapey, not to mention firmly tannic. Best to cellar this one until 1996 or 1997 and hope it softens.

84 NAPA RIDGE Cabernet Sauvignon Central Coast Oak Barrel 1991 **$8.00** Supple and generous, with pretty wild berry and cherry flavors. Mildly tannic; you can drink now or cellar for a year or so to allow it to soften.

84 PARDUCCI Cabernet Sauvignon Mendocino 1991 **$8.00** Smooth and polished, with more depth and character than this wine's had in recent vintages; shows off ripe plum and smoky oak flavors.

84 RAYMOND Cabernet Sauvignon California Amberhill California Selection 1991 **$8.00** Pleasantly balanced, with spicy, toasty oak and supple currant and cherry flavors.

84 SEGHESIO Cabernet Sauvignon Sonoma County 1992 **$9.00** Firm and intense, showing a pretty core of grapey Cabernet fruit and finishing with hints of currant and cherry. Best after 1996.

84 SILVER RIDGE Cabernet Sauvignon Napa Valley 1989 **$10.00** A good 1989 with ripe currant, spice and oak shadings. Best to drink soon.

83 CANYON ROAD Cabernet Sauvignon California 1992 **$7.00** Pleasantly balanced with ripe cherry, plum and raspberry flavors. Not too tannic, so you can enjoy it now.

83 CASTORO Cabernet Sauvignon Paso Robles The Wine 1991 **$10.00** Trim and compact, with a narrow band of earthy plum and cherry flavors.

83 DOMAINE ST. GEORGE Cabernet Sauvignon Russian River Valley Premier Cuvée Reserve 1989 **$10.00** Spicy, with a cedary oak frame and chewy tannins; it delivers just enough ripe Cabernet fruit to keep in balance.

83 FOREST GLEN Cabernet Sauvignon Sonoma County Barrel Select 1992 **$10.00** Earthy, with a narrow range of spicy currant and Cabernet flavors; turns tannic on the finish. Best after 1997.

83 HAYWOOD Cabernet Sauvignon California 1991 **$8.00** Firm and intense, compact and young, with spice, currant and light oak shadings. Finishes with a tannic edge. Best now through 1998.

83 HUSCH Cabernet Sauvignon Mendocino La Ribera Red 1992 **$8.00** Tight and firm, with a narrow band of spicy currant Cabernet fruit. Best to drink now through 1997.

83 MONTPELLIER Cabernet Sauvignon California 1990 **$8.00** An earthy style that pulls through with supple currant and berry flavor and finishes with a coffee and floral edge.

83 RODNEY STRONG Cabernet Sauvignon Sonoma County 1992 **$10.00** A rustic style marked by cedary oak, currant and berry flavors, with firm tannins. Best after 1996.

83 THORNHILL Cabernet Sauvignon Napa Valley 1991 **$10.00** Ripe and pruny, this compact young Cabernet shows currant, black cherry and spice notes before turning austere and tannic on the finish. Lacks finesse and polish, but at this price delivers plenty of flavor.

82 BEAULIEU Cabernet Sauvignon Napa Valley Beautour 1991 **$9.00** Crisp and austere, with an herb and bell pepper tone to the ripe flavor notes. Close to maturity now.

82 BELVEDERE Cabernet Sauvignon Sonoma County 1991 **$10.00** Lean and a bit green, with cedar, tart plum and black cherry notes that pick up tobacco and light oak flavors on the finish. Ready now through 1998.

82 CORBETT CANYON Cabernet Sauvignon Napa Valley Reserve 1991 **$9.00** A grapey style of Cabernet with a coarse, tannic edge. Packs intense flavors but is short on finesse. Ready now through 1997.

82 ESTANCIA Cabernet Sauvignon Alexander Valley 1992 **$10.00** Earthy, dry and tannic, with just enough fruit coming through to hold your interest.

82 FOSS CREEK Cabernet Sauvignon Sonoma County 1991 **$7.00** Simple but pleasing, with cedar, coffee, herb and currant flavors that finish with a tannic edge.

82 INDIAN SPRINGS Cabernet Sauvignon Nevada County 1991 **$9.00** Strikes a nice balance between cedary oak and ripe currant flavors. Picks up a hint of coffee on the finish before the tannins kick in.

82 J. LOHR Cabernet Sauvignon California Cypress 1991 **$8.00** Shows off its toasty, buttery oak and has enough Cabernet fruit to match. A good value.

82 LAWRENCE J. BARGETTO Cabernet Sauvignon Central Coast Cyrpress 1991 **$9.00** Light and fruity, with an herbal edge to the Cabernet flavors.

82 NORMAN VINEYARD Cabernet Sauvignon Paso Robles No Nonsense Red 1992 **$9.00** Herb, cedar, currant and berry flavors are tight and compact, finishing with firm tannins. Best after 1996.

82 ROBERT MONDAVI Cabernet Sauvignon California Woodbridge 1992 **$6.75** An herbal style, with spicy currant and berry notes. Simple but appealing.

82 SILVER HORSE Cabernet Sauvignon Paso Robles 1990 **$10.00** Simple but pleasant enough, with light berry and cola notes.

82 WENTE BROS. Cabernet Sauvignon Livermore Valley 1991 **$10.00** Leans toward the earthy, leathery spectrum, turning dry on the finish. A good 1991 that's ready to drink now.

81 CRESTON Cabernet Sauvignon San Luis Obispo 1990 **$10.00** Firm and intense, with a narrow band of cranberry flavor that bows to the tannins.

81 MONTERRA Cabernet Sauvignon Monterey 1991 **$7.00** Earthy and spicy, displaying bell pepper and herb flavors. Finishes on the short side, with drying tannins.

81 RUTHERFORD ESTATE Cabernet Sauvignon Napa Valley 1991 **$7.00** Austere and tannic, with flavors of modest depth and proportion. Tough and chewy; perhaps some age will soften it.

81 SUTTER HOME Cabernet Sauvignon California 1991 **$6.00** Dry and tannic, with herb and cedar flavors. A solid everyday Cabernet.

81 VIANO Cabernet Sauvignon California Reserve Selection 1988 **$9.50** Mature, with a cedary aroma and austere currant and spice notes that turn tannic on the finish. Best in 1996.

80 FOPPIANO Cabernet Sauvignon Russian River Valley 1990 **$9.50** Looks and tastes mature for a wine this young. Finishes with stewed plum and spice notes and soft tannins.

80 HAHN Cabernet Sauvignon Santa Lucia Highlands 1991 **$10.00** An herbaceous style with modest fruit and gritty tannins.

80 ROUND HILL Cabernet Sauvignon California 1991 **$7.00** Simple but correct with mature Cabernet and oak flavors. Firmly tannic, but best consumed soon.

Oregon

85 SEVEN HILLS Cabernet Sauvignon Oregon 1991 **$10.00** A sturdy red, showing some pretty plum and berry flavors and finishing with a simple impression. Should get more supple by 1997.

84 EOLA HILLS Cabernet Sauvignon Oregon 1992 **$9.00** Firm and ripe, with the bright flavors of blackberry and currant shining through the nicely modulated tannins. Best after 1996.

82 FORIS Cabernet Sauvignon Rogue Valley 1991 **$9.00** Simple, supple and appealing, a gentle red with black cherry and peach flavors that linger nicely on the finish.

Washington

87 PAUL THOMAS Cabernet Sauvignon Columbia Valley 1993 **$9.00** Ripe and nicely focused, showing nicely defined plum, currant and spice flavors that linger on the smooth, elegant finish.

86 STE. CHAPELLE Cabernet Sauvignon Washington Canyon 1992 **$7.00** An Idaho Cabernet Sauvignon made from Washington grapes that's ripe but a little chunky and firm-textured. Has black cherry, currant and cedar flavors that echo on the finish. Best from 1996.

84 COLUMBIA CREST Cabernet Sauvignon Columbia Valley 1991 **$9.00** Crisp and a little spicy, with enough plum and currant fruit to keep it interesting. Drinkable now, maybe best from 1996-1997.

83 STE. CHAPELLE Cabernet Sauvignon Washington 1992 **$10.00** Tough and chewy, a little syrupy with its berry and currant flavors, finishing soft and tannic enough to keep until 1998.

83 STONE CELLARS Cabernet Sauvignon Columbia Valley 1993 **$5.00** Youthful, bursting with fruit, crossed with a little tannin that should round out nicely by 1997-1998.

Merlot

CALIFORNIA

88 ESTANCIA Merlot Alexander Valley 1992 **$10.00** Supple and complex, with pretty herb, currant and cedary oak flavors that are well focused and long on the finish. Drinks well now but has the richness and depth to cellar.

87 NAPA RIDGE Merlot North Coast Coastal 1992 **$9.00** Chewy, with a pretty core of herb, currant and vanilla flavors that fold together nicely, finishing with a pretty cherry and spice edge.

85 CHATEAU JULIEN Merlot Monterey County Private Reserve 1991 **$9.00** Supple and elegant, with a ripe core of cherry, currant and cedary oak flavors that linger on the finish. This winery continues to make a fine value Merlot. Ready now through 1997.

85 LA CROSSE Merlot Napa Valley 1993 **$8.00** Supple and fruity, with a pleasant band of herb, black cherry and spicy notes that turn smooth on the finish, where the tannins are mild.

84 BOCAGE Merlot Monterey Proprietor's Cuvée 1990 **$10.00** Leans toward the weedy, herb and bell pepper spectrum of Merlot, but it's balanced and appealing on those counts.

84 MIRASSOU Merlot Central Coast Fifth Generation Family Selection 1992 **$9.00** Bright and floral; the currant flavors sneak in on the slightly tannic finish. Best from 1997.

84 POPPY HILL Merlot Napa Valley Founder's Selection 1991 **$10.00** Ripe and inviting, with a pretty core of supple currant, cherry and herb flavors.

84 RAVENSWOOD Merlot North Coast Vintners Blend 1992 **$10.00** Well proportioned, with supple earthy berry and cherry flavors that pick up a spicy edge.

84 THE NEGOCIANTS Merlot Napa Valley Reserve 1992 **$8.00** Focused with herb, cherry and currant notes that shorten up with firm tannins. Best after 1996.

83 BOGLE Merlot California 1992 **$8.00** Supple and fruity, nicely balanced and contained, a wine that shows some reserve and polish. Drinkable now.

83 FOPPIANO Merlot Russian River Valley 1992 **$10.00** Firm and compact, with a tight, narrow band of cherry and currant flavors that pick up an herb and spice edge on the finish.

83 KINDERWOOD Merlot California 1992 **$6.00** Intense with grapey, floral- and currant-laced fruit. An excellent value in everyday Merlot.

83 NOMINEE Merlot Napa Valley 1992 **$8.00** Crisp and flavorful, a chunky wine with a nice plum-and-currant streak, finishing generous and unfocused.

83 VICHON Merlot California Coastal Selection 1992 **$10.00** Crisp and fruity, with simple cherry and currant flavors and mild tannins.

82 ARROWOOD Merlot Sonoma County Domaine du Grand Archer 1991 **$9.00** Lean and firm with a tight band of currant and cherry fruit; turns hard and tannic on the finish.

82 BEAULIEU Merlot Napa Valley Beautour 1991 **$10.00** Tough and chewy, with firm tannins overriding the berry, herb and cherry flavors. Best after 1997.

82 BUTTERFLY CREEK Merlot Sierra Foothills Mariposa County 1991 **$10.00** A rough and chunky style with ripe chewy cherry and currant notes and gritty tannins. Drinkable now.

82 CLOS DANIELLE Merlot Napa Valley 1993 **$10.00** Forward and fruity with a wild berry edge to the flavors. Appealing now.

82 CORBETT CANYON Merlot California Coastal Classic 1992 **$7.00** Simple and fruity, more like a light style of Zinfandel than Merlot, but pleasant and quaffable.

82 DUNNEWOOD Merlot North Coast Barrel Select 1992 **$7.00** Very ripe, almost pruny, with gobs of currant and blackberry fruit, finishing soft but persistent. Drinkable now for its individuality.

82 FOREST GLEN Merlot California 1992 **$10.00** Simple and direct, with grapey currant and cherry notes that turn tannic on the finish. Good value; ready now.

82 GLEN ELLEN Merlot California Proprietor's Reserve 1992 **$5.00** Pleasing for its light and fruity cherry and vanilla flavors.

82 J. PEDRONCELLI Merlot Dry Creek Valley 1991 **$10.00** Dense and earthy, with a pungent, funky, leathery edge. Finishes with chewy tannins. Best after 1996.

82 LOUIS M. MARTINI Merlot North Coast 1991 **$8.00** Simple and fruity, with a cranberry and cherry streak that becomes tart and a bit earthy on the finish. Drinkable now.

82 M.G. VALLEJO Merlot California Harvest Select 1992 **$6.00** Ripe and fruity with simple cherry, berry and spice notes.

82 RUTHERFORD RANCH Merlot Napa Valley 1992 **$10.00** Lean and a little chewy, showing a beam of blackberry and tar flavors that extend into the finish. Best from 1997.

81 COOK'S Merlot California Captain's Reserve 1992 **$5.00** Light and fruity, a pretty wine with appealing currant and berry flavors. Drinkable now.

81 FETZER Merlot California Eagle Peak 1992 **$8.00** Lean and crisp, a chewy wine with modest berry and plum fruit. Tannic enough to be best after 1996.

81 FOXHOLLOW Merlot California 1992 **$10.00** Herbal, floral overtones give this crisp, slightly tannic red a little extra interest.

81 GRAND CRU Merlot California Premium Selection 1992 **$8.00** Light and fruity with grapey cherry and currant notes. Drinks easy now.

81 HACIENDA Merlot California Clair de Lune 1992 **$8.00** Light and fruity, with currant and strawberry notes and mild tannins.

81 HAHN Merlot Monterey 1992 **$10.00** Chewy, tannic and hard to get a handle on. The modest currant flavors struggle to breathe free. May improve after 1997.

81 MICHAEL SULLBERG Merlot California Barrel Reserve 1991 **$7.00** Soft and fruity, a chunky wine with modest flavor intensity.

80 MONTEREY VINEYARD Merlot Monterey County 1992 **$6.00** Hard-edged, a lightish wine with modest plum and berry fruit, a bit tannic on the finish.

80 MONTPELLIER Merlot California 1992 **$8.00** Offers spicy strawberry and raspberry flavors in a light and simple style.

80 OAK FALLS Merlot Napa Valley 1992 **$9.00** Light in texture and not very concentrated; it should be nice when the currently coarse tannins subside. Try in 1997-1998.

OREGON

85 VALLEY VIEW Merlot Rogue Valley Jazz Label 1992 **$10.00** Soft and gently fruity, showing a modest level of currant, vanilla and spice flavor that firms up and focuses on the finish.

WASHINGTON

87 COLUMBIA CREST Merlot Columbia Valley 1992 **$10.00** Light and zingy, a lively wine that puts some zip behind its raspberry and currant fruit, finishing with a pleasant touch of vanilla and spice. Tasty to drink now.

87 PAUL THOMAS Merlot Columbia Valley 1992 **$9.00** Earthy, spicy black cherry and blackberry flavors come through strongly in this chewy, cellar-worthy wine. Drinkable now, best in 1997.

83 STONE CELLARS Merlot Columbia Valley 1993 **$6.00** Crisp and flavorful, generous with its meaty black cherry and berry flavors. Tannins are a little chewy, may be best from 1997.

81 WASHINGTON HILLS Merlot Columbia Valley 1992 **$9.00** Firm, spicy and toasty in texture, a lightweight wine with a modest level of plum fruit to balance. Drinkable now.

OTHER U.S.A.

85 STE. CHAPELLE Merlot Idaho 1992 **$10.00** Intense with bright, lively wild berry and cherry fruit that's ripe and focused. Finishes with firm tannins and smoky oaky notes. Impressive for its flavor and balance. Best after 1996.

Pinot Noir

CALIFORNIA

86 LOUIS M. MARTINI Pinot Noir Carneros Napa Valley 1992 **$7.50** Smooth and ripe with appealing plum, cherry and anise notes and a delicate aftertaste with mild tannins.

86 SHOOTING STAR Pinot Noir Mendocino 1993 **$9.50** Well oaked, with vanilla and toasty oak flavors that complement the black cherry and spice flavors.

84 ESTANCIA Pinot Noir Monterey County 1993 **$10.00** A lighter style with strawberry jam and spicy flavors made in a fruity, delicate style.

84 NAPA RIDGE Pinot Noir North Coast Coastal 1993 **$8.00** Leans toward the herb and tea side of Pinot Noir, but it holds together, finishing with a nice touch of toasty oak and black cherry notes. A solid value.

84 PEPPERWOOD GROVE Pinot Noir California Cask Lot 3 1992 **$5.50** Lightly fruity, with herb, tar and spice notes that add dimension to the plum and berry flavors. Another terrific value from this producer.

83 CHRISTOPHE Pinot Noir Napa Valley Los Carneros 1992 **$8.00** Pleasant with peppery plum and currant flavors that are supple.

83 PEPPERWOOD GROVE Pinot Noir California 1993 **$6.00** Simple with fleshy herb and cedary notes, finishing with spicy cherry flavors.

83 VILLA MT. EDEN Pinot Noir California Cellar Select 1993 **$8.00** Simple and correct, with a nice band of herb, cola, cherry and spice notes.

82 CARNEROS CREEK Pinot Noir Carneros Fleur de Carneros 1993 **$9.50** Light and simple cherry, herb and strawberry flavors are a bit cloying.

82 CHARLES KRUG Pinot Noir Carneros Napa Valley 1992 **$9.00** Tart and earthy; a spicy wild raspberry edge turns funky on the finish.

82 CORBETT CANYON Pinot Noir Santa Barbara County Reserve 1992 **$9.00** Simple but pleasant, with light cherry, earth and spice notes.

82 YORK MOUNTAIN Pinot Noir San Luis Obispo County 1990 **$10.00** Tart, lean and a bit green, with tea, herb and tobacco flavors dominating the fruit. Turns earthy and tannic on the finish, where it picks up a cola cherry edge. Try now.

81 BOUCHAINE Pinot Noir California Q.C. Fly 1992 **$8.50** Lean and simple, with a narrow band of spice and plum notes. Turns tannic on the finish.

81 MICHAEL SULLBERG Pinot Noir Anderson Valley 1992 **$6.00** Supple and spicy, this is a medium-bodied Pinot Noir with modest cherry and oak flavors.

81 NEWLAN Pinot Noir Napa Valley Napa-Villages 1991 **$10.00** A light but pleasant wine, with strawberry and cranberry notes, picking up an earthy, smoky edge on the finish.

81 RUTHERFORD ESTATE Pinot Noir Napa Valley 1992 **$7.00** Supple and fruity, with simple plum and cherry notes.

New York

80 MILLBROOK Pinot Noir Central Coast Mistral Vinyard 1993 **$9.00** A ripe and fruity Pinot with black cherry and tea flavors and a touch of leather. Full-bodied and balanced, but a little murky.

Oregon

89 ARGYLE Pinot Noir Willamette Valley 1993 **$9.50** A smooth, elegant, lively Oregon Pinot displaying ripe berry, spice and currant flavors beautifully. Finishing supple and glowing. Stylish and drinkable now through 1998.

87 DUCK POND Pinot Noir Willamette Valley Unfiltered 1992 **$7.00** Smooth, elegant and clean, generous with its nicely focused currant and blackberry flavors shaded by a toasty note on the finish.

87 TUALATIN Pinot Noir Willamette Valley 1992 **$10.00** Smooth, generous and spice-scented, showing enough concentrated currant and plum flavors to finish nicely.

86 HENRY Pinot Noir Oregon Umpaqua Cuvée 1992 **$9.00** Bright, fruity and chewy, with nicely focused blackberry and currant flavors plus a touch of toast on the solid finish.

86 SCHWARZENBERG Pinot Noir Willamette Valley 1992 **$10.00** Black cherry and currant flavors linger nicely on the textured, oak-scented finish.

83 AMITY Pinot Noir Oregon 1992 **$10.00** Very light color, with more tea leaf that fruit in the aroma, but the bright raspberry and wild berry flavors remain light through the finish. Ultimately simple; drink soon.

83 BRIDGEVIEW Pinot Noir Oregon Reserve 1990 **$10.00** Smooth and lively, showing some bright black cherry with smoky, earthy overtones; nicely balanced and generous on the finish. Drinkable now.

83 FIRESTEED Pinot Noir Oregon 1993 **$7.00**
Light, soft and spicy, a distinctive Pinot Noir that
picks up a floral edge on the finish. Drinkable now.

83 OREGON VINEYARDS Pinot Noir Oregon
1992 **$9.00** Medium-weight, spicy and simple, a
sturdy red with toasty black cherry flavors.

82 FORIS Pinot Noir Rogue Valley 1992 **$10.00**
Ripe and chewy, a chunky red with firm tannins and a
modest level of black cherry and mint-spice overtones. Best from 1996 or 1997.

81 AUTUMN WIND Pinot Noir Oregon 1992
$10.00 Firm in texture, with modest plum and berry
flavors pushing through the hard edge of tannin on the
finish. May be best by 1997.

81 SCHWARZENBERG Pinot Noir Willamette
Valley Dry Blanc de Pinot Noir 1992 **$9.00** Light
and refreshing, a simple wine with a slightly earthy
edge to the soft, berryish flavors.

80 SOKOL BLOSSER Pinot Noir Yamhill County
1991 **$10.00** Simple and chewy, chunky, with mod-
est cherry and toast flavors struggling to break
through.

80 VERITAS Pinot Noir Willamette Valley 1989
$9.00 Light and a bit earthy, with toasty, tobacco-
scented currant flavor; slightly rough in texture.
Drinkable now.

W ASHINGTON

81 WHITE HERON Pinot Noir Washington 1990 **$7.00** Light, soft and mature, modest berry and plum flavors echoing against the spicy overtones. Drinkable now.

Rhône-Style Blend

C ALIFORNIA

86 BRINDIAMO Rhône Blend South Coast Rosso Vecchio Limited Bottling 1993 **$10.00** Combines intensity and finesse with a solid core of currant, anise and cedary oak flavors that fold together nicely. A new brand from Thornton in Temecula.

86 SOBON ESTATE Rhône Blend Shenandoah Valley Rhône Rouge 1992 **$8.00** Intensely spicy, with an earthy, tarry, bell pepper edge to the currant and cherry notes underneath.

85 PRESTON Rhône Blend Dry Creek Valley Faux 1993 **$9.00** Smooth and generous, a spicy edge adding character to the black cherry and berry fruit that lingers on the solid finish in this medium-weight wine. Blend includes Syrah, Grenache and Mourvèdre.

82 RABBIT RIDGE Rhône Blend California Allure 1991 **$7.00** A touch herbaceous, but it serves up enough pleasant fruit flavors to keep it in balance.

Zinfandel

CALIFORNIA

92 GUNDLACH BUNDSCHU Zinfandel Sonoma Valley 1992 **$10.00** A claret style that's fresh and vibrant, with black cherry, plum and buttery toast flavors. Folded neatly together in complex and enticing style. Drinks well now.

89 SAUSAL Zinfandel Alexander Valley 1992 **$9.00** A big wine but smooth and ripe in flavor, oozing plum and blackberry fruit on a satiny texture. Impressive now, best from 1996.

88 E. & J. GALLO Zinfandel Northern Sonoma 1990 **$5.00** Lots of ripe, juicy black cherry, blueberry and raspberry flavors that pick up a spicy, buttery oak note on the finish. Crisp, with lean tannins. Drinks well now, but should hold through 1997.

88 SEGHESIO Zinfandel Sonoma County 1992 **$9.00** Clean, flavorful and youthful, with bright, fresh black cherry, wild berry and raspberry flavors that are crisp and focused. Deftly balanced.

88 TRENTADUE Zinfandel Sonoma County 1992 **$10.00** Firm, ripe and intense, with a solid core of spicy mint and wild cherry fruit that picks up pretty earthy, gamy notes on the finish. Well balanced and easy to drink while maintaining the zesty personality of the grape.

87 CHATEAU SOUVERAIN Zinfandel Dry Creek Valley 1992 **$9.00** Smooth and smoky, with a spicy core of raspberry and black cherry. Intense and lively. Delicious now, but should hold through 1997.

87 HOP KILN Zinfandel Sonoma County Marty Griffin's Big Red Reserve NV **$8.00** Tightly wound and compact, with rich, sharply focused cherry and raspberry flavors. Finishes with a burst of ripe fruit; the tannins should settle sometime in 1996.

87 SHOOTING STAR Zinfandel Lake County 1993 **$8.50** Supple and polished, with pretty wild berry, raspberry and blueberry flavors that are ripe and appealing. Drinks well now through 1997.

86 BERINGER Zinfandel Napa Valley 1991 **$7.50** Solid and well balanced, with a tight core of cherry, wild berry and spice flavors. Finishes with firm tannins and good length.

86 ELIZABETH Zinfandel Mendocino 1992 **$10.00** Smooth, ripe and complex, with layers of supple black cherry, plum and wild berry flavors. Thick but polished tannins let the fruit glide through. Ready now through 1997.

86 FETZER Zinfandel Mendocino County Barrel Select 1992 **$9.00** Firm and compact, with spicy cherry, earth and raspberry flavors that pick up a buttery oak flavor on the finish.

86 JOYA Zinfandel Napa Valley 1992 **$9.00** A big, ripe, jammy style with tannins to match. A wild, juniper berry flavor gives it an earthy edge. Finishes with crisp tannins. Drinkable now.

86 PEIRANO ESTATE Zinfandel Lodi 1992 **$10.00** Ripe and juicy, with intense, jammy wild berry, cherry and plum flavors that hang with you.

85 HIDDEN CELLARS Zinfandel Mendocino 1992 **$10.00** Solid and rustic, with bright, ripe cherry, spice and earthy raspberry flavors, finishing with firm tannins.

85 MILANO Zinfandel Mendocino County Sanel Valley Vineyard 1990 **$8.00** Ripe, supple, fruity flavors with notes of maturity. Turns soft and fleshy on the finish. Ready now through 1997.

85 SANTA BARBARA WINERY Zinfandel Santa Ynez Valley Lafond Vineyard 1992 **$10.00** Ripe and spicy, with a rustic core of tarry Zinfandel fruit that turns dry and tannic on the finish. Some cellaring will soften the cherry and wild berry notes. Try now.

85 STONE CREEK Zinfandel California 1991 **$6.00** Firm, tannic and dry, with a compact band of black cherry and wild berry flavors that are tart and persistent. Finishes with a tannic edge.

85 TROQUATO Zinfandel Santa Clara County 1991 **$8.00** Ripe and jammy, with bright cherry and blackberry flavors. Tart and intriguing; best with food. Drinkable now through 1998.

85 WHITE OAK Zinfandel Sonoma County 1992 **$9.00** Firm, tight and gamy, with wild berry, cherry and plum flavors. Try now.

84 BOEGER Zinfandel El Dorado 1992 **$10.00** The buttery oak and the spicy, tarry raspberry flavors make this complex and intriguing, despite some rough edges.

84 BOGLE Zinfandel California 1992 **$6.50**
Dense and chewy, but the ripe plum and berry jam
notes rise to the forefront, giving it balance and depth.
Better than bottles previously tasted.

84 CASTORO Zinfandel Paso Robles The Wine
1991 **$9.25** Crisp and intense, with earthy spice, tar
and wild berry flavors, finishing with firm tannins.

84 CLINE Zinfandel Contra Costa County 1992
$10.00 Zesty, spicy, chunky oregano flavors, but not
much in the way of fruit. Finishes with gritty tannins
and complex flavors. Drinkable now.

84 FREY Zinfandel Mendocino 1992 **$8.00** Very
ripe and fruity, with layers of cherry, raspberry and
plum. Drinkable now through 1998.

84 MEEKER Zinfandel Sonoma County Sonoma
Cuvée 1992 **$10.00** Smooth and polished, with ele-
gant wild berry and cherry flavors. A solid Zin that is
best now to 1998.

84 TOPOLOS Zinfandel Sonoma County 1992
$8.50 Firm, tight, compact and earthy, but enough
spicy raspberry flavor sneaks through to hold interest.
May be better with another year in the bottle.

84 VILLA MT. EDEN Zinfandel California Cellar
Select 1992 **$8.00** Firm and compact, with a tight
band of earthy, tarry fruit flavors and a shade of light
oak. Drinks well now.

84 WELLINGTON Zinfandel Sonoma Valley
Casa Santinamaria 1992 **$10.00** Dark, ripe and
intense, with jammy cherry and wild berry flavors

that turn supple and earthy on the finish. Drinks well now through 1998.

84 WHALER Zinfandel Mendocino 1992 **$10.00** Firmly tannic, with a supple wild berry and blueberry flavor profile that's pleasing.

83 J. PEDRONCELLI Zinfandel Dry Creek Valley 1991 **$7.50** Medium-bodied, with earthy raspberry and cherry flavors. Finishes with crisp tannins and a touch of spice.

83 LOLONIS Zinfandel Mendocino County 1991 **$10.00** Ripe, with a berry jam character, finishing with crisp tannins.

83 MARTIN BROTHERS Zinfandel Paso Robles La Primitiva 1992 **$10.00** Simple and fruity, with a light color and modest berry flavors.

83 RAVENSWOOD Zinfandel North Coast Vintners Blend 1992 **$8.00** Simple and fruity, with plum and cherry flavors that turn spicy and earthy on the finish. Mild tannins make it drinkable now.

83 ROSENBLUM Zinfandel Contra Costa County 1992 **$10.00** Lean, earthy and gamy, with some fruit coming through on the finish. May never lose its gamy edge. Try now.

83 SEBASTIANI Zinfandel Sonoma County 1991 **$8.00** Has a shallow band of spicy flavors that picks up hints of cherry and raspberry on the finish.

83 SHENANDOAH Zinfandel Amador County Special Reserve 1992 **$8.50** Smells floral and fruity, but tastes a bit earthier, with anise and wild berry notes before the tannins close in.

83 SUTTER HOME Zinfandel Amador County Centennial Selection Reserve 1990 **$10.00** Strikes a nice balance between intense, spicy fruit flavors and buttery oak notes. Drinks well now, but could stand some cellaring.

82 KARLY Zinfandel Amador County 1992 **$9.50** Intense and a bit raw, but with enough spicy cherry and raspberry flavors to hold your interest.

82 PARDUCCI Zinfandel Mendocino County 1992 **$6.00** Crisp and a bit woody, with the oak overshadowing the light berry flavor. Still, it comes together on the finish.

82 SANTA BARBARA WINERY Zinfandel Santa Ynez Valley Beaujour 1994 **$9.00** Ripe and grapey, a Beaujolais style that's best served chilled.

81 ALEXANDER VALLEY FRUIT AND TRADING CO. Zinfandel Dry Creek Valley 1992 **$9.00** Lean and tannic, with a narrow band of spicy strawberry flavors, but it's diluted on the finish.

81 BUEHLER Zinfandel Napa Valley 1993 **$10.00** Austere with an earthy, gamy edge to the spice and wild berry flavors. Needs food.

81 CHARLES KRUG Zinfandel Napa Valley 1992 **$7.00** Simple, with earthy notes of modest proportion and distinction.

81 CHATOM Zinfandel Calaveras County 1991 **$8.00** Well mannered, with toasty, buttery, intense wild berry flavors, but it's also quite gritty and tannic on the finish; best after 1996.

81 C.K. MONDAVI Zinfandel California 1992 **$5.25** A solid Zin, with an earthy, barnyardy edge that adds an interesting dimension.

81 CLAUDIA SPRINGS Zinfandel Mendocino 1992 **$10.00** Firm and tannic, with a lean band of earthy, tarry fruit flavors that turn dry on the finish.

81 HOP KILN Zinfandel Sonoma County Marty Griffin's Big Red 1992 **$8.50** Austere with a thin, earthy band of dried cherry fruit. Finishes with a metallic edge.

81 PELLEGRINI FAMILY Zinfandel Sonoma County Old Vines 1993 **$9.00** Crisp and compact, with a narrow band of simple berry fruit.

81 ROSENBLUM Zinfandel California Vintners Cuvée IX NV **$8.00** Supple and elegant, with light strawberry and cherry notes. Drinks well now.

80 DUNNEWOOD Zinfandel Sonoma Valley Barrel Select 1992 **$10.00** Austere with an earthy, cedary edge to the muted berry flavors.

80 KONRAD Zinfandel Mendocino 1991 **$9.00** Crisp and austere, with more drying tannins than fruit showing through. Drinkable now.

80 MONTEREY PENINSULA Zinfandel Amador County Ferrero Vineyard 1991 **$9.00** Intense and tannic, with earthy, tarry raspberry flavor. Could use short-term cellaring to soften.

80 VALLEY OF THE MOON Zinfandel Sonoma Valley Reserve 1990 **$10.00** Firm and austere, with spicy fruit; finishes on a tar and herb note.

80 VIANO Zinfandel Contra Costa County Sand Rock Hill Reserve 1991 **$8.00** A very ripe and oaky style that somehow hangs together. The cherry and raspberry flavors border on jammy and it's tannic and hot on the finish.

80 WILDHURST Zinfandel Clear Lake 1992 **$9.00** Intense and tannic, with drying fruit flavors that have an earthy, briary edge.

Other Red

California

87 PRESTON Gamay Beaujolais Dry Creek Valley 1994 **$8.50** Dark in color, effusively fruity, with bright berry flavors and smooth texture. Drink it while it's fresh and zingy.

85 BOGLE Petite Sirah California 1992 **$7.00** Spicy, earthy, barnyard notes add a little extra to the soft plum and berry fruit that lingers through the finish. Tannins are soft.

84 PARDUCCI Petite Sirah Mendocino County 1991 **$7.00** A little chewy, with vanilla-scented strawberry and plum flavors that linger sweetly on the finish. Drinkable now.

83 MARIETTA Sonoma County Old Vine Red Lot Number Fourteen NV **$8.00** Ripe with sweet cherry and berry fruit that turns soft and supple. Appealing now.

83 NAVARRO Mendocino Petits Villages 1993 **$8.50** Very light and fruity, a Beaujolais-style wine with appealing berry and watermelon characters. A blend of several varieties, including Grenache, Pinot Noir and Gamay.

82 BONNY DOON Grenache California Clos de Gilroy 1994 **$8.00** A wine marked by soft banana and berry fruit, with good concentration. An easy-drinking summer quaffer.

81 CONCANNON Petite Sirah Central Coast Selected Vineyard 1991 **$10.00** An earthy, barn-yard edge colors the basic black cherry fruit, finishing soft and a little short.

81 MIRASSOU Petite Sirah Monterey County Fifth Generation Family Selection 1991 **$9.00** A little coarse in texture, but the flavors of berry and pepper are true.

80 JORY California Red Zeppelin Bon Jory Red 1991 **$10.00** Light and gamy; shows more earthy flavor than fruit.

WASHINGTON

87 WORDEN Washington Cascade Claret 1992 **$9.00** Light and brightly fruity, nicely balanced and immensely appealing, echoing berry and spice on the long finish. Just delicious for drinking now.

85 COLUMBIA CREST Columbia Valley Gamay Beaujolais 1993 **$7.00** Light and fruity, delicately spicy, too, and very pleasant and long on the finish. Best served slightly chilled.

84 KIONA Lemberger Yakima Valley 1992 **$10.00** Smoky, almost burnt on the nose, but the flavors are polished and generously fruity, echoing raspberry and spice. Drinkable now.

82 HOGUE Lemberger Yakima Valley 1992 **$9.00** Crisp and fruity, with a strong herbal-anise streak running through the berry flavors. Drinkable now.

81 KNIPPRATH Lemberger Yakima Valley Pleasant Vineyards 1992 **$8.00** Dark, dense and spicy, with a modest level of blackberry fruit sneaking in to balance the toasty spice flavors. Drinkable now.

80 COVEY RUN Lemberger Yakima Valley 1993 **$7.00** Light and fruity, but dark in flavor, with more black cherry and blackberry than anything lighter. Drinkable now.

WHITE

Chardonnay

CALIFORNIA

87 BELVEDERE Chardonnay Alexander Valley 1992 **$9.00** Serves up attractive pear, apple and spice notes that gain a honeyed edge on the finish. Light oak adds dimension.

87 CHATEAU DE BAUN Chardonnay Russian River Valley 1993 **$10.00** Appealing for its tangerine and nectarine flavors, it turns smooth and creamy, picking up a buttery edge on the finish.

87 CLOS DANIELLE Chardonnay Carneros Private Reserve 1993 **$9.00** A ripe, honeyed and rich-textured California Chardonnay, with beautifully delineated flavors that last and last on the finish.

87 ESTANCIA Chardonnay Monterey County 1993 **$9.00** Pleasantly fruity with elegant pear, toast and spice flavors that fan out and turn complex on the finish.

87 SEBASTIANI Chardonnay Sonoma County 1993 **$10.00** Smooth and creamy, with appealing apple, pear and vanilla shadings that unfold and hang together on the finish, where it picks up a toasty edge.

87 THE NEGOCIANTS Chardonnay Central Coast 1992 **$6.00** Lean and trim, but the smoky pear and spice flavors fan out on the finish, where they get more interesting, finishing with a toasty aftertaste. Tremendous value.

86 BEAULIEU Chardonnay Napa Valley
Beautour 1993 **$9.00** Strikes a nice balance
between apple and pear-laced fruit and subtle creamy
oak flavors, turning elegant and refined on the finish.

86 CHATEAU WOLTNER Chardonnay Howell
Mountain 1993 **$10.00** Light and fruity, with fresh
pear and apple notes that pick up a spicy citrus edge
on the finish. Drinks well now but can age another
year or so.

86 FOSS CREEK Chardonnay Central Coast
Barrel Fermented 1992 **$7.00** Smooth and fruity,
sliding its apple, earth and honey flavors nicely
through the lingering finish.

86 HESS SELECT Chardonnay California 1993
$9.50 Firm and lively, with intense grapefruit, citrus
and pear-laced fruit. Turns complex and supple on the
finish, where the flavors linger on.

86 LOUIS M. MARTINI Chardonnay Napa Valley
1992 **$8.00** Very fruity and forward, with ripe,
creamy pear, apple and spice flavors that are rich and
focused. Finishes with a long, fruity aftertaste that
gains complexity.

86 ROUND HILL Chardonnay California 1993
$7.00 Young and tart, with a green edge to the pear
and apple flavors, but fans out on the finish, holds its
fruit and gains complexity.

86 RUTHERFORD RANCH Chardonnay Napa
Valley 1992 **$9.00** Fresh, lively and focused; bright
with apple and pear fruit that keeps bouncing through
the finish.

86 RUTHERFORD VINEYARDS Chardonnay Napa Valley 1993 **$8.00** Light and easy to drink, with a passion fruit edge to the pear and toast flavors.

86 TAFT STREET Chardonnay Sonoma County 1993 **$9.50** Smooth and creamy, with ripe pear, apple and spice flavors and aromas that turn elegant and soft on the finish.

85 GEYSER PEAK Chardonnay Sonoma County 1993 **$10.00** Ripe and juicy, with spicy pear, apple and nutmeg flavors that smooth out on the finish.

85 HAHN Chardonnay Monterey 1993 **$10.00** Young and fruity, with ripe pear and apple notes that pick up a spice edge on the finish. Ready now.

85 MACKINAW Chardonnay California 1993 **$10.00** Ripe and generous, built around a core of pear and citrus fruit, displaying a touch of spice and honey as counterpoint.

85 MERIDIAN Chardonnay Santa Barbara County 1993 **$10.00** Medium weight, with ripe pear, apple and spice notes that are pleasing.

85 NAPA RIDGE Chardonnay Central Coast Coastal Vines 1993 **$8.00** Lightly fruity, with spicy pear and grapefruit, notes that are harmonious. Easy to drink.

85 R.H. PHILLIPS Chardonnay California Barrel Cuvée 1993 **$7.00** Well balanced, with pretty pear, spice and light oak shadings, all focused with a lingering aftertaste.

85 VILLA MT. EDEN Chardonnay California Cellar Select 1993 **$8.00** Ripe and fruity, with good depth and intensity to the pear and apple notes, turning elegant on the finish.

85 WENTE BROS. Chardonnay Central Coast Wente Family Estate Selection 1993 **$9.00** Crisp with a slightly coarse texture, but appealing pear and apple flavors.

85 WILSON DANIELS Chardonnay Napa Valley 1992 **$10.00** Lean and a bit green, displaying spice, tart pear and apple notes of modest proportions and finishing with light oak shadings.

84 BELVEDERE Chardonnay Sonoma County 1993 **$9.00** Medium weight with a spicy, nutty edge to the ripe pear flavors.

84 BOUCHAINE Chardonnay California Q.C. Fly 1992 **$8.50** A spicy style, with appealing pear, apple and light oak shadings.

84 COTES DE SONOMA Chardonnay Sonoma County 1993 **$8.00** Fresh and flavorful, simple, and brimming with pear and nectarine character that lingers on the finish.

84 FETZER Chardonnay Mendocino County Bonterra Organically Grown Grapes 1993 **$9.00** Smooth and spicy, generous with its pear and nutmeg flavors, gliding gently into the finish.

84 GLASS MOUNTAIN QUARRY Chardonnay California 1993 **$9.00** Well oaked, with toasty buttery aromas and just the right mix of ripe pear and spice notes to achieve balance.

84 GROVE STREET Chardonnay Sonoma County Vintage Select 1992 **$7.00** Intense and a bit earthy, with a grassy edge to the pear and pineapple flavors. Drinks well now. A second label from the owner of Belvedere Winery.

84 M.G. VALLEJO Chardonnay California Harvest Select 1992 **$6.00** Light and fruity, with a spicy edge that gives it some extra zing.

84 MORRO BAY Chardonnay Central Coast Special Edition 1993 **$10.00** Soft and pleasantly fruity, with pear, apple and light spice shadings.

84 ORFILA Chardonnay California Barrel Fermented 1992 **$10.00** Lean and spicy, with a trim band of citrus and pear laced flavors that finish with a honeyed note.

83 BUENA VISTA Chardonnay Carneros 1992 **$10.00** Lightly fruity, with simple pear, apple and pineapple notes that finish with a soft aftertaste.

83 CALLAWAY Chardonnay Temecula Hawk Watch Classic Sur Lie Style Calla-Lees 1992 **$8.00** Ripe and fruity, with complex apple, pear and spice flavors that turn elegant and supple.

83 FOREST GLEN Chardonnay Sonoma County Barrel Fermented 1993 **$10.00** Clean and lightly fruity, with pear, spice and vanilla notes.

83 HACIENDA Chardonnay California Clair de Lune 1993 **$6.00** Soft and ripe, shows off pear and floral flavors with delicacy.

83 LA CROSSE Chardonnay Napa Valley 1993 **$7.00** Well oaked, with subdued pear and apple flavors that turn soft on the finish.

83 STEPHEN ZELLERBACH Chardonnay California 1993 **$8.50** A lightly fruity style; ripe pear, apple and melon flavors finish with a trace of oak.

82 BOGLE Chardonnay California 1993 **$6.25** Crisp and fruity, lively; simple and appealing for its nectarine flavor.

82 HAYWOOD Chardonnay California Vintner's Select 1993 **$8.00** Tastes off-dry, with a spicy Riesling-like edge to the subtle pear and apple notes.

82 LAWRENCE J. BARGETTO Chardonnay Central Coast Cypress 1992 **$9.00** Ripe and fruity with spicy pear and apple notes.

82 SHOOTING STAR Chardonnay Mendocino 1993 **$9.50** An odd style, with an earthy edge to the pear and spice-laced Chardonnay flavors. This young wine may need more time in the bottle to settle out.

82 STEVENOT Chardonnay Sierra Foothills 1993 **$8.00** Crisp with a flinty, earthy edge to the pear and apple notes.

82 VICHON Chardonnay California Coastal Selection 1993 **$10.00** Clean and fruity, with a citrus note that holds the pear and spice flavors together.

81 CORBETT CANYON Chardonnay Santa Barbara County Reserve 1993 **$9.00** Simple, rather like canned pears in flavor, with a fresh finish.

81 FOSS CREEK Chardonnay Sonoma County 85% Barrel Fermented 1992 **$6.00** Lean and lively with citrusy apple and pear flavors.

81 PARDUCCI Chardonnay Mendocino County 1993 **$8.00** Tart and green with crisp pear and apple notes. For fans of non-oaked Chardonnay.

80 BONVERRE Chardonnay California Lot Number 14 1992 **$7.00** Bright and fruity, a simple wine with lively citrus and peach fruit that echoes on the finish.

80 CLOS ST. THOMAS Chardonnay California 1993 **$7.50** A simple, fruity style with spice, pear and apple notes of modest proportion.

80 CORBETT CANYON Chardonnay Central Coast Coastal Classic 1993 **$5.00** Light and fruity; displaying a slight metallic edge to the peach and pear flavors.

80 DOMAINE ST. GEORGE Chardonnay California Vintage Reserve 1993 **$6.00** Tastes sweet beyond ripeness, with cloying pear and apple flavors.

80 DUNNEWOOD Chardonnay North Coast Barrel Select 1993 **$8.00** Simple and fruity, with hints of pear, apple and spice, turning grassy on the finish.

80 THE NEGOCIANTS Chardonnay Central Coast Barrel Fermented 1992 **$7.00** Lean and simple, with pear, spice and cedary oak flavors.

New York

89 MILLBROOK Chardonnay Central Coast Mistral Vineyard 1993 **$8.00** A serious Chardonnay from the toasty aromas to the ripe and layered fruit to the lasting finish. Fine balance, a touch of oak flavor and velvety texture add to its appeal.

81 GLENORA Chardonnay Finger Lakes 1991 **$9.00** A pleasant, harmonious Chardonnay with a soft texture, nicely ripe flavors and good balance. Attractive, if fairly straightforward.

Oregon

86 BRIDGEVIEW Chardonnay Oregon Barrel Select 1992 **$10.00** Gentle, offering crisp apple and lemon flavors, softened around the edges by spicy vanilla notes, all ringing nicely on the finish. Lovely to drink now.

86 KNUDSEN ERATH Chardonnay Willamette Valley 1993 **$10.00** A bright and fruity Oregon Chardonnay. Nicely balanced, with a greenish, floral edge to the appealing apple and pear flavors. Drinkable now.

86 SOKOL BLOSSER Chardonnay Yamhill County 1992 **$10.00** Bright, fruity and appealing, with a supple texture and nicely focused apple and apricot flavors. Drinkable now.

86 WILLAMETTE VALLEY Chardonnay Oregon 1992 **$9.00** Bright and fruity, with lingering green apple, pear and spice flavors. A charming white that offers lovely fruit notes right through the finish.

85 MONTINORE Chardonnay Willamette Valley 1992 **$10.00** Lean, earthy and crisp, picking up some lemony pear flavor as the finish smooths. Drinkable now.

84 HENRY Chardonnay Oregon Umpqua Cuvée 1992 **$9.00** Floral and citrusy, distinctive, with more rose petal and honey flavor than fruit. Nicely balanced and smooth on the finish. Drinkable now.

84 SHAFER VINEYARD CELLARS Chardonnay Willamette Valley NV **$7.50** Light and a bit tart, a lively little white with modest apple and spice flavors that turn lemony on the crisp finish.

83 VERITAS Chardonnay Yamhill County 1991 **$10.00** Earthy, mineral flavors dominate, shouldering past the modest pear notes. Shows some appealing honey on the finish. Might be best from 1996.

82 SPRINGHILL Chardonnay Oregon 1991 **$10.00** Simple, fruity and generous, echoing nectarine and mineral flavors on the finish. Drinkable now.

81 VALLEY VIEW Chardonnay Rogue Valley Barrel Select 1991 **$10.00** A sturdy, chunky sort of Chardonnay with mineral, pear and apple flavors that sneak in on the finish.

80 FORIS Chardonnay Rogue Valley Barrel Fermented 1992 **$10.00** Aggressively earthy and tarry on the palate; a little tart and gangly but crisp enough to finish nicely. Drinkable now.

80 VALLEY VIEW Chardonnay Rogue Valley Jazz Label 1992 **$9.00** Crisp and straightforward with fresh, biting-into-the-fruit pear and nectarine flavors and texture. Drinkable now.

WASHINGTON

90 PAUL THOMAS Chardonnay Columbia Valley 1993 **$10.00** Fresh, fruity and appealing, a supple wine with gorgeous fruit flavors that keep getting juicier with every sip, echoing grapefruit, peach and pear flavors on the smoothly balanced finish.

89 CATERINA Chardonnay Columbia Valley 1993 **$10.00** Fruity and vibrant, delicious from the first sip to the last echo of peach, apple and grapefruit flavors.

89 HOGUE Chardonnay Columbia Valley 1993 **$10.00** Beautifully articulated pear and apple fruit picks up a citrusy, spicy edge as the finish zings and zings. A lively wine that's utterly beguiling to drink while it's fresh.

88 COLUMBIA CREST Chardonnay Columbia Valley Barrel Select 1992 **$10.00** Spicy, toasty flavors fold together nicely with the pear and grapefruit at the core, making this an appealing wine to drink now for its range of flavors.

88 COLUMBIA CREST Chardonnay Columbia Valley 1993 **$8.00** A bright and fresh Washington white that's distinctive for its spicy nectarine and pear flavors that remain lively through the ripe finish. Tasty now; should improve through 1996.

88 LATAH CREEK Chardonnay Washington 1993 **$10.00** Smooth, supple and generous, folding some nice spicy notes in with the nicely articulated pear and peach fruit. Immensely appealing to drink now.

88 WATERBROOK Chardonnay Columbia Valley 1993 **$9.00** A lean and intensely focused Washington white. A deftly balanced wine that shows nice hints of nectarine and pear flavors on the lively finish.

86 ARBOR CREST Chardonnay Columbia Valley Cameo Reserve 1993 **$9.50** Brightly fruity and distinctly spicy, fresh and lively, and rounded off with a nice tang of smoky oak.

86 BOOKWALTER Chardonnay Washington 1992 **$8.00** Bright and fruity, not a flashy wine but brimming with crisply defined pear and apricot fruit, echoing on the finish. Tasty stuff.

86 W.B. BRIDGMAN Chardonnay Yakima Valley 1992 **$9.00** Ripe, round and a little grassy at the edge, an earthy wine that unfolds some nice nectarine and apple fruit on a smooth frame. Ready now.

85 GORDON BROTHERS Chardonnay Washington 1992 **$9.00** Smooth and generous, a little spicy and toasty around the edges, shining a bright beam of apple and pear fruit right through the finish.

85 WASHINGTON HILLS Chardonnay Columbia Valley 1992 **$8.00** Round and generous, a full-bodied wine that leans distinctly in the direction of fruit, offering bright nectarine and apple on the lively finish. Drinkable now.

83 HYATT Chardonnay Yakima Valley 1992 **$10.00** Crisp and fresh, not especially rich or complex, but it has a little spiciness to accent the citrusy flavors. Drinkable now.

83 WORDEN Chardonnay Washington 1991 **$10.00** Crisp and earthy, a lean wine with a mineral edge to the modest apple fruit.

82 LATAH CREEK Chardonnay Washington Feather 1993 **$7.00** Simple and fruity, lively enough to show off the Mâcon-like apple and mineral flavors. Drinkable now.

81 STONE CELLARS Chardonnay Columbia Valley 1993 **$5.00** A subdued, subtle white exhibiting nice nectarine and spice flavors that linger on the delicate finish.

81 TAGARIS Chardonnay Columbia Valley 1993 **$6.00** Nicely fruity, with apricot, nectarine and pear notes, but the texture comes off as a little coarse and simple.

OTHER U.S.A.

85 OASIS Chardonnay Virginia Bleu Rock Vineyard 1992 **$10.00** This lively, tightly-wound wine shows bright, lemony fruit, sweet vanilla oak and crisp acidity. It's still young and fresh. A clean, well-made wine.

84 STE. CHAPELLE Chardonnay Idaho 1992 **$10.00** Bright and fruity, a light-textured wine that picks up some nice pear and spice flavors.

82 OASIS Chardonnay Virginia 1993 **$10.00** A good, serviceable and fruity wine whose flavors are on the lean side. Rather tart, too.

Chenin Blanc

CALIFORNIA

87 WHITE OAK Chenin Blanc California 1993 **$7.00** Bright, fruity and utterly charming, unfolding its melon, mint and pear flavors with grace and style.

85 CHAPPELLET Chenin Blanc Napa Valley Dry 1992 **$7.50** Bright and fruity, dry and spicy enough to weave some nice nuances around the delicate apple fruit.

85 DURNEY Chenin Blanc Carmel Valley 1993 **$9.00** Light, simple and fruity, off-dry but nicely balanced to show off the melon and apple fruit.

85 HUSCH Chenin Blanc Mendocino La Ribera Vineyard 1994 **$8.00** Light, charming and generous with its green apple and sweet pear fruit. Not too sweet.

85 MIRASSOU Chenin Blanc Monterey County Fifth Generation Family Selection Dry 1993 **$6.00** Lively, citrusy, generous, a dry wine with appealing orange and pear flavors that linger.

84 DANIEL GEHRS Chenin Blanc Monterey County Le Chenay 1993 **$8.50** Gehrs adds 20% Chardonnay to this cuvée which gives it a little more body, but it's still a trim, compact wine with tart apricot and pear-laced flavors.

84 KENDALL-JACKSON Chenin Blanc California Vintner's Reserve 1992 **$10.00** Light and direct, off-dry, showing fresh apple and leafy flavors, polished on the finish.

83 DANIEL GEHRS Chenin Blanc Santa Barbara County Le Cheniere 1993 **$8.00** This barrel fermented wine strives for complexity with its toasty oak outline and makes for an interesting wine. Serves up spicy pear and apple notes that ring true for Chenin Blanc.

82 DRY CREEK Chenin Blanc California Dry 1993 **$7.00** Smooth, off-dry, a generous wine with nicely compact pear and melon fruit.

81 VENTANA Chenin Blanc Monterey 1993 **$6.00** Soft and fragrant, a leafy, minty character carrying through stronger than the fruit.

WASHINGTON

87 KIONA Chenin Blanc Yakima Valley 1993 **$6.00** Fruity, spicy and lively, a mouthful of citrusy peach and melon flavor that keeps spilling over on the finish. A wonderful sipper.

86 PAUL THOMAS Chenin Blanc Washington 1993 **$6.00** A charming wine, crisp and fruity; a delicious mouthful of peach, pear and melon flavors, off-dry but not too sweet. Drink while fresh.

86 WORDEN Chenin Blanc Washington 1993 **$7.00** Silky-smooth, oozing with melon and pear flavors, a generously fruity wine that finishes light and deftly balanced with a touch of sweetness.

84 CHATEAU STE. MICHELLE Chenin Blanc Columbia Valley 1993 **$7.00** Bright and fruity, slightly off-dry and bursting with melon and pear flavors that keep singing on the finish. Drink soon for the fruit.

84 HOGUE Chenin Blanc Columbia Valley 1993 **$6.00** Light and fruity, centered around pear and apple, finishing with a silky texture and lingering fruit.

83 HOODSPORT Chenin Blanc Washington 1992 **$8.00** Fresh and fruity, on the dry side but showing plenty of grassy melon and pear flavors. Drink soon, while it's fresh.

82 HOGUE Chenin Blanc Columbia Valley Dry 1993 **$6.00** Fruity and simple, with fine melon and apple flavors and a strong floral note.

80 BOOKWALTER Chenin Blanc Washington 1993 **$6.50** Frankly sweet, a simple wine with melon and peach fruit.

Gewürztraminer

California

88 CLAIBORNE & CHURCHILL Gewürztraminer Central Coast Dry Alsatian Style 1993 **$10.00** Crisp and a little austere, a dry wine that shows a little reserve and a haunting whiff of spice on the long finish.

87 Z MOORE Gewürztraminer Russian River Valley Barrel Fermented Dry 1992 **$9.50** A dry, fruity style from California that favors citrus, pineapple and melon flavors—until the finish, which echoes spice.

85 BOUCHAINE Gewürztraminer Russian River Valley Dry 1993 **$8.50** Bright and floral, a generous wine with a spicy edge to the pear and cream flavors.

85 HANDLEY Gewürztraminer Anderson Valley 1993 **$8.00** On the dry side, but the nectarine and melon fruit flavors are appealing. Should make a wonderful apéritif.

84 DE LOACH Gewürztraminer Russian River Valley Early Harvest 1993 **$8.50** Bright and citrusy, smooth-textured, with a nectarine note to the lemon and grapefruit flavors.

84 GEYSER PEAK Gewürztraminer North Coast 1993 **$6.00** Soft, smooth and bubbling with fresh fruit flavors, centering on pear, floral and sweet orange.

84 MILL CREEK Gewürztraminer Dry Creek Valley 1993 **$7.00** Soft and lively, a bright, fruity wine with pear and spicy floral aromas and flavors.

84 NAVARRO Gewürztraminer Anderson Valley Dry 1993 **$9.50** Light, with a touch of grapefruit and pear sneaking in behind the floral, spicy notes, finishing a little flat.

84 PARAISO SPRINGS Gewürztraminer Monterey County Santa Lucia Highlands 1993 **$7.00** With its rose petal and pear aromas and flavors, this dryish wine performs lightly and appealingly through the fine finish.

82 HOP KILN Gewürztraminer Russian River Valley M. Griffin Vineyards 1993 **$7.50** Dry, modest in scope, with rose petal and apple flavors that emerge gently on the finish.

82 KENDALL-JACKSON Gewürztraminer California Vintner's Reserve 1993 **$10.00** Bright, refreshing and simple with pleasant pear and spice flavors.

81 HUSCH Gewürztraminer Anderson Valley 1993 **$9.00** Light and soft, an airy-textured white featuring simple citrus and peach flavors.

80 ADLER FELS Gewürztraminer Sonoma County 1993 **$9.00** Lightly sweet, resiny and floral with smooth orange and pear notes.

80 BUENA VISTA Gewürztraminer Carneros 1993 **$7.50** Soft and fruity, simple in flavor, a little sweet and apricot-like on the finish.

80 GRAND CRU Gewürztraminer California Premium Selection 1993 **$7.00** Brassy color, modest flavors, soft and sweet, hitting a touch of peach on the finish.

80 LAWRENCE J. BARGETTO Gewürztraminer Monterey County 1993 **$9.00** A little sweet and gentle, offering a spicy edge to the simple melony flavor.

New York

85 WAGNER Gewürztraminer Finger Lakes 1991 **$8.00** What we like in Gewürztraminer, with fresh fruit and floral aromas and slightly sweet flavors that become more complex as you sip. Has great balance and appeal.

Oregon

88 DUCK POND Gewürztraminer Willamette Valley 1993 **$7.00** Crisp in texture and distinctively floral and spicy in flavor; fragrantly varietal and zingy on the finish. Built to be dry and charming. Drinkable now.

86 MONTINORE Gewürztraminer Willamette Valley 1992 **$6.00** Distinctively varietal and lightly sweet in a lovely apéritif style, showing rose petal, grapefruit and green apple flavors that linger on the finish.

85 BRIDGEVIEW Gewürztraminer Oregon Dry Vintage Select 1991 **$7.00** Definitely varietal, with rose petal and spice grace notes to the modest pear and citrus flavors that linger on the aftertaste.

83 HENRY Gewürztraminer Umpqua Valley Dry 1993 **$8.00** Soft and fruity, charming and dry; shows more pear and apple flavor than Gewürztraminer spice. Drinkable now.

82 BETHEL HEIGHTS Gewürztraminer Willamette Valley 1993 **$7.00** Light and modestly spicy, a soft white with an appealing varietal edge.

81 FORIS Gewürztraminer Rogue Valley 1992 **$7.00** Light and floral; simple but charming and easy to drink.

WASHINGTON

85 COLUMBIA Gewürztraminer Yakima Valley 1993 **$6.00** Floral, a succulent wine that pours out distinctive rose petal and pineapple flavors.

85 COLUMBIA CREST Gewürztraminer Columbia Valley 1993 **$6.00** Soft and refreshingly fruit-oriented, showing litchi, pear and grapefruit flavors that pick up a touch of rose petal on the finish. Lovely to drink now.

84 HOGUE Gewürztraminer Columbia Valley 1993 **$6.00** Bright and fruity with a welcome edge of rose petal and spice that reflects the varietal character in spades. A little soft on the finish, but otherwise nicely done.

82 COVEY RUN Gewürztraminer Yakima Valley 1993 **$7.00** On the dry side, a modestly flavorful wine with enough spicy notes to let you know it's Gewürztraminer.

81 WASHINGTON HILLS Gewürztraminer Columbia Valley 1993 **$6.00** Light and soft, with appealing rose petal-scented melon flavors, finishing light and a little sweet.

Pinot Gris

OREGON

88 MONTINORE Pinot Gris Willamette Valley 1993 **$10.00** Bright, fresh and appealing from the first whiff to the last echo of the nectarine, pear and apple flavors. Delightful to drink by itself or with lighter foods.

86 CRISTOM Pinot Gris Willamette Valley 1993 **$10.00** Ripe with melon flavors, a fruity white that offers a little more richness than most.

86 REX HILL Pinot Gris Oregon Kings Ridge 1993 **$9.50** Rich and flavorful, with an earth and mineral streak cutting through the basic nectarine and apricot flavors. Drinkable now.

85 OAK KNOLL Pinot Gris Willamette Valley 1992 **$9.00** A little spicy around the edges, but it has richness and bright nectarine and pear flavors. Charming and tasty.

83 AUTUMN WIND Pinot Gris Oregon 1993 **$10.00** Bright and forward, with a lively, gamy edge to the pear flavor. Finishes refreshingly.

83 BETHEL HEIGHTS Pinot Gris Willamette Valley 1993 **$10.00** Firm, focused and balanced with a strong earth-mineral component. Unusual; finishes a little spicy.

83 KRAMER Pinot Gris Willamette Valley Estate Bottled 1993 **$10.00** Crisp and fruity, with lively peach and pear flavors, finishing a little spicy. Drinkable now.

82 CHEHALEM Pinot Gris Oregon Ridgecrest Vineyards 1992 **$10.00** Distinctively spicy and aromatic, sweeter and softer than most; not typically dry. Would make a pleasant apéritif or between-meals sipper.

82 VERITAS Pinot Gris Yamhill County 1993 **$8.50** Solidly built, with generous nectarine and mineral aromas and flavors. Drinkable now.

80 BRIDGEVIEW Pinot Gris Oregon Cuvée Speciale 1993 **$9.00** Soft and a little watery, but pleasantly flavored with fresh melon. Drinkable now.

80 YAMHILL VALLEY Pinot Gris Willamette Valley 1993 **$10.00** Simple and fruity, dry, slightly coarse in texture; enjoyable for its freshness and youthful charm.

Riesling

CALIFORNIA

86 HAGAFEN Johannisberg Riesling Napa Valley 1994 **$8.00** Fresh, fruity and appealing. Lightly sweet and loaded with peach, nectarine and floral flavors.

86 HIDDEN CELLARS Johannisberg Riesling Mendocino 1993 **$8.00** Fragrant and distinctly floral. A nice beam of apricot flavor carrying through the off-dry finish. Tasty now.

85 BONNY DOON Riesling California Pacific Rim 1993 **$8.00** Light and crisp, a lively, floral, slightly resiny wine that keeps singing pretty on the finish.

85 GREENWOOD RIDGE White Riesling Anderson Valley 1993 **$8.50** Bright and fruity, a light wine that is a little spritzy on the palate, which balances the sweet peach and nectarine fruit. An appealing wine from the first whiff to the finish.

85 RENAISSANCE Riesling North Yuba Dry 1992 **$9.00** Light and refreshing flavors centered around grapefruit, finishing a tad sweet.

84 BOEGER Johannisberg Riesling El Dorado 1992 **$7.50** Light and fragrant, bright with apple and floral aromas and flavors, slightly sweet and appealing.

84 FESS PARKER Johannisberg Riesling Santa Barbara County 1993 **$9.00** Light and refreshing, a little sweet, with appealing peach and apple fruit prominent.

84 VENTANA Johannisberg Riesling Monterey White Riesling 1993 **$6.00** Smooth and appealing, a soft wine with modest apple and pear flavors that linger on the finish.

83 GRAND CRU Johannisberg Riesling California Premium Selection 1993 **$7.00** Odd sappy, citrus-peel flavors won't be to everyone's taste, but this off-dry wine has character and style, finishing with a touch of apricot.

83 GUNDLACH BUNDSCHU Riesling Sonoma Valley Dresel's Sonoma Riesling 1993 **$9.00** Light and fruity, showing nice pear and nectarine flavors that linger softly on the finish.

83 HOP KILN Johannisberg Riesling Russian River Valley M. Griffin Vineyards 1993 **$8.00** Frankly sweet but balanced with a sort of austerity that keeps the peach, honey and floral flavors in check. Tasty now.

83 NAVARRO White Riesling Anderson Valley 1992 **$8.50** Light and slightly sweet, with apricot and floral flavors that extend into a solid finish. Could be a little more delicate.

82 CLAIBORNE & CHURCHILL Riesling Central Coast Dry Alsatian Style 1993 **$10.00** Sharply focused pear and peach fruit on a light, simple frame. Could use a smoother texture.

80 KENDALL-JACKSON Johannisberg Riesling California Vintner's Reserve 1993 **$9.50** Soft, a little sweet, with modest apple and citrus flavors.

NEW YORK

86 DR. KONSTANTIN FRANK Johannisberg Riesling New York Semi-Dry 1993 **$8.00** A very complete and harmonious wine, with bright, ripe fruit flavors, great balance and acidity, a smooth, rich texture and not enough sweetness to make it cloying.

85 DR. KONSTANTIN FRANK Johannisberg Riesling Finger Lakes Dry 1993 **$8.00** Generous in texture, ripe in flavor, firm in acidity, showing crisp apple and peach notes accented by grassy aromas. Overall it's clean, fruity and easy to drink.

83 LAMOREAUX LANDING Riesling Finger Lakes Dry 1993 **$8.00** A dry, clean-tasting Riesling with nice floral and piney aromas, crisp acidity and light body. Brisk, fruity and nicely balanced, clean on the finish.

83 SWEDISH HILL Riesling Finger Lakes Dry 1992 **$8.00** A rich style of dry Riesling, showing peachy, slightly piney aromas, plenty of body, smooth texture and honest, appley flavors.

83 WAGNER Johannisberg Riesling Finger Lakes 1991 **$8.00** Grapey, spicey aromas and nearly dry flavors of apple and herbs make this an interesting, complex wine that is evolving well with age. Could use more harmony, but the balance and drinkability is good.

82 DR. KONSTANTIN FRANK Riesling New York Salmon Run NV **$7.00** Just like some German Rieslings, with a distinct aroma of kerosene and crisp, slightly sweet fruit flavors that remind us of peach.

O R E G O N

87 TUALATIN Riesling Willamette Valley 1993 **$6.00** Light, sweet and aromatic, with grapefruit, apple and floral flavors. Delicious now as an apéritif or with foods that don't mind some sweetness.

86 CHAMPOEY White Riesling Willamette Valley 1992 **$6.00** Lightly sweet, but lively with zingy acidity to support the apricot, honey and floral aromas and flavors.

85 ELK COVE Riesling Willamette Valley 1993 **$7.00** Light and floral, a crisp, lightly sweet white with green apple and wildlflower flavors.

85 SEVEN HILLS White Riesling Oregon 1993 **$6.00** Light and fruity, slightly sweet, tasty for its fresh apple and apricot flavors; finishes with some richness.

84 KRAMER Riesling Willamette Valley Estate Bottled 1993 **$6.00** Barely off-dry, crisp and lively, focusing its green apple and floral flavors nicely on a zingy finish. Drinkable now.

84 VIENTO White Riesling Columbia Gorge Vineyard 1993 **$7.00** Light and fruity, lightly sweet, with pleasant apple, pear and floral flavors in modest proportions. Drinkable now.

83 AIRLIE Riesling Oregon 1993 **$7.00** More floral and piney than fruity, this off-dry Riesling has plenty of flavor and pizzazz. Drinkable now.

83 ARGYLE Riesling Oregon Dry Reserve 1991 **$8.00** Light, fruity and soft enough for easy drinking, echoing peach, apple and floral notes on the finish.

82 BRIDGEVIEW Riesling Oregon Blue Moon NV **$6.00** Light, off-dry and pleasantly fruity, reflecting peach and apple flavors on the clean finish.

81 SPRINGHILL Riesling Willamette Valley 1993 **$8.00** Surprisingly dark in color and rich-textured, although flavors soften up on the finish and it comes off as simple and lightly spicy.

81 TUALATIN Riesling Willamette Valley Dry 1991 **$7.00** Crisp and sappy, with a floral edge to the piney aromas and flavors. Drinkable now.

Washington

87 COLUMBIA CREST Johannisberg Riesling Columbia Valley 1993 **$6.00** Bright and fruity, light on its feet, deftly balancing a real mouthful of spicy nectarine and peach fruit on an easy-drinking frame.

87 KIONA White Riesling Yakima Valley 1993 **$6.00** Soft, lightly sweet and fruity, offering a ripe apricot note to the fresh pear and apple fruit, generous and delicious to drink now.

87 PAUL THOMAS Johannisberg Riesling Washington 1993 **$6.00** With its bright beam of apricot-peach fruit, this one is immediately likeable and fresh, finishing off-dry.

86 KIONA White Riesling Yakima Valley Dry 1993 **$6.00** Lightly sweet (despite the label) and pleasantly fruity. A polished wine with appealing melon and apple flavors that pick up a citrusy tinge on the finish.

86 PAUL THOMAS Riesling Washington Dry 1993 **$6.00** Bright and fruity, an apricot edge indicating ripeness despite the dry finish. Drink now while it's fresh.

86 WASHINGTON HILLS Johannisberg Riesling Columbia Valley 1993 **$6.00** Off-dry and smooth, a silky wine that shows very pretty apple and apricot fruit, finishing generously.

86 WASHINGTON HILLS White Riesling Columbia Valley Special Harvest 1993 **$6.00** Lightly sweet and delicately honeyed, not a rich wine but it offers creamy pineapple and floral flavors. Drinkable now.

85 CHATEAU STE. MICHELLE Riesling Columbia Valley Dry 1993 **$7.00** Light and lively, showing an airy texture and a bright core of floral and apple flavors that echo on the finish. Not sweet.

85 COLUMBIA Johannisberg Riesling Columbia Valley Cellarmaster's Reserve 1993 **$7.00** Frankly sweet, with a spicy, honeyed edge to the apricot and pear fruit. Drinkable now.

85 SUNCREST Johannisberg Riesling Washington 1992 **$7.00** Fruity and generous, a mouthful of pretty peach and apple fruit, plus a touch of honey on the finish.

83 ARBOR CREST Riesling Columbia Valley Dry Dionysus Vineyard 1993 **$5.50** Light and piney; on the dry side, with just enough green apple fruit to keep it in balance.

83 HOGUE Johannisberg Riesling Yakima Valley 1993 **$6.00** Soft and fruity, generous with its peach and apple fruit, hinting at honey on the finish.

82 COLUMBIA Johannisberg Riesling Columbia Valley 1993 **$6.00** Soft, a little sweet, showing lots of pleasant apple and floral flavors.

82 SILVER LAKE Riesling Columbia Valley Dry 1992 **$7.00** Light and sappy, with piney notes adding an extra touch to the simple melon and peach fruit.

81 COVEY RUN Riesling Yakima Valley Dry 1993 **$7.00** Fresh and lively, showing some nice green apple and floral flavors, but could be finer in texture. Drinkable now.

81 HOGUE Johannisberg Riesling Yakima Valley Dry 1993 **$6.00** Dry, but not particularly crisp or lively, a simple wine with modest pear fruit.

81 HYATT Johannisberg Riesling Yakima Valley 1992 **$5.00** Sweet and fruity, a simple wine with a hint of apricot to the melon fruit. Finishes a little sweet.

81 WORDEN Johannisberg Riesling Washington 1992 **$7.00** Light and fruity, with a slightly spicy edge to the apple flavors. Drinkable now.

80 ARBOR CREST Johannisberg Riesling Columbia Valley Dionysus Vineyard 1992 **$5.25** Light and fruity, a little bit sweet, mostly showing fresh grapefruit and pear aromas and flavors.

80 HOODSPORT Johannisberg Riesling Washington 1993 **$8.00** Soft and refreshing, a simple wine with a piney edge to the melon flavors.

OTHER U.S.A.

85 RAPIDAN RIVER Riesling Virginia Dry 1992
$9.00 A light wine with pretty floral, peach and apple
flavors singing brightly over the crisp structure.

83 RAPIDAN RIVER White Riesling Virginia
Semi-dry 1992 **$9.00** Off-dry and flavorful, a light
wine, peppery and floral, with a distinctive range of
flavors.

Sauvignon Blanc/Fumé Blanc

CALIFORNIA

90 CHATOM Sauvignon Blanc Calaveras
County 1993 **$8.50** Smooth and generous, showing
nicely defined pear and floral flavors that just keep
coming and coming on the finish. A terrific
Sauvignon Blanc that tones down the varietal
character but keeps just enough of it.

89 MARKHAM Sauvignon Blanc Napa Valley
1993 **$8.00** Floral, spicy and juicier than most
1993s, with a passion fruit character running through
it and lingering on the finish.

89 VENTANA Sauvignon Blanc Monterey 1993
$8.00 Ripe and refreshing, a round, harmonious
example of fruit-centered Sauvignon that lavishes
spice and tobacco nuances on the pear, fig and honey
character.

88 NAVARRO Sauvignon Blanc Mendocino Cuvée 128 1993 **$10.00** Light and smooth in texture, vibrant in flavor with melon, pear and floral notes competing for attention on the citrusy finish.

88 ROBERT MONDAVI Fumé Blanc Napa Valley 1993 **$10.00** Crisply flavorful, harmonizing its pear, citrus, toast and herb flavors, hinting at anise on the lively finish.

88 SEGHESIO Sauvignon Blanc Sonoma County 1993 **$7.50** Crisp and lively, grapefruit at the core and distinctly herbal at the edges, a bright, appealing wine that keeps pumping out the flavor.

88 VOSS Sauvignon Blanc Napa Valley 1993 **$10.00** Fresh and lively, with a fruity center and nice anise and herbal overtones, distinctly varietal and nicely balanced. Drink soon while it's fresh.

87 BERNARDUS Sauvignon Blanc Monterey County 1993 **$9.00** Broad, ripe and spicy, a toasty, honey-scented style that weaves its oaky flavors among the pear and apple fruit. There's a lot going on here, but it doesn't quite come together as harmoniously as it could. Try now.

87 CHATEAU SOUVERAIN Sauvignon Blanc Alexander Valley Barrel Fermented 1993 **$7.50** Fresh and lively, with snappy pear, sweet pea, fig and citrus notes. Medium-bodied with good depth and richness.

87 FIELDBROOK Sauvignon Blanc Mendocino County Webb Vineyard 1993 **$9.00** Bright and fruity, flavors centered around grapefruit and sweet vanilla, echoing nicely on the crisp, smoothly balanced finish. Drinkable now for its fresh liveliness.

86 J. LOHR Fumé Blanc California Cypress 1993 **$7.00** Ripe, round, generous and smooth-textured, with nice honey and fig notes on the finish. A little sweet, but balanced.

86 MERIDIAN Sauvignon Blanc California 1993 **$8.50** Bright and fragrant, lively with apple and pear flavors, shaded with a touch of herb, finishing smooth.

86 MILL CREEK Sauvignon Blanc Dry Creek Valley 1993 **$8.00** Smooth and spicy, balancing crisp grapefruit against spicy oak in a light- to medium-weight wine. Drinkable now.

86 MURPHY-GOODE Fumé Blanc Alexander Valley Dry 1993 **$10.00** Light and slightly herbal, a crisp wine with bright grapefruit and sage flavors, drinkable now.

86 PRESTON Sauvignon Blanc Dry Creek Valley Cuvée de Fumé 1993 **$9.50** Lean and crisp, a racy wine that has a green edge to the tobacco-scented pear.

86 ROBERT PEPI Sauvignon Blanc Napa Valley Two-Heart Canopy 1993 **$9.50** Bright and fruity, offering generous pear and vanilla flavors and a slight oniony, varietal edge.

86 WILLIAM WHEELER Fumé Blanc Sonoma County 1992 **$7.50** Smooth and distinctly herbal, with a minty note that carries through the finish against a citrusy pear background. Drinkable now.

85 CANYON ROAD Sauvignon Blanc California 1993 **$6.00** Lively and citrusy, a mouthfilling wine showing exuberant fruit and bright acidity. Delicious to drink now.

85 CHATEAU POTELLE Sauvignon Blanc Napa Valley 1993 **$9.00** Fruity and bright, lively and exuberant; echoes citrus and pear flavors.

85 CHATEAU ST. JEAN Fumé Blanc Sonoma County Dry 1992 **$8.00** Crisp and citrusy, the herbal overtones adding a nice dimension to the lemony flavors.

85 COTES DE SONOMA Sauvignon Blanc Sonoma County 1993 **$7.00** A gentle wine, showing plenty of pear and a touch of herb flavor, echoing a bit of anise on the finish. Drinkable now.

85 FIELDBROOK Sauvignon Blanc California Trinity County Meredith Vineyard 1992 **$9.00** Soft, fruity and appealing, echoing pear and spice flavors, not very varietal but fun to drink.

85 HANDLEY Sauvignon Blanc Dry Creek Valley 1992 **$9.00** Soft, fruity and pleasant, its slightly citrusy overtones adding a nice extra touch.

85 HANNA Sauvignon Blanc Sonoma County 1993 **$10.00** Crisp and lemony, a spicy wine with polished texture, finishing light but persistent.

85 HIDDEN CELLARS Sauvignon Blanc Mendocino 1993 **$8.00** Smooth, round and more complex than most Sauvignons, with an earthy, mineral edge to the honeyed pear flavors.

85 MEEKER Fumé Blanc Dry Creek Valley Gold Label Cuvée 1993 **$9.00** Light and distinctly herbal, a little pear flavor at the core and a hint of sweet peas around the edges. Drinkable now.

85 MOUNT KONOCTI Fumé Blanc Lake County 1993 **$7.00** Lean and citrusy, with distinct grapefruit character running through the finish.

85 QUAIL RIDGE Sauvignon Blanc Napa Valley 1992 **$10.00** Soft, floral and fruity, a generous wine with a profile that includes pear, honey and oak.

85 RODNEY STRONG Sauvignon Blanc Northern Sonoma Charlotte's Home Vineyard 1993 **$10.00** Soft and fruity, spicy and generous, echoing nectarine and spicy vanilla flavors.

85 VICHON Sauvignon Blend Napa Valley Chevrignon 1993 **$8.50** Smooth, harmonious and delicately herbal atop a layer of pretty apple and pear fruit.

85 WENTE BROS. Sauvignon Blanc Livermore Valley Wente Family Estate Selection 1993 **$7.00** Smooth and spicy, with pineapple and herb flavors that extend into a generous finish.

85 WOODBRIDGE Sauvignon Blanc California Barrel Aged 1993 **$5.00** Smooth and appealing, with generous pineapple, passion fruit and citrus flavors that persist on the lively finish.

84 BENZIGER Fumé Blanc Sonoma County 1994 **$10.00** Lean and nicely focused, centering around spice, pear and herb flavors.

84 BRANDER Sauvignon Blanc Santa Ynez Valley 1994 **$10.00** Lean and even a little austere, with herbal flavors edging past the modest apple fruit, and finishing with a green leafy edge.

84 DE LOACH Fumé Blanc Russian River Valley Dry Sauvignon Blanc 1993 **$10.00** Strongly varietal, with herbal, vegetal flavors that keep playing on the finish.

84 JOULLIAN Sauvignon Blanc Carmel Valley 1992 **$7.50** Sturdy, spicy and round, maybe a little sweet, but balanced and drinkable.

84 KENWOOD Sauvignon Blanc Sonoma County 1993 **$9.50** Crisp, floral and lively, with smoothly integrated apple fruit character.

84 LAKEWOOD Sauvignon Blanc Clear Lake 1993 **$9.00** Lean and crisp, with hints of herb, melon and grassy notes.

84 SILVERADO Sauvignon Blanc Napa Valley 1993 **$9.50** Crisp and grapefruity up front, a refreshing wine that fades a little as it approaches the finish.

83 ADLER FELS Fumé Blanc Sonoma County 1992 **$9.50** So floral it could even pass as a Riesling; an appealing wine with nice fruit. Drinkable now.

83 BEAULIEU Sauvignon Blanc Napa Valley 1992 **$9.50** Light and fragrant, a perfumey wine with a citrusy tang.

83 BEAULIEU Sauvignon Blanc California Beautour 1994 **$7.00** Lean and harmonious, showing lots of nice pear and herb flavors that zip through the finish.

83 BERINGER Fumé Blanc Napa Valley 1992 **$8.50** A sturdy white wine with floral flavors and chunky fruit character.

83 BOEGER Sauvignon Blanc El Dorado 1993 **$8.00** Light, floral and lively, with a core of green apple and pear flavor that carries through the finish.

83 BOGLE Fumé Blanc Lake County Dry 1993 **$5.50** Crisp and citrusy, a light herbal edge adding a touch of complexity.

83 CHRISTOPHE Sauvignon Blanc Napa Valley 1993 **$6.50** Bright and fresh, a soft, fruity wine with pleasant apple and herb flavors.

83 DANIEL GEHRS Sauvignon Blanc Monterey County Fumé En Vogue 1993 **$9.50** Another Loire-style wine, this Sauvignon Blanc has grapey, racy flavors that pick up a honey and pear flavor on the finish.

83 GAN EDEN Sauvignon Blanc Sonoma County 1993 **$8.50** Crisp and lively, a fruity wine with green apple at the core and distinctive nuances of celery and sweet peas.

83 KARLY Sauvignon Blanc Amador County 1993 **$8.50** Smooth and fruity, generous and definitive; leafy, herbal overtones add to the pear and melon flavors.

83 LAKESPRING Sauvignon Blanc Napa Valley Yount Mill Vineyard 1993 **$8.50** Fresh and herbal, with a nice core of peach and melon fruit to keep it lively.

83 MERRYVALE Sauvignon Blanc Napa Valley 1993 **$10.00** Simple and fruity, sturdy enough to carry through the spicy pineapple flavors on the finish.

83 OCTOPUS MOUNTAIN Sauvignon Blanc Anderson Valley 1991 **$8.50** Crisp and fruity, lively with sweet pear and spice flavors.

83 RENAISSANCE Sauvignon Blanc North Yuba 1992 **$10.00** Aggressively floral aromas and flavors mark this as an unusual style, but there is some nice pear and apple fruit behind it. Drinkable now.

83 RIVERSIDE VINEYARDS Fumé Blanc Sonoma County 1992 **$6.00** Smooth but dominated by earthy-floral flavors around a lean core of apple and spice flavor.

83 ROBERT PECOTA Sauvignon Blanc Napa Valley 1993 **$7.00** Sturdy, fruity and spicy, drinkable now for its freshness.

83 WHITE OAK Sauvignon Blanc Sonoma County 1993 **$9.00** Light and spicy, a lean wine with pear and herb flavors that soften on the finish. Drinkable now.

82 AMADOR FOOTHILL Fumé Blanc Shenandoah Valley Amador Fumé 1992 **$8.00**

Crisp and refreshing, a solid wine with an earthy edge
to the decent pear fruit.

82 DE LORIMIER Sauvignon Blend Alexander
Valley Spectrum 1991 **$10.00** Lean and herbal,
with a greenish edge to the citrusy apple flavors.

82 ESTANCIA Sauvignon Blanc Monterey
County 1993 **$7.00** Soft and fruity, a nicely bal-
anced wine for drinking while it's still fresh.

82 GAINEY Sauvignon Blanc Santa Ynez Valley
1992 **$9.00** Crisp and lively, with a generous layer of
pear and spice aromas and flavors, hinting at herbs on
the finish.

82 IVAN TAMAS Fumé Blanc Livermore Valley
Figoni Ranch 1992 **$7.00** Light and crisp, with
simple green apple and lemon flavors. Drinkable now.

82 KENDALL-JACKSON Sauvignon Blanc
California Vintner's Reserve 1993 **$9.50** Sturdy,
simple and lightly herbal, softly fruity at the core.

82 MONTPELLIER Sauvignon Blanc California
1992 **$7.00** Herbal and peppery, but it's smooth and
graceful enough to remain in balance.

82 NICHELINI Sauvignon Blanc Napa Valley
Joseph A. Nichelini Vineyards 1993 **$9.00** Ripe
and floral, a creamy, supple wine with a modest level
of pear and vanilla flavors, echoing floral notes.

82 SHENANDOAH Sauvignon Blanc Amador
County 1993 **$8.00** Smooth and polished, a silky
wine with citrusy pear and mineral flavors.

82 SUTTER HOME Sauvignon Blanc California 1993 **$5.00** Light, fruity and simple, sturdy enough to display appealing apple and spice flavors.

82 V. SATTUI Sauvignon Blanc Napa Valley 1993 **$10.00** Brightly focused and flavorful; earthy, herbal notes echo only a touch of grapefruit to balance it.

81 DE LOACH Sauvignon Blanc Russian River Valley 1993 **$10.00** Lean in texture, a floral wine with a sweet edge to the modest pear fruit.

81 DOMAINE NAPA Sauvignon Blanc Napa Valley Michel A. Perret 1992 **$9.50** Lean and a bit austere, with an earthy edge to the modest vanilla and pear fruit.

81 FIRESTONE Sauvignon Blanc Santa Ynez Valley 1992 **$7.00** Soft and fruity, with a strong earthy-weedy streak. Not for everyone.

81 FOPPIANO Sauvignon Blanc Dry Creek Valley 1992 **$8.25** Crisp and straightforward, a simple wine with bright fruit.

81 LAMBERT BRIDGE Sauvignon Blanc Sonoma County Fumé 1993 **$8.00** Light, fruity and appealing, with pear and smoky herbal flavors lingering on the delicate finish.

81 NAPA RIDGE Sauvignon Blanc North Coast Coastal 1993 **$4.00** Simple and appealing, offering peach and pear fruit with an earthy, herbal edge.

81 RANCHO SISQUOC Sauvignon Blanc Santa Maria Valley 1992 **$9.00** Ripe and broad, with flavors that lean more toward pineapple and grapefruit than herbs, and finishing a little chunky.

81 RED HILL Sauvignon Blanc California 1993 **$3.00** Light and crisp, distinctly fruity but ultimately fairly simple.

81 SUMMERFIELD Sauvignon Blanc California 1993 **$4.00** Pleasant, with simple, muddled flavors on a soft frame, a vanilla edge to the pear fruit.

81 WHITEHALL LANE Sauvignon Blanc Napa Valley Barrel Fermented 1993 **$10.00** Herbal, foxy aromas and flavors are distinctive but could be off-putting to some.

80 AUDUBON Sauvignon Blanc Napa Valley Dry Juliana Vineyards Audubon Collection 1992 **$9.00** Flavorful but a bit raucous and coarse in texture, finishing with a nice array of pear and herb character. Drinkable now.

80 BYINGTON Fumé Blanc San Luis Obispo French Camp Vineyard Dry 1992 **$8.50** A pleasant wine, soft and a little sweet, with an herbal edge to the pear fruit.

80 CALLAWAY Sauvignon Blanc Temecula Hawk Watch 1993 **$7.00** Soft, a little sweet, with apple and spice flavors that linger.

80 CHATOM Fumé Blanc Calaveras County Calaveras Fumé 1991 **$6.00** Lean, simple and refreshing, a lighter style of Sauvignon with some floral overtones and a hint of honey on the finish.

80 CLOS DU BOIS Sauvignon Blanc Alexander Valley Barrel Fermented 1993 **$8.00** Simple and subdued, a pleasant wine with pear and modest spice flavors.

80 ESTRELLA RIVER Sauvignon Blanc California Proprietor's Reserve 1993 **$5.25** Soft and fragrant, spicy enough make the slightly buttery pear flavors interesting. Drinkable now.

80 FALLENLEAF Sauvignon Blanc Sonoma Valley 1991 **$9.00** Frankly vegetal, with more celery and pepper than fruit, but it finishes crisp and refreshing.

80 GLEN ELLEN Sauvignon Blanc California Proprietor's Reserve 1993 **$5.00** Lean, fruity and spicy, a simple wine with modest flavors.

80 JOSEPH FILIPPI Sauvignon Blanc Monterey Winemaker's Reserve Limited Release 1992 **$6.00** Aggressively vegetal and earthy, not for the faint of heart, but soft and fruity enough overall to stay in bounds.

80 KUNDE Sauvignon Blanc Sonoma Valley Magnolia Lane 1993 **$10.00** Smooth and distinctly herbal, a light wine with a resiny edge.

80 STERLING Sauvignon Blanc Napa Valley 1993 **$9.00** Clean and bright, with just a narrow streak of tobacco and herb running through the modest pear and peach flavors.

80 STEVENOT Sauvignon Blanc Calaveras County Barrel Fermented 1992 **$7.50** Lean and spicy, with an earthy-mineral undertone to the peachy fruit.

OREGON

87 VALLEY VIEW Fumé Blanc Rogue Valley Anna Maria 1993 **$10.00** Immensely appealing, fresh and fruity, shining with nectarine and spice flavors that keep glowing on the long finish. Drinkable now.

86 AUTUMN WIND Sauvignon Blanc Oregon 1992 **$8.00** Shows a lot of personality. Strongly floral and herbal in flavor, soft in texture, echoing caramel on the long finish.

81 ASHLAND VINEYARDS Sauvignon Blanc Rogue Valley 1992 **$9.00** Soft and buttery, a drinkable style that emphasizes smooth texture and keeps the flavors from becoming too aggressive.

WASHINGTON

88 COVEY RUN Fumé Blanc Washington 1993 **$8.00** Bright, fruity and spicy, a lively wine with polished edges that allow the citrusy pear and apple fruit to shine. There's a hint of herb on the finish.

88 HOGUE Fumé Blanc Columbia Valley Dry 1993 **$7.50** A brilliantly fruity Sauvignon, brimming with peach, apricot, pear and citrus flavors that keep vibrating on the lively finish.

86 WATERBROOK Sauvignon Blanc Columbia Valley 1993 **$9.00** Soft and creamy, with tasty, slightly leafy apple and vanilla flavors that stay upright through the finish. Echoes a touch of oak. Drinkable now.

83 BARNARD GRIFFIN Fumé Blanc Columbia Valley Dry 1993 **$9.00** Soft and fruity, light enough to sip by itself, generous enough with its citrusy pear fruit to match up with dinner. Drinkable now.

82 W.B. BRIDGMAN Sauvignon Blanc Yakima Valley 1992 **$8.00** Light and spicy, a creamy-textured wine with low-level pear and vanilla flavors at the finish.

81 HYATT Fumé Blanc Yakima Valley 1992 **$7.00** Crisp and refreshing, a simple wine with appealing peach and slightly herbal aromas and flavors.

Other U.S.A.

84 LLANO ESTACADO Sauvignon Blanc Texas 1992 **$8.00** Crisp and lightly spicy, a lively wine with modest flavors.

82 STE. CHAPELLE Fumé Blanc Idaho 1993 **$7.00** Simple, bright and fruity, showing green-edged peach and vanilla flavors that linger.

Sémillon

California

87 CHATOM Sémillon Calaveras County 1993 **$8.00** Bright, focused and layered with appealing fruit aromas and flavors, centering around peach, pear and pineapple. Lasts on the finish.

86 FENESTRA Sémillon Livermore Valley 1992 **$9.00** Round and generous, very pretty for its honey-scented pear and apricot fruit, tasty to drink now.

OREGON

85 WEISINGER'S Rogue Valley Sémillon 1993 **$9.00** Light and crisp, a soft-textured white with pleasant pear and pineapple notes.

WASHINGTON

86 COLUMBIA Sémillon Columbia Valley 1993 **$8.00** Crisp and fruity, fragrant with tobacco and hay-like notes to the bright lemon and pear fruit. Appealing to drink now while fresh.

86 HOODSPORT Sémillon Washington 1992 **$8.00** Crisp and nicely herbal, a lively wine with very pretty pear and floral flavors that extend into a fresh finish.

85 ARBOR CREST Sémillon Columbia Valley Dionysus Vineyard 1993 **$6.25** Lean and austere at first, a little earthy but bright enough to balance with some pear and honey notes. Finishes a little sweet.

85 HOGUE Sémillon Columbia Valley 1993 **$8.00** Light and fragrant, with a tobacco edge to the nicely defined citrusy pineapple fruit, finishing fresh.

84 COLUMBIA CREST Sémillon Columbia Valley 1993 **$6.00** Light and fruity, simple and appealing for its citrusy pear flavors. Drinkable now. Tasted twice.

84 SNOQUALMIE Sémillon Columbia Valley 1993 **$7.00** Light and perfumy, a refreshing wine with delicate herb and floral overtones to the citrusy pear fruit. Drinkable now.

80 COLUMBIA Sémillon Columbia Valley Chevrier Sur Lie 1992 **$10.00** Kind of flat and stale tasting at first, but it picks up some nice honey and caramel notes on the long finish. That stale note persists, however.

80 PAUL THOMAS Sémillon Columbia Valley 1993 **$6.00** Simple and modestly fruity, showing some nice fig and herb flavors.

Other White

CALIFORNIA

89 DE LORIMIER Alexander Valley Meritage Spectrum 1992 **$10.00** Delicate with understated fig, melon, cigar box and butterscotch flavors that fold together nicely.

88 CRONIN Napa Valley Sauvignon Blanc and Chardonnay 1992 **$10.00** Very ripe and buttery, spicy and mouth-filling, with rich oak notes, pear flavor and a little bit of an herbal edge. Drinkable now.

88 RABBIT RIDGE Sonoma County Mystique 1992 **$7.00** Smooth and creamy, a mouthfilling wine that spills its vanilla- and spice-scented citrusy pear flavors gently through the long and appealing finish. Sauvignon Blanc, Sémillon, and Gewürztraminer blend.

86 NAVARRO Mendocino Edelzwicker 1993 **$6.50** A little sweet, but the snappy acidity balances nicely, showing off the appealing apple, citrus and spice flavors.

85 CA' DEL SOLO Monterey Malvasia Bianca 1993 **$8.50** Soft and floral, an earthy wine with a nice core of pear and almond flavor that lingers nicely on the finish.

85 RABBIT RIDGE North Coast Mystique 1993 **$7.00** Light and bright, simple and straightforward, showing off its buttery pear fruit with freshness.

84 DANIEL GEHRS Monterey County Muscadet 1993 **$8.50** Part of Gehrs Loire-style wines, this is a crisp, flinty wine with a narrow band of spice, tart pear and mineral tones. Drinks well now.

84 MONTE VOLPE Mendocino Pinot Bianco 1993 **$9.00** Bright and fruity, a zingy wine with lively pear and resin flavors that linger on the finish.

83 CA' DEL SOLO California Big House White 1993 **$7.50** Smooth and ripe, a simple, appealing wine with a citrusy edge to the gentle fruit.

83 JOYA Pinot Blanc Napa Valley 1991 **$8.00**
Smooth and buttery, with a floral edge to the modest
flavors, finishing soft and a little spicy.

82 MOUNT KONOCTI Lake County Sémillon-
Chardonnay 1993 **$7.50** Simple and a little herbal,
with a sappy edge to the basic apple fruit.

82 PARAISO SPRINGS Pinot Blanc Monterey
County 1991 **$8.00** Crisp and spicy around a light
core of pear and apple fruit.

81 DANIEL GEHRS Pinot Blanc Monterey County
1993 **$10.00** Simple with fruity pear and herb notes;
the least interesting of the new Gehrs wines.

81 GEYSER PEAK California Semchard 1993
$7.50 Herbal, almost vegetal flavors sneak in around
the edges of the mostly apple and leafy flavors, finishing crisp.

81 MASO Napa Valley White Table Wine 1992
$8.00 Oak, oak and more oak. A spicy, toasty, round-
textured wine that finally gets around to some honey
and pear notes on the finish. Try now. Primarily
Chardonnay.

81 MIRASSOU Pinot Blanc Monterey County
Fifth Generation Family Selection White
Burgundy 1993 **$7.00** Light but sturdy, with a tarry,
spicy edge to the basic pear fruit.

81 TRIBAUT DEVAVRY Blanc de Noirs
(Sparkling) California NV **$9.00** Lean and trim,
with a hint of cherry and spice in an otherwise crisp,
narrow wine.

81 TRIBAUT DEVAVRY Brut (Sparkling) California NV **$9.00** Tastes off-dry with a metallic edge to the pear and citrus notes. Simple but serviceable.

NEW YORK

83 LAMOREAUX LANDING Finger Lakes 1992 **$7.00** There is lots of sweet oak in this lush-textured, lavish-tasting Chardonnay-Riesling blend. Doesn't have much fruit flavor, but it's enjoyable for its opulence and style. Nicely priced, too.

80 HUNT COUNTRY VINEYARDS Vignoles Finger Lakes 1992 **$7.00** A sweet, flavorful white that smells herbal and tastes like sweetened rhubarb or peaches. Try it as an apéritif or with a fruit dessert.

OREGON

87 TUALATIN Willamette Valley Müller Thurgau 1993 **$6.00** Brilliantly ripe, focusing its pure apricot notes in a supple, gently appealing style that keeps flashing the flavor on the finish. Very nicely done.

83 AIRLIE Oregon Müller-Thurgau 1993 **$7.00** Light and fruity; off-dry but crisp enough to display delicate pear and floral flavors.

83 MONTINORE Willamette Valley Müller Thurgau 1993 **$6.00** Light and frankly sweet, a touch of honey enlivening the basic pear flavor. Drinkable now.

Washington

87 COLUMBIA Columbia Valley Sémillon-Chardonnay 1993 **$8.00** Firm and fruity, nectarine flavors taking the forefront, finishing with a flair of fresh fruit. Drinkable now.

85 HOGUE Columbia Valley Sémillon Chardonnay 1993 **$7.50** Crisp and refreshing, a lively wine with spicy pear and vanilla flavors that linger nicely on the citrusy finish.

84 COLUMBIA CREST Columbia Valley Sémillon Chardonnay 1993 **$7.00** Smooth and a little sweet, with a fruit cocktail-pear character that hangs on through the bright finish. Drinkable now.

83 COLUMBIA CREST Columbia Valley Sémillon Sauvignon 1992 **$7.00** Bright and fruity, with a spicy-pineapple streak running through the pear flavors. Fresh and appealing to drink now. Tasted twice.

80 HEDGES Washington Fumé Chardonnay 1993 **$8.00** Sweet and fruity, crisp enough to balance the sweetness and pleasant to drink by itself. The melon and apple fruit is appealing.

80 WASHINGTON HILLS Columbia Valley Sémillon Chardonnay 1992 **$7.00** Sturdy, fresh floral, medium weight, finishing slightly bitter.

BLUSH

CALIFORNIA

87 JOSEPH PHELPS Grenache California Vin du Mistral Rosé 1993 **$10.00** A pretty rosé, bright with strawberry and raspberry flavors that extend into a lively finish. Drink it fresh.

86 BONNY DOON California Vin Gris De Cigare 1993 **$8.00** Broader and richer than most rosés, but it keeps the lively strawberry, leather and watermelon flavors in delicate balance.

84 SWANSON Sangiovese Napa Valley Rosato 1994 **$9.00** Dominated by new oak, this wine has loads of cherry fruit to match. Nuances of vanilla and butter add up to a tasty mouthful. The finish lingers.

83 BONNY DOON California Le Canard Froid Pinot Meunier 1993 **$9.00** Soft, fruity and a little sweet and floral, but the berry flavors make this Pinot Meunier sparkler an enjoyable between-meal sipper.

83 MCDOWELL Grenache Rosé Mendocino 1993 **$7.00** There's plenty of dried fruit and spice in the aromas and flavors, underscored by lively acidity. Vibrant and refreshing, with a substantial finish.

83 RUTHERFORD ESTATE White Zinfandel California 1994 **$7.00** Off-dry with nice cherry and berry flavors. It has some body and balance, with loads of good fruit aromas and flavors. Clean, well-made, with a good dose of apricot on the finish.

82 BONNY DOON California Vin Gris de Cigare Pink Wine 1994 **$7.50** A rosé-style with a little spritz. Very dry and almost austere with dried currant and herbal flavors. Well-balanced.

82 HEITZ Napa Valley Grignolino Rosé 1994 **$5.50** A serious wine that tastes like a rosé, with a wild side dominated by earthy, spicy and berry flavors. It's extremely pungent and dry as well as full-bodied.

82 MIRASSOU White Zinfandel California 1994 **$10.00** Very fruity with some body and zippy acidity. Only a hint of sweetness, with nice strawberry and cherry flavors.

81 BERINGER White Zinfandel California 1994 **$5.50** A flavorful wine that's sweet and fruity with decent cherry and berry flavors. There's enough acidity in this wine to make it balanced.

81 VENDANGE White Zinfandel California Autumn Harvest 1994 **$6.00** A wine with some character. Smells and tastes like Muscat with an herbal note. The flavors linger on the finish.

80 FETZER White Zinfandel California 1994 **$7.00** A sweeter style with strawberry flavors and a hint of butter on the finish. It has enough acidity to balance the sugar.

80 M.G. VALLEJO White Zinfandel California 1994 **$6.00** A well-made wine that tastes of tea and cherries. Quite dry, well-balanced, but fairly soft.

DESSERT
CALIFORNIA

86 VIANO Zinfandel Late Harvest Contra Costa County Reserve Selection 1988 **$8.50** Dense, dark and chewy, showing off complex tar, smoke and toasty oak flavors with lots of fresh, ripe, bright cherry, raspberry and plum notes. Drinks well now, but has the balance to hold until 1997.

85 CA' DEL SOLO Moscato Monterey Moscato del Solo 1993 **$9.00** A disarmingly fresh and appealing dessert wine, not very aromatic, but the spicy, peppery flavors float lightly and keep lingering on the sweet, honeyed finish. Ready and willing.

84 TOBIN JAMES Zinfandel Paso Robles Solar Flair 1992 **$10.00** Sweet and ripe, with cherry, berry and spicy flavors. A very appealing late harvest Zin that doesn't overpower you with tannins.

83 QUADY Orange Muscat California Electra 1993 **$9.00** Light and sweet, with orange and peach flavors that glide smoothly across the palate.

82 MADDALENA Muscat Canelli Central Coast 1993 **$6.00** Spicy and exotic, with a peppery-allspice-clove character that is unusual and appealing; not too sweet.

81 QUADY Port California LBV 1991 **$9.00** Light in color, lightly plummy and spicy in flavor. A smooth wine that is ready to drink.

81 SHENANDOAH Late Harvest Sierra Foothills Zinfandel/Sirah 1991 **$8.00** Bold, ripe and Port-like, with dense, dry, chewy tannins. The ripe plum flavor doesn't quite fight through. Best after 1998, but likely to remain tannic.

80 GAN EDEN Black Muscat San Joaquin County 1993 **$7.50** Soft, sweet, with plum and spice flavors that linger lightly on the finish.

O REGON

85 MONTINORE Willamette Valley Late Harvest Gewürztraminer 1993 **$6.00** Ripe and sweet but stops short of unctuous, showing moderate levels of apricot, honey and floral flavors.

84 MONTINORE Willamette Valley Late Harvest White Riesling 1993 **$6.00** Light and delicate but definitely sweet and soft-textured, with a modest level of apricot and pear flavors.

W ASHINGTON

93 COLUMBIA CREST Sémillon Late Harvest Columbia Valley 1992 375ml **$8.00** Beautifully rich, focused and exquisitely balanced, dealing out its honey-scented pear, pineapple and apricot fruit that swirls and echoes on the finish, supported by just the right amount of zingy acidity. Ready now, but should improve through 2001-2005.

89 KIONA Gewürztraminer Late Harvest Yakima Valley 1993 **$6.25** Sweet and unctuous, a spicy, floral wine that picks up some melon, apricot and vanilla notes on the long, supple finish.

89 KIONA Muscat Late Harvest Yakima Valley 1993 375ml **$7.00** Fruity; a fresh, direct and clean-tasting example of pure varietal fruit, sweet but not unctuous. Beautifully balanced.

88 COVEY RUN White Riesling Late Harvest Yakima Valley 1993 **$7.00** Sweet and rich, a little on the sugary side, but shows enough bright pear and vanilla flavor to make a delicious dessert wine on its own terms. Finishes long and sweet.

87 TEFFT Sauvignon Blanc Late Harvest Yakima Valley River Mist 1992 **$10.00** Sweet and floral with a bit of a honey edge that picks up some black fig and toast notes on the finish. Nicely made, not too sweet, but rich enough. Tasty now.

87 THURSTON WOLFE Port Washington JTW's Port 1991 500ml **$10.00** A classically built Port, sweet and juicy with black currant, black cherry and spice flavors that linger on the finish. Could use a little more grip, but should be fine from 1998-2000.

86 KIONA White Riesling Late Harvest Yakima Valley 1991 **$6.25** Sweet but balanced with enough acidity to taste almost delicate, showing appealing honey-scented floral, peach and almond flavors.

85 HOGUE White Riesling Late Harvest Columbia Valley 1993 **$6.00** Sweet and ripe without being unctuous. Melon and nectarine flavors echo right through the finish, which is not too sweet. Nicely balanced.

85 THURSTON WOLFE Muscat Washington Black Muscat 1992 **$9.00** Sweet and fruity, a little plum and black cherry sneaking in amidst the lightly spicy citrusy flavors.

85 THURSTON WOLFE Yakima Valley Sweet Rebecca Late Harvest 1992 **$10.00** Tastes very sweet and honeyed, with a wild, herbal edge to the orange and apricot fruit. Balanced toward sweetness, but doesn't try to be too rich.

83 WORDEN Gewürztraminer Late Harvest Washington 1992 **$7.50** Sweet and pleasantly floral, with a slightly bitter edge to the apricot and pear fruit, finishing sweet and snappy. Drinkable now.

82 HYATT Muscat Yakima Valley Black Muscat Royale 1993 **$7.00** Off-dry, soft and lively, with a peppery-spicy streak running through the modest apple fruit. Drinkable now.

80 BOOKWALTER Muscat Washington Blanc 1993 **$8.00** Very light and soft, with floral overtones to the modest melon and cream flavors.

Other Countries

Outside the traditional appellations of Europe and the more established New World regions such as California and even Chile, there are many more places in the world where wine bargains can be found.

One of the best is Argentina. While close to Chile's major wine producing regions, Argentina's vineyards are just now emerging amid a more open and stable political system. Meanwhile, look for wines with the Mendoza appellation, including the Trapiche Malbec Oak Cask Vintner's Selection and Finca Flichman's Cabernet Sauvignon Proprietors Reserve.

Central and eastern Europe also have some values. Look for the Servus Burgenland Cuvée from Austria and from Bulgaria try Chardonnay from Chateau Dalina.

Argentina

RED

86 TRAPICHE Malbec Mendoza Oak Cask Vintner's Selection Lujan de Cuyo County 1990 **$8.00** This round, vivid wine shows good depth and polish, with deep black cherry fruit and appealing notes of smoke, toast and spice. It's a sturdy, basic red that stays with you. Drink now through 1996.

84 FINCA FLICHMAN Cabernet Sauvignon Mendoza Proprietors Private Reserve 1990 **$8.00** Oozing with ripe, soft fruit flavors; very fresh and light in tannins. Drink now for its charm and exuberance.

81 VALENTIN BIANCHI Malbec Mendoza Elsa's Vineyard 1992 **$5.00** A lively wine, with black pepper notes perking up the black cherry fruit. The tannins are a bit strong for the fruit, but it can handle simple meat dishes.

80 BODEGAS ESMERALDA Cabernet Sauvignon Mendoza Trumpeter 1992 **$7.00** A core of sweet cherry fruit is appealing but dry tannins and an earthy note detract a bit from the pleasure. It's maturing already and should be drunk now.

80 TRAPICHE Cabernet Sauvignon Mendoza Oak Cask Maipu County 1991 **$8.00** An odd mix of tart cranberry fruit, musty, earthy notes and oaky vanilla flavors keeps this wine off-balance. It's rich, though, ripe and concentrated. Try in 1996.

WHITE

84 BODEGAS ESMERALDA Chardonnay Mendoza Trumpeter 1993 **$7.00** Harmonious and balanced, this soft-textured wine offers light oak and ripe fruit flavors. It's supple and complete, in a lower key, and shows finesse and length.

84 VALENTIN BIANCHI Chenin Blanc Mendoza Elsa's Vineyard 1994 **$5.00** This pleasantly fruity wine is soft yet refreshing. Clean floral and peach aromas give way to smooth flavors of peach and pear with a slight honey note. A lovely apéritif.

83 TRAPICHE Chardonnay Mendoza Oak Cask Vintner's Selection Tupungato Valley 1992 **$8.00** A plump, generous wine with plenty of oak, this offers ripe tropical fruit and lots of creamy vanilla flavor. A bit exaggerated, but tasty.

Austria

83 SERVUS Burgenland Cuvée 1992 **$5.00** This crisp, clean white shows citrus and light herbal flavors enlivened by a keen edge of acidity. It's a light-bodied, refreshing apéritif.

Bulgaria

84 VINPROM Sliven Bulgare Merlot & Pinot Noir 1993 **$4.00** A great value. Generous in flavor, easygoing in texture, with light tannins and good fruit flavors. This has fresh cherry and raspberry accents and an enticing balance.

82 NAZDRAVE Russe Country Red NV **$4.00** A pleasant, well-rounded, easy-drinking red with jammy, plummy flavors. Low in tannin, soft in texture and ready to drink now.

80 CHATEAU DALINA Chardonnay Russe 1993 **$4.00** Thick and soft, with top-heavy pear and vanilla flavors, this is an entry-level wine without any hard edges or scary depths.

Hungary

80 VINUM BONUM Chardonnay Etyeki 1993 **$10.00** This big, showy wine falls cleanly within the new international style, with its tropical fruit flavors, crisp acidity and sweet vanilla accents.

Romania

80 LEGACY Murfatlar Special Reserve Muscat Ottonel 1992 **$10.00** Very aromatic, nicely fruity and a moderately sweet dessert wine, with appealing peach and apricot flavors and a soft, smooth texture.

Index of
Winery Names

Adam, J.B., 66
Adler Fels, 189, 206
Age, 122, 123, 127
Agricola de Borja, 126
Airlie, 197, 219
Alameda, 39, 45
Alexander Valley Fruit and Trading Co., 168
Alexis Lichine, 74
Alois Lageder, 98
Alsace Willm, 67
Amador Foothill, 208
Amity, 160
Andre-Michel Bregeon, 71
Anselmi, 98
Antinori, 95, 100, 101
Antonio Barbadillo, 128
Arbor Crest, 183, 199, 200, 215
Argyle, 160, 197
Arrowood, 142, 153
Ashland Vineyards, 213
Ashwood, 22, 24, 30
Audubon, 211
Augey, 68
Aujoux, Jean-Marc, 60
Autumn Wind, 161, 192, 213
Aveleda, 106

B. Chereau, 72
Backsberg, 113, 115
Bandiera, 143
Barbadillo, Antonio, 128
Barbi, 100

Bargetto, Lawrence J., 148, 178, 190
Barnard Griffin, 141, 214
Baron Herzog, 143
Barone Cornacchia, 94
Barone Ricasoli, 96
Barton & Guestier, 69, 75, 76
Beaulieu, 147, 153, 174, 206
Becker, J., 67
Belvedere, 147, 173, 176
Benziger, 205
Berberana, Bodegas, 123
Beringer, 164, 207, 222
Bernardus, 202
Bethel Heights, 191, 192
Beyer, Leon, 65
Bleasdale, 22, 23, 30
Bocage, 152
Bodegas Berberana, 123
Bodegas Corral, 122
Bodegas Esmeralda, 228, 229
Bodegas Faustino Martinez, 124
Bodegas Lan, 123
Bodegas Manuel Sancho, 125
Bodegas Martinez Bujanda, 123
Bodegas Montecillo, 122
Bodegas Senda Galiana, 124
Bodegas Sierra Cantabria, 123
Boeger, 165, 194, 207
Bogle, 153, 166, 170, 178, 207
Boisset, Jean Claude, 62

Bolla, 90, 93, 97, 98

Bonnet, Chateau, 67

Bonnigal, M., 72

Bonny Doon, 171, 194, 217, 221

Bonverre, 179

Bookwalter, 183, 187, 226

Boschendal, 114

Bouchaine, 159, 176, 188

Brander, 205

Bregeon, Andre-Michel, 71

Bridgeview, 160, 180, 190, 193, 197

Bridgman, W.B., 183, 214

Brindiamo, 162

Brown Brothers, 20, 21, 26, 31, 32

Buehler, 168

Buena Vista, 177, 189

Bujanda, Bodegas Martinez, 123

Butterfly Creek, 154

Byington, 211

Ca' De Monte, 92, 101

Ca' Del Solo, 217, 218, 223

Ca'vit, 92

Cadeaux, 77

Callaway, 177, 211

Canaletto, 94, 98

Canepa, 38, 40, 41, 45, 48

Canyon Road, 146, 204

Capezzana, 91, 95

Carmen, 38, 42-45, 47

Carneros Creek, 158

Carta Vieja, 41, 45

Casa Lapostolle, 43, 45, 48

Casablanca, 47, 49

Castellare di Castellina, 100

Castello Banfi, 96

Castello D'albola, 92

Castello Di Volpaia, 92

Castello Romitorio, 95

Castoro, 146, 166

Caterina, 182

Cathedral Cellar, 116

Catherine de St.-Juery, 64

Cavalchina, 101

Caves Alianca, 106, 107

Caves Dom Teodosio, 107, 108

Caves Velhas, 107, 108

Cecchi, 91, 96

Cedar Brook, 144

Champoey, 197

Chantefleur, 74-76

Chappellet, 185

Charles Krug, 158, 168

Chateau Bonnet, 67

Chateau Dalina, 230

Chateau de Baun, 173

Chateau de Jau, 64

Chateau de la Chesnaie, 71

Chateau de la Ragotiere, 70

Chateau du Coing de St.-Fiacre, 70

Chateau Haut-Mazieres, 61, 67

Chateau Julien, 152

Chateau Lagrezette, 64

Chateau Le Bouscat, 62, 68

Chateau Mont-Redon, 62

Chateau Pech de Jammes, 65

Chateau Pitray, 62

Chateau Potelle, 204

Chateau Reynella, 22

Chateau Routas, 64, 72

Chateau Souverain, 163, 202

Chateau St. Jean, 204

Chateau Ste. Michelle, 187, 199

Chateau Tahbilk, 30

Chateau Woltner, 174

Chatom, 169, 201, 211, 215

Chehalem, 193

Cheneau, Paul, 129

Chereau, B., 72

Chiarlo, Michele, 90

Christophe, 158, 207

Cielo, 93, 98

C.K. Mondavi, 169

Claiborne & Churchill, 188, 195

Claudia Springs, 169

Cline, 166

Clos Daniell 154, 173

Clos Du Bois, 212

Clos St. Thomas, 179

Cocora Ortona, 94

Codorniu, 128

Coldridge, 21, 29

Collavini, 93, 96

Columbia, 191, 199, 200, 215, 216, 220

Columbia Crest, 151, 156, 172, 182, 191, 198, 216, 220, 224

Concannon, 144, 171

Concha Y Toro, 41-43, 45, 48

Cono Sur, 39, 41, 44

Cook's, 155

Corbett Canyon, 148, 154, 159, 179

Cornacchia, Barone, 94

Corral, Bodegas, 122

Cotes de Sonoma, 176, 204

Covey Run, 172, 191, 200, 213, 225

Crane Lake, 38

Creston, 149

Cristom, 192

Cronin, 216

Cune, 124

Dalina, Chateau, 230

Daniel Gehrs, 186, 207, 217, 218

Dario d'Angelo, 94

De Baun, Chateau, 173

De Jau, Chateau, 64

De la Chesnaie, Chateau, 71

De la Ragotiere, Chateau, 70

De Loach, 188, 205, 210

De Lorimier, 209, 216

De Martino, 41

De Wetshof, 113

Deinhard, 82

Delas, 74

Deschaux, Lucien, 63, 68

Dickerson, 140

Domaine Barre, 72

Domaine de la Batardiere, 70

Domaine de la Coste, 64

Domaine de la Mordorée, 63

Domaine de la Quilla, 70

Domaine Deletang, 72

Domaine des Fontanelles, 75, 77

Domaine Maurice Protheau, 69

Domaine Napa, 210

Domaine Rabat, 39

Domaine St. George, 143, 144, 146, 179

Domaines Schlumberger, 65, 66

Dona Sol, 39, 45, 47

Donatien Bahuaud, 72

Dr. Konstantin Frank, 195, 196

Drayton's, 32

Dry Creek, 186

Du Coing de St.-Fiacre, Chateau, 70

Duboeuf, Georges, 59-61, 63, 64, 68, 69, 73, 74, 76, 77

Duck Pond, 160, 190

Dunnewood, 145, 154, 169, 179

Durney, 185

E. & J. Gallo, 163

E. Guigal, 62

Elizabeth, 164

Elk Cove, 197

Eola Hills, 150
Esmeralda, Bodegas, 228, 229
Estancia, 148, 151, 158, 173, 209
Estrella River, 212
Evans & Tate, 24

Fallenleaf, 212
Farina, 126, 128
Fazi-Battaglia, 99
Fenestra, 215
Fess Parker, 194
Fetzer, 155, 164, 176, 222
Fieldbrook, 202, 204
Filippi, Joseph, 212
Finca Flichman, 228
Firesteed, 161
Firestone, 210
Fleur du Cap, 113, 116
Fontana Candida, 96
Fontanafredda, 90
Foppiano, 150, 153, 210
Forest Glen, 146, 154, 177
Foris, 150, 161, 182, 191
Fortant de France, 73, 75-77
Foss Creek, 148, 174, 179
Fossi, 95
Foxhollow, 155
Frank, Dr. Konstantin, 195
Freixenet, 128, 129
Frescobaldi, 96
Frey, 166

Gaierhof, 98
Gainey, 209
Galiana, Bodegas Senda, 124
Gallo, E. & J., 163
Gallula, Lionel, 73
Gan Eden, 207, 224
Garofoli, 99
Gehrs, Daniel, 186, 207, 217, 218

Georges Duboeuf, 59-61, 63, 64, 68, 73-77
Geyser Peak, 175, 188, 218
Glass Mountain Quarry, 176
Glen Ellen, 154, 212
Glenora, 180
Gordon Brothers, 183
Graf Von Neipperg, 84
Grand Cru, 155, 190, 194
Greenwood Ridge, 194
Groot Constantia, 114, 115
Grove Street, 177
Guigal, E., 62
Gundlach Bundschu, 163, 195

Hacienda, 155, 178
Hagafen, 193
Hahn, 150, 155, 175
Handley, 188, 204
Hanna, 204
Hanwood, 23, 27
Hardy's, 20, 21, 23, 25, 27, 28, 32
Haut-Mazieres, Chateau, 61, 67
Haywood, 146, 178
Hedges, 141, 220
Heitz, 222
Henri Poiron, 71
Henry, 160, 181, 191
Heritiers Guilbaud, 70
Herzog, Baron, 143
Hess Select, 143, 174
Hidden Cellars, 165, 194, 204
Hijos de Antonio Barcelo, 125
Hogue, 172, 182, 187, 191, 199, 200, 213, 215, 220, 225
Hoodsport, 187, 200, 215
Hop Kiln, 164, 169, 189, 195
Hope Farms, 140, 145
Hugel, 66
Hunt Country Vineyards, 219

Husch, 147, 185, 189
Hyatt, 141, 184, 200, 214, 226

Indian Springs, 148
Infernotto, 95
Ivan Tamas, 209

J. Becker, 67
J. Lohr, 148, 203
J. Pedroncelli, 154, 167
J.B. Adam, 66
Jabiru, 22, 27
Jaboulet Aîné, Paul, 63
Jadot, Louis, 60
James, Tobin, 223
Jean Claude Boisset, 62, 69
Jean-Marc Aujoux, 60
Jean-Pierre Moueix, 75
Jory, 171
Joseph Filippi, 212
Joseph Phelps, 221
Joullian, 206
Joya, 164, 218
Julien, Chateau, 152

Karly, 168, 207
Kendall-Jackson, 186, 189,
    195, 209
Kenwood, 206
Kinderwood, 153
Kiona, 172, 186, 198, 224,
    225
Knipprath, 172
Knudsen Erath, 180
Konrad, 169
Kookaburra, 25, 28
Kramer 193, 197
Kreusch, Leonard, 83
Krug, Charles, 158, 168
Kunde, 212
KWV, 116, 117

La Bouverie, 63
La Crosse, 152, 178
La Porcii, 76
La Sorte, 94
La Vieille Ferme, 63, 73
Lageder, Alois, 98
Lagrezette, Chateau, 64
Lakespring, 208
Lakewood, 206
Lambert Bridge, 210
Lamoreaux Landing, 196, 219
Lan, Bodegas, 123
Latah Creek, 183, 184
Laurel Glen, 142
Lawrence J. Bargetto, 148,
    178, 190
Le Bouscat, Chateau, 62, 68
Leasingham, 24, 28
Leflaive, Olivier, 62
Legacy, 230
Lehmann, Peter, 25, 29
Leon Beyer, 65
Leonard Kreusch, 82, 83
Les Freres Couillaud, 71
Les Jamelles, 73, 76
Lichine, Alexis, 74
Lindemans, 22, 24, 25, 27, 29
Lionel Gallula, 73
Llano Estacado, 142, 214
Lohr, J., 148, 203
Lolonis, 167
Lorinon, 122
Los Vascos, 39
Louis Jadot, 60
Louis M. Martini, 154, 157,
    174
Lucien Deschaux, 63, 68
Lungarotti, 97, 100

M. Bonnigal, 72
M.G. Vallejo, 155, 177, 222
Mackinaw, 175

Maddalena, 223

Marienberg, 30

Marietta, 171

Markham, 201

Marques De Caceres, 124, 127

Marques De Grinon, 122

Marques De Murrieta, 128

Marques De Riscal, 127

Marquis De Goulaine, 71

Martin Brothers, 167

Martinez, Bodegas Faustino, 124

Martini, Louis M., 154, 157, 174

Mas Ste.-Berthe, 65

Masciarelli, 93

Masi, 90, 94, 99

Maso, 140, 218

McDowell, 221

McGuigan Brothers, 26

McLarens, 25, 29

Meeker, 166, 205

Meridian, 175, 203

Merryvale, 208

Meyer-Fonne, 66

Michael Sullberg, 156, 159

Michele Chiarlo, 90

Miguel Torres, 40, 49

Milano, 165

Mill Creek, 188, 203

Millbrook, 159, 180

Mirassou, 152, 171, 185, 218, 222

Mitchelton, 21, 24, 28

Mommessin, 61

Mondavi, C.K., 169

Mondavi, Robert, 148, 202

Mont-Redon, Chateau, 62

Monte Antico, 96

Monte Volpe, 217

Montecillo, Bodegas, 122

Monterey Peninsula, 145, 170

Monterey Vineyard, 156

Monterra, 149

Montes, 40, 45

Montinore, 181, 190, 192, 220, 224

Montpellier, 147, 156, 209

Moreau, 74, 77

Morro Bay, 177

Mosca, 91, 94

Moselland, 82

Moueix, Jean-Pierre, 75

Mount Konocti, 140, 145, 205, 218

Mouton-Cadet, 68

Murphy-Goode, 203

Napa Ridge, 145, 152, 158, 175, 210

Navarro, 171, 189, 195, 202, 217

Nazdrave, 230

Nederburg, 115

Negociants, The, 152, 173, 180

Newlan, 159

Nichelini, 209

Nominee, 153

Norman Vineyard, 148

Normans, 22, 26, 28

Oak Falls, 156

Oak Knoll, 192

Oasis, 184, 185

Octopus Mountain, 208

Olivier Leflaive, 62

Onix, 125

Oregon Vineyards, 161

Orfila, 177

Pallavicini, 100

Paraiso Springs, 189, 218

Parducci, 145, 168, 171, 179

Paul Cheneau, 129

Paul Jaboulet Aîné, 63

Paul Thomas, 141, 150, 156, 182, 187, 198, 216

Pech de Jammes, Chateau, 65

Pecota, Robert, 208

Pedroncelli, J., 154, 167

Peirano Estate, 164

Pellegrini Family, 169

Penfolds, 20, 27, 29, 30

Pepi, Robert, 203

Pepperwood Grove, 158

Peter Lehmann, 25, 29

Phelps, Joseph, 221

Phillips, R.H., 175

Pierre Sparr, 65-67

Pighin, 97

Pio Cesare, 90, 92, 97

Pitray, Chateau, 62

Plozner, 101

Poiron, Henri, 71

Poppy Hill, 152

Potelle, Chateau, 204

Preston, 162, 170, 203

Quady, 223

Quail Ridge, 205

Queen Adelaide, 21, 28

Quinta do Cotto, 106

R.H. Phillips, 175

Rabbit Ridge, 162, 217

Rancho Sisquoc, 210

Rapidan River, 201

Ravenswood, 152, 167

Raymond, 145

Red Hill, 211

Renaissance, 194, 208

Renato Ratti, 92

Renzo Masi, 91

Rex Hill, 192

Reynella, Chateau, 22

Riverside Vineyards, 208

Robert Mondavi, 148, 202

Robert Pecota, 208

Robert Pepi, 203

Rodney Strong, 147, 205

Rooiberg, 113, 114, 116

Rosemount, 20, 22, 24, 28-30

Rosenblum, 167, 169

Round Hill, 150, 174

Routas, Chateau, 64

Rutherford Estate, 149, 159, 221

Rutherford Ranch, 143, 155, 174

Rutherford Vineyards, 175

Saccardi, 91

Sancho, Bodegas Manuel, 125

Santa Barbara Winery, 165, 168

Santa Carolina, 40, 43, 44

Santa Monica, 46, 49

Santa Rita, 40, 42 47, 48

Santa Sofia, 99

Sattui, V., 210

Sausal, 163

Scala Dei, 125, 126

Schmitt Sohne, 82-84

Schwarzenberg, 160, 161

Seaview, 26, 31

Sebastiani, 144, 167, 173

Seghesio, 146, 163, 202

Segura Viudas, 129

Seltz, 67

Seppelt, 20, 23

Servus, 229

Seven Hills, 150, 197

Shafer Vineyard Cellars, 181

Shenandoah, 142, 168, 209, 223

Shooting Star, 140, 157, 164, 178

Sichel Sohne, 82
Sierra Cantabria, Bodegas, 123
Silver Horse, 149
Silver Lake, 200
Silver Ridge, 146
Silverado, 206
Snoqualmie, 141, 216
Sobon Estate, 162
Sogrape, 106-108
Sokol Blosser, 161, 180
Solana, 126
Sonsierra, 124, 124
Souverain, Chateau, 163, 202
Spalletti, 91
Springbok, 113, 114
Springhill, 181, 198
St. Francis, 144
St. Jean, Chateau, 204
Ste. Chapelle, 151, 157, 182, 214
Ste. Michelle, Chateau, 187, 199
Stellenryck, 113
Stephen Zellerbach, 178
Sterling, 212
Stevenot, 178, 212
Stone Cellars, 151, 157, 184
Stone Creek, 165
Strong, Rodney, 147, 205
Sullberg, Michael, 156, 159
Sumarroca, 129
Summerfield, 211
Suncrest, 199
Sutter Home, 149, 168, 210
Swanson, 221
Swedish Hill, 196

Taft Street, 175
Tagaris, 184
Tahbilk, Chateau, 30
Tamas, Ivan, 209
Tefft, 141, 225

Tenute Colue, 90
Terra de Lobos, 107
Terrale, 95
Thomas, Paul, 141, 150, 156, 182, 187, 198, 216
Thornhill, 147
Thurston Wolfe, 225, 226
Tiefenbrunner, 97
Tobin James, 223
Topolos, 166
Torres, Miguel, 40
Tosti, 101
Trapiche, 228, 229
Trefethen, 140
Trentadue, 163
Tribaut Devavry, 219
Troquato, 165
Tualatin, 160, 196, 198, 219
Tyrrell's, 20, 23-27, 31, 32

Umani Ronchi, 99
Undurraga, 38, 40, 46

V. Sattui, 210
Valentin Bianchi, 228, 229
Vallejo, M.G., 155, 177, 222
Valley of the Moon, 170
Valley View, 156, 181, 182, 213
Vallformosa, 129
Vendange, 222
Ventana, 186, 194, 201
Veritas, 161, 181, 193
Viano, 149, 170, 222
Vicente Gandia, 126
Vichon, 143, 153, 178, 205
Viento, 197
Vignalta, 100
Villa Cervia, 93
Villa Frattina, 100
Villa Mt. Eden, 158, 166, 176
Villa Pigna, 95
Villard, 42, 44, 48

Villiera Estate, 114
Vina Magana, 125
Vina Porta, 38
Vina Segu Olle, 49
Vinas del Vero, 127
Vinos de Chile, 48
Vinprom, 229
Vinum Bonum, 230
Von Hovel, 82
Von Neipperg, Graf, 84
Voss, 202

W.B. Bridgman, 183, 214
Wagner, 190, 196
Walnut Crest, 43
Washington Hills, 141, 157, 184, 192, 199, 200
Waterbrook, 183, 214
Weingut Klein, 83
Weinstock, 144
Weisinger's, 219
Wellington, 166
Wente Bros., 149, 176, 205
Whaler, 167
Wheeler, William, 203

White Heron, 142, 162
White Oak, 165, 185, 208
Whitehall Lane, 211
Wildhurst, 170
Willamette Valley, 181
William Wheeler, 203
Willm, Alsace, 67
Wilson Daniels, 176
Woltner, Chateau, 174
Woodbridge, 205
Woodley, 31
Worden, 172, 184, 187, 200, 226
Wyndham, 23, 26, 28

Xenius, 129

Yalumba, 21, 27
Yamhill Valley, 193
York Mountain, 159

Z Moore, 188
Zellerbach, Stephen, 178
Zonin, 93